T0150635

THE END OF
SUKARNO

A Coup that Misfired:
A Purge that Ran Wild

THE END OF
SUKARNO

A Coup that Misfired:
A Purge that Ran Wild

JOHN HUGHES

By the same author

THE NEW FACE OF AFRICA

© John Hughes 1967, 2002

All rights reserved. No part of this publication may be reproduced
or transmitted in any form or by any means, electronic or mechanical,
including photocopying, recording or any information storage and retrieval system,
without the prior written permission of the copyright owner.

This fourth edition published in 2014
Editions Didier Millet
78 Jalan Hitam Manis
Singapore 278488

www.edmbooks.com

Reprinted 2017

First edition published in the USA in 1967 by David McKay Company,
New York, under the title *Indonesian Upheaval*
Second edition published in Great Britain in 1968 by Angus & Robertson (UK) Ltd,
54 Bartholomew Close, London

ISBN 978-981-4385-75-6

Photo Credits

All photographs except those of the murdered generals and of the Djakarta victory parade are by courtesy of the Indonesian Government agency, Deppen

Contents

Part Three: The Fall

Who's Who

SUKARNO

President of Indonesia for nearly 22 years. Stripped of his powers on March 12, 1967. Died on June 21, 1970.

SUHARTO

President of Indonesia from 1967 to 1998. Catapulted into prominence as leader of the troops that smashed the 1965 coup.

NASUTION, Abdul Haris

Army hero and senior general; narrowly escaped assassination in the 1965 coup. Became chairman of the People's Consultative Congress, supreme policymaking body. Died in 2000.

SUBANDRIO

Former foreign minister and Sukarno's right-hand man. For his involvement in the 1965 coup, he was given the death sentence, but this was subsequently commuted to life. Died in 1995.

SUPARDJO, Mustafa Sjarif

Army general; one of the ringleaders of the 1965 coup. Executed in 1967.

UNTUNG

Lieutenant Colonel of the presidential palace guard; one of the ringleaders of the 1965 coup. Executed in 1967.

DHANI, Omar

Former chief of the Indonesian Air Force; played a key role in the 1965 coup. Executed in 1967.

MALIK, Adam

Foreign minister and implacable foe of Sukarno. Member of the post-coup ruling triumvirate with Suharto and Hamengku Buwono. Became Vice President of Indonesia in 1978. Died in 1984.

HAMENGKU BUWONO

Sultan of Jogjakarta; charged with rebuilding Indonesia's stricken economy. Died in 1988.

YANI, Achmad

Indonesian Army commander; murdered with five other leading generals during the 1965 coup attempt.

SARWO EDHY

General commanding the army's crack para-commandos; played a key role in suppressing the coup and the Indonesian Communist Party. Died in 1972.

Preface
to the Third Edition

When I was a foreign correspondent visiting Indonesia in the sixties, I would arrive in Jakarta (formerly Djakarta), take an ancient taxi or *betjak* pedicab, sprinkle my visiting cards around at the homes of generals, cabinet ministers, politicians and old friends I wanted to see, then go back to my hotel and wait for a few days.

There was no point in trying to reach these sources at their offices. In part it was because Indonesia was then so poverty-wracked they were all moonlighting at other jobs, but in part because in Indonesia's easy-going culture, they had their own way of making contact.

Eventually, the invitations would trickle back, sometimes circuitously: drop in for Sunday breakfast with general so-and-so; maybe afternoon tea with the foreign minister; maybe a late night tête-à-tête with someone who did not want to be seen with a foreign journalist.

All this was immensely frustrating to hustle-and-bustle American businessmen, flying in, expecting instant appointments, trying to close deals overnight, then on to the next Asian country.

But it was the Indonesian way, and in it there is perhaps a lesson worth pondering as we observe Indonesia today at something of a crossroad. The lesson for Westerners is patience, and a recognition that things in this mystic land are not always what they seem. Sometimes they are as complex as the wayang, the popular Indonesian shadow play in which puppets are manipulated behind a back-lit curtain.

One of the most populous countries in the world, an island archipelago home to nearly 230 million people, Indonesia is for the most part overlooked in the world scheme of things. Outside Asia, except for occasional eye-catching upheavals and eruptions, it rarely leads the TV network news or makes the front pages of the newspapers.

After declaring independence from the Dutch after World War II, President Sukarno ruled Indonesia for 20 years. He badly mismanaged the country, but as late as the sixties I watched him still exerting his mesmeric control over audiences of many thousands. An abortive communist coup against the military in 1965 led to his downfall, a savage bloodletting, and the installation of army general Suharto. For the next three decades Suharto ruled Indonesia with an iron hand, amid widespread corruption, without realizing either the economic potential or the democratic gains for which many had hoped after Sukarno's exit. Suharto himself was ousted in 1998, was succeeded briefly by two weak presidents, and finally in 2001 by Megawati Sukarnoputri, Sukarno's daughter. Megawati is not the politically messianic figure that her father was, but she is popular and has the support of the Indonesian army which has long played a critical political role in the country.

Thus Indonesia finds itself at a critical turning point.

Will it make up for the lost opportunities of the past, utilizing its rich natural resources for the economic advancement of all its people?

Will a period of political turbulence be followed by stability and steady democratic progress?

Will the Indonesian army, recovering from its tarnished reputation following human rights abuses in East Timor, assume a more conventional and less political role?

Perhaps most critically of all, will Indonesia be taken hostage by the kind of religious extremism which would move it away from the world's mainstream and ally it with the least developed nations of Islam?

With the advent of international terrorism, the existence of pockets of Muslim extremists in parts of Indonesia has captured the attention of the outside world, particularly the United States.

Here cool analysis is needed. Indonesia is the largest Muslim country in the world. But it is not an Arab country. Nor do the majority of Indonesia's Muslims follow Islam with the hard-line fervour that is prevalent in many Arab countries. Nevertheless, the sprouting of a variety of extremist cells and groups, some professing sympathy with Osama bin Laden, is cause for concern.

Foreign aid, particularly American, in arresting this ominous growth should not be intrusive, lest on the one hand it inflames the extremists and on the other hand alienates the moderates in Indonesia. I was one of the few foreign journalists in Indonesia covering the overthrow of Sukarno in 1965–7. His downfall derived from massive student dissatisfaction and demonstrations, coupled with the enthusiasm of the army for purging the country of the Indonesian Communist Party with which he had allied himself. Though the United States was clearly delighted at the Communist Party's eclipse, it was either unable or unwilling to intervene in any substantial way, leaving Indonesians to work an outcome that obviously was not unwelcome.

The same diplomatic deftness is required now. The skill with which Indonesia's rulers tackle their challenges, and the sensitivity with which Indonesia's foreign friends assist, may determine whether Indonesia veers towards the radical, or remains moderate. Indonesia may have been ignored in the past but the stakes now are high. The direction of large, non-Arab, Muslim countries like Indonesia and Pakistan and Turkey versus the more extreme Muslim lands of the Arab Middle East will have a major impact on the future of Islam and its relations with the rest of the world.

I hope this book may have some relevance to your understanding of Indonesia today. As the Far Eastern correspondent of *The Christian Science Monitor*, I spent a good deal of time in Indonesia both before and after the violent upheaval of 1965, and was fortunate to be an eyewitness to events. Much of the information contained herein was gathered during the heat of daily reporting, moving through crowds sometimes friendly and mobs sometimes hostile. Sometimes I could reach key players like President Sukarno, and some of the generals and political and student leaders involved, and some of the time they were incommunicado. My dispatches were daily snapshots of moments of history in the making. Once the country had returned to relative calm, I had many unanswered questions and returned to Indonesia, taking my family with me, to live there for several months seeking the answers to those questions, clarifying who did what when, what their thought processes were at the time, who hid from whom, which generals moved which units where, who were the killers, and who were the killed. This complete story was much longer than could be told in any series of newspaper dispatches and so emerged this book, first published in 1967.

It is the story of a critical chapter in the history of a country for which I have a great affection. I hope it will contribute in some measure to your understanding of Indonesia's challenges and promise today.

JOHN HUGHES
September 2002

Part One: The Coup

1. Beginning of the End

For almost twenty-two years, President Sukarno cast the spell of his political magic across Indonesia. Abroad, he strutted through foreign lands a figure of political consequence, if also of controversy. Leader of the fifth most populous country in the world, he was watched warily from Washington, London, Moscow, Peking.

But in the Indonesian capital of Djakarta on a hot, soggy day in March of 1967, the spell was finally broken, the magic ran out, the legend was shattered. Sukarno was stripped, by the representatives of his people, of the last vestiges of his authority. Instead, a 46-year-old army general named Suharto was sworn in as Acting President.

Perhaps time would anyway have caught up with Sukarno. But the specific cause of his downfall was the drama of one single night, the abortive coup of September 30/October 1, 1965. Sukarno's actions during the coup and his reactions after it were his undoing. For eighteen months more, Sukarno clung to office, but his power was steadily whittled away, his influence eroded, his image discredited. The coup triggered a sequence of events from which he never recovered.

For a night destined to change the course of history, September 30, 1965, began innocently enough.

As the day's heat ebbed, a misty blue twilight settled over the Indonesian capital of Djakarta in brief, mellow transition before the onrush of tropical darkness. The moon that rose with nightfall was peaceful, pale, and full. As the day's gasoline fumes faded, the liberated evening air took on a gentle fragrance peculiar to Indonesia, an exotic blend of jasmine, frangipani, and the smoke from locally made cigarettes spiced with cloves.

In the harsh light of tropical day, Djakarta is not one of Indonesia's most captivating cities. Bleached and dusty under the equatorial sun, it simmers in a swampy coastal plain, an unworthy introduction to the lush, eye-shocking beauty of much of the rest of the country.

When the Dutch ruled Indonesia they tried to mold the capital in the image of some cool little town left reluctantly behind in the European Lowlands. They cut canals through the city's heart and shaded them with trees. Then, overlooking them, they set sturdy little houses, prim, gabled and tight- windowed, whose occupants worked hard and loyally for their government masters and the big trading and shipping companies back in Amsterdam, Rotterdam, and The Hague.

Perhaps for a while, with their doughty European industry, the Dutch did succeed in impressing an artificial air of order on Batavia, as the capital then was called. But since Indonesia wrested control of its destiny from the Dutch, all this has been allowed to run down, through a combination of cheerful tropical casualness, the ravages of the climate, and outright economic neglect. Thus there is an air of peeling seediness about buildings once quaint. Public lawns have become small jungles. And while for some the canals have become a public bathhouse, for others they are sewers.

President Sukarno, a man of grand ambitions and a compulsive artistic tinkerer, himself frequently exploded in impatience at some of the capital's more tawdry aspects. In twenty years of rule he sought to give Djakarta a face-lifting. But the result has a curiously half-finished air about it, for Sukarno's eye was drawn to the spectacular. He had little interest in, or patience with, the humdrum details of steady, long-term development plans. His option, therefore, was for a series of one shot spectaculars—buildings, monuments, palaces—intended as eye-catching diversions from an economy grinding steadily downhill.

Thus Djakarta is left with a face irregular and disjointed. An impressive new government building is bordered by shanties and approached via a cratered cart-track. There are fountains, but no sidewalks. To the chagrin of Indonesian officials, the visiting photographers from *Life* and *Paris-Match* monotonously shoot such buildings as the luxurious Hotel Indonesia, designed to impress foreign visitors, amid a frieze of tawdry surrounding shacks.

And the statues favored by President Sukarno, strident as they break their chains and cry death to the imperialists atop their austere concrete blocks, all in the style of Soviet realism, are sadly alien to so cultured and artistic a people as the Indonesians.

But with the coming of dusk, the harshness of both monuments and Djakarta itself seems to fade. Floodlit in their reflecting pools, the statues take on softer tones. Around the fountains, people gather to sniff the freshness off the tumbling water.

The city begins to unclog and untangle from its daylong traffic snarl. According to the governor of Djakarta, eighty percent of the city's buses are off the streets for lack of spare parts. Those remaining are groaning, overloaded testimony both to the skill of their makers and the ingenuity of Indonesian mechanics who keep them stuttering along on bits of bent wire, string, and metal salvaged from beer cans. But by nightfall this tatterdemalion old fleet has coughed, spluttered, and belched its way homeward, laden to the long-suffering gills with Indonesian workers clutching their bags of rice, issued as vital supplement to their salaries.

Then the streets are left to the tattered *betjak*-drivers, the lean, hard-muscled men who hunt the streets anxiously with their bicycle-driven rickshaws for the fares that will buy them their evening meal of rice.

And as the *betjak*-drivers clang their deep gongs, and the little kerosene lanterns flare up on the street-corner stalls under the gardenia trees, Djakarta at night seems touched a little by the magic of Java, the strange and mystical island on which it is set, the heartland of the 3,000-mile-long Indonesian archipelago.

Such a night was it on September 30, 1965, as the city began to take what seemed to be its innocent ease.

At his high-ceilinged official residence on Taman Suropati, a square in the exclusive diplomatic quarter of Djakarta, American Ambassador Marshall Green prepared that evening for a diplomatic party of unusual character. It was given by the New Zealand minister, who entertained some seventy-five diplomatic guests from 7:30 P.M. till the early hours of next morning with traditional Indonesian music. It was performed by a *gamelan* orchestra of gongs and xylophones in a nearby *kampong*, or village community. The entertainment included a traditional Indonesian *wayang*, or shadow play. Ambassador Green, newly arrived in Indonesia, had been finding his job tough going, at least insofar as his relations were concerned with President Sukarno, the dominant political figure in the country. The new Ambassador, a brisk, red-haired career officer and Far Eastern specialist, had succeeded Howard Jones, a gentle, silver-haired diplomat who had been Ambassador to Indonesia for seven years, during which time he had come closer to President Sukarno than any other foreigner.

Despite the friendship, the last months of Mr. Jones's tenure had been marred by an ugly and mounting anti-American crusade in Indonesia, including a string of savage attacks on American buildings and property certainly permitted by President Sukarno, if not actually ordered by him.

Mr. Green, it was widely speculated by the diplomatic

correspondents, was the apostle of the State Department's new tough line toward Indonesia. There would be no diplomatic break unless it became impossible to avoid, but, it was said, Mr. Green was under orders to stand no nonsense from Sukarno.

Perhaps predictably in the face of these rumors, President Sukarno took an instant dislike to the new American Ambassador, or at least declared to those around him that he had.

From the day he presented his credentials, Mr. Green was met with abusive demonstrations. He was compelled as part of his first duties in Indonesia to lodge a series of protests against new anti-American incidents.

Now, with another day's work behind him, the Ambassador was preparing to relax at the evening's coming party. There is no clue that either he or any other American official had the slightest hint of the drama about to begin elsewhere in the capital that night. One embassy official recalls that at a staff meeting the previous day, someone had mentioned that truckloads of young Indonesians wearing empty pistol belts had been passing his house in the morning and returning at night. The road past his house led to Halim air base, on the outskirts of the city, and as became evident later, the youths were young Communists spending their days at Halim for military training and indoctrination. At the time, the incident was dismissed as vaguely puzzling, and there is no evidence that the American Embassy had any foreknowledge of what was to come.

While half the diplomatic corps spent the night listening to soothing *gamelan* music, other diplomats were at a jovial reception following the wedding of the counselor at the Italian Embassy to a pretty secretary from the Dutch Embassy. For the isolated little Western community it was a lively event. One of the guests invited to the reception was Sara Ratna Dewi, a Japanese beauty who had become one of Moslem President Sukarno's several wives. The bride recalls that Dewi arrived late, about nine o'clock, thus holding up the cake-cutting ceremony. Afterwards many of the party went on to the Nirwana nightclub, atop the Hotel Indonesia, to continue celebrating.

Dewi was among them, her dinner partner being the Iranian Ambassador.

Meanwhile, at the rambling white presidential palace that dominates Merdeka (Freedom) Square, a huge, open green space in the center of the city, there was the bustle that traditionally preceded President Sukarno's departure. In the elegant reception rooms the crystal chandeliers were ablaze. Aides scurried across the marble floors, dotted with Oriental rugs and groupings of gilt tables and chairs. In his private quarters, Sukarno was shrugging into his custom-made uniform jacket, ready to leave for a political meeting in the suburb of Senajan. Waiting at the steps beyond one of the palace's wide, high verandas was his big black Chrysler. Chatting quietly against the backdrop of the immaculate lawns, lily ponds, and statues in the palace grounds were the white-helmeted and gauntleted police motorcycle outriders, ready to roar out in front of his car with sirens screaming. The jeep-loads of heavily armed men from the crack presidential bodyguard, the Tjakrabirawa regiment, had taken up their customary protective positions in the presidential convoy.

Other leading Indonesian figures were variously dispersed. The President's right-hand man, Subandrio, deputy premier and foreign minister, was on a speaking tour in remote northern Sumatra, having left two days previously. A week before that, another deputy premier, Chairul Saleh, had departed the capital with a 45-man delegation en route to Peking, there to celebrate China's national day on October 1.

The army commander, Lieutenant General Achmad Yani, recently returned from an inspection tour of Timor and eastern

Indonesia, played golf, to which he had become addicted, in the capital during the afternoon. Much of the evening he spent with Major General Basuchi Rachmat, who had been given permission to fly in from his command in East Java to report to General Yani on Communist disturbances and agitation in his area. General Yani told the visiting General that he had been summoned to report to President Sukarno at his weekend palace at Bogor, 40 miles south of Djakarta, at eight o'clock the next morning. He warned Basuchi Rachmat to accompany him in order to retell his story of Communist intrigue to the President himself.

Another general, named Suharto, then commander of KOSTRAD, the army's strategic reserve, and relatively obscure, spent part of his day inspecting troops who had been moved in from Central and East Java. Quartered at the Senajan sports complex, the huge project built for the Indonesians by the Soviet Union, they were practicing for a big army march-past to be held the following week on Armed Forces Day, October 5.

Yet though the evening of September 30 began quietly enough, the calm was a deceptive one. For over the preceding weeks and months, political tension in Indonesia had been mounting.

A year previously, during his Independence Day speech on August 17, 1964, President Sukarno had lashed out publicly for the first time against the United States. The speech was the starting signal for a virulent anti-American campaign in the months following. American oil companies were threatened, American movies banned, American libraries and buildings attacked, and the American flag was ripped to shreds on all too many occasions. American correspondents were barred. American aid dribbled to a halt; the United States Information Service was virtually run out of town; the Peace Corps was invited to leave. The dwindling number of Americans left in the country found themselves in lonely political quarantine. Old friends stopped calling, and to most Indonesians,

American connections were clearly an embarrassment, sometimes even a danger. Communist trade unions saw to it that mail deliveries to American homes were stopped, and telephone and water and electricity supplies were cut off. Along Djakarta's main boulevards, huge propaganda posters were set up, usually depicting burly Indonesians ramming sharpened stakes down the gullet of a cringing Uncle Sam.

Already, of course, President Sukarno had thrust Indonesia into a hysterical anti-British campaign, ostensibly because of Britain's backing of the concept of a new Malaysian federation, to which Sukarno himself was opposed.

But the new intensity of the anti-Western campaign that developed in 1964 and 1965 was clearly much more than presidential pique at one or two Western countries. As is now obvious in retrospect, it was part of a headlong Indonesian slide toward the left, both at home and in foreign policy.

At loggerheads with the United States and Britain, hopelessly in debt to the Soviets, and a figure of increasing embarrassment to the Afro-Asian neutrals, Sukarno turned more and more, either from necessity or from conviction, to the militant world of Communist China and its cohorts.

Increasingly he talked of a Peking-Djakarta axis and huddled with Chinese leaders. To Chinese acclaim, he crooked his finger and summoned home the Indonesian delegation to the United Nations, abruptly terminating his country's membership.

Into his speeches there crept more and more frequently references to "turning the steering wheel" of his country, and "swinging the helm over." Though he spurned the representatives of the West, the Chinese Communist Ambassador to Djakarta, Yao Chung-ming, was a frequent and welcome visitor to the presidential palace. For advice on foreign affairs, Sukarno leaned more and more on Dipa Nusantara Aidit, leader of the Indonesian Communist

Party, which had thrown its weight, in the Sino-Soviet wrangle, firmly behind Communist China. For help in drafting his 1965 Independence Day speech he summoned home from abroad Njoto, another Communist Party leader. And though this was revealed only long afterwards, Sukarno in mid-September sent his Communist-sympathizing air force chief, Omar Dhani, on a secret mission to Peking. One of the objects was to clinch a deal under which the Chinese Communists would deliver 100,000 small arms to Indonesia, through unorthodox channels of the President's choosing and without informing the army or regular defense ministry officials.

Also in September he left little doubt about the direction of his sentiments when he cabled North Vietnam's President Ho Chi Minh expressing confidence that the North Vietnamese and Vietcong would record still greater successes in "the patriotic self-defense struggle against recent provocations by the United States imperialists."

In this favorable climate, the Indonesian Communist Party, already third largest in the world (after the Soviet Union's and China's), blossomed and preened itself in the belief that power, or at least a substantial share of it, might now be near.

Confidently and militantly the Communists pressed their cause, assuming greater influence and demanding, and often getting, the hobbling of their political opponents. But one major obstacle remained: the army. Though infiltrated by the Communists, its senior officers were largely anti-Communist.

For years the army and the Communists had circled each other warily and with mutual distrust. The two most powerful forces in the country, they had traditionally balanced each other, while Sukarno, the master manipulator, remained supreme above.

But now the Communists were impatient with this standoff. They wanted guns, specifically to arm the peasantry as a so-called "fifth force," in addition to the army, the navy, the air force, and the police. Also they sought to introduce into the army a system of political commissars. From the President they got support. Indeed, in his speech on August 17 that year he indicated that the fifth force was his own brainchild. He deplored some of the negative reaction to the idea that had come from army leaders. But, he said, "the facts are that the Necolim [a word coined to describe the neo-colonialists and imperialists, or in other words, the West] are leveling their sword points and gun barrels at us. The defense of the state demands a maximum effort from us all, while according to our constitution 'Every citizen shall have the right and the duty to participate in the defense of the state.' After an even more thorough consideration of this question, I will take a decision on this matter in my capacity as Supreme Commander of the Armed Forces."

Although the army could not know it, soon after this speech President Sukarno was dispatching his air force commander on that secret mission to Peking to tie up delivery of 100,000 small arms. It is difficult to believe those arms could have been intended for anything else but equipping the fifth force which Sukarno favored but which the army opposed.

The army, however, was under no illusions as to the character of the peasant militia the Communists and Sukarno appeared so anxious to arm. In army eyes, the fifth force would be a Communist one, destroying the old balance concept, ending the army's influence, and putting the country within Communism's grasp.

Throughout September political tension rose. The army generals' suspicions were hardly allayed by a series of fiery speeches demanding the crushing of the "capitalist bureaucrats." The phrase deceived nobody. In the tortuous phraseology of Indonesian politics, everybody knew that it meant the army generals blocking the Communists', and apparently the President's, way.

During the week prior to September 30 for example, the Communist-backing Front Pemuda demanded mass action against "corruptors, capitalist bureaucrats, pilferers, and charlatans." They should be "dragged to the gallows," or "shot in public," said a Front statement.

Communist Party leader Aidit himself said publicly that the counterrevolutionaries were at bay, but he warned that they might therefore resort to desperate actions. They were making "jumps into the dark by acts of terrorism," he charged. And then he counseled, 'The progressive revolutionary people must be ready at any time to respond with matching actions to barbarous acts."

Not only the Communists pounded away at the theme. In his August 17 speech, President Sukarno pointed a not-too-subtle finger at the generals. "Those who were progressive yesterday," he said, "are possibly retrogressive, anti-progressive today. Those who were revolutionary yesterday are possibly counterrevolutionary today. Those who were radical yesterday are possibly soft and resistless [sic] today. Even if you were formerly a bald-headed general in 1945 [during Indonesia's fight for independence], if you split the revolutionary national unity today, if you are an enemy of the main pillars of the revolution today, then you have become a force of reaction."

According to the Communist Party newspaper *Harian Rakjat*, the President followed this up with a speech on September 29 to the Communist university students' association in which he said, "Earlier there were persons who were revolutionary, but now they have become counterrevolutionary. As explained in my August 17 speech, there were loyal generals, but now they have become protectors of counterrevolutionary elements. These we must crush."

Meanwhile Dr. Subandrio during September could hardly stay away from the anti-capitalist, bureaucrat theme. On September 2 he told an audience in Menado, "If the leadership in Indonesia were corruptors, the people have the right to take over from them. Power must be in the hands of the people, and it is you who will determine the destruction of the corruptors."

On September 9 he urged a student gathering to "smash the exploiters and capitalist bureaucrats, annihilate the pilferers of the state's wealth." On September 14 he told the national council of SOBSI, the Communist trade union organization, that the present stage of the revolution demanded fighters not only against Necolim, but also against the capitalist bureaucrats. Then he confided, "The eyes and ears of Indonesians at present are sharper than those of the government."

A week later he said in yet another speech that the Indonesian revolution had given birth to a lot of heroes, but that a lot of these had now turned into traitors. These heroes-turned-traitors had not been strong enough to face the trials of the present era.

And again a few days later, at the opening session of the Immigration Directorate, Dr. Subandrio said, "The people no longer want empty cries and big talk. A great number of heroes present during the physical revolution have collapsed during the present stage."

To all this political tension was added a further unsettling factor: the uncertainty of the President's health. Sukarno's kidneys had for months featured in the political dispatches of various embassies in Djakarta to their foreign ministries. That he had kidney trouble there was no disputing, but just how serious it was, and thus how much of a political factor, nobody could be sure. Some observers, noting his full program and active demeanor, dismissed his ailment. Others argued that it could take a sudden and serious turn.

The political experts settled down to watch carefully and record every presidential cough, splutter, and hiccup that might be of significance. Sukarno himself, undoubtedly aware of the stir his health was causing, did little to dampen the speculation. On several occasions, while addressing large rallies, he paused and ostentatiously slipped off his shoes because, as he confided to the crowds, his "feet were hurting." The observers scuttled off to the medical reference books, there to discover that one of the symptoms of kidney disease is swollen feet—a fact duly telegraphed to their foreign ministries.

But like many Indonesians, Sukarno had long had a penchant for slipping off his shoes. Once, when he did so at a dinner party given by an Asian ambassador in Djakarta, he confided absolutely seriously to the fascinated guests that it was "to let the electricity out of my body."

Serious or not, however, his illness had become a political factor and a major topic for discussion in Djakarta. To treat it he had imported a team of specialists in acupuncture, the practice of sticking sharp needles into selected parts of the body, from Communist China. It is widely believed that the Chinese doctors reported to Communist Party leader Aidit on the state of the President's health. There is no reason to doubt this. If they reported that Sukarno's illness was serious, and that he could die soon, this was obviously information of tremendous significance that might have impelled the Indonesian party to emergency action.

Communist leaders captured after the abortive coup admit that the President's health was discussed at central committee meetings of the party. But of course, almost every other group of political significance in Indonesia was discussing it, too. The army kept careful note of developments. Air force chief Omar Dhani had his special informer check on new reports early in August that Sukarno had taken a turn for the worse and canceled several engagements.

It is hardly surprising that this unsettled atmosphere spawned whispers of coups and plots. The army distrusted the Communists; the Communists distrusted the army. With the President in uncertain health it is inconceivable that both of them did not have contingency plans for moving against each other in the event of his death.

Privately the Communists began to spread the word that a "Council of Generals" was plotting against the President. Aidit reported this to Sukarno. Sukarno challenged army commander Yani about it. But Yani explained calmly that it was a group concerned only with promotions of colonels to the ranks of the generals. Nevertheless, there are some indications that Communist leaders were tense and nervous as September drew on, some of them moving around the city and sleeping at different houses on different nights.

For its part, there is abundant evidence that the army was warned of a Communist coup against it. Long after the events of 1965, various generals in separate interviews assured me they had warned General Yani. One said Yani replied with the statement, "That's old news you're telling me—we've heard it many times before." Another general, Brigadier General Sugandhi, now on the staff of defense headquarters, says he was approached about the Council of Generals by an old school friend, Sudisman, who had become a Communist and risen to membership in the party's politburo. Sugandhi also says he talked to Yani and warned him that the Communists were using the generals' "Council" as a pretext for plotting a coup. But Yani, he says, told him, "That's Communist psychological warfare," and waved the warning aside.

It may be, of course, that some generals so long after the event have come to believe they were more prescient at the time than they really were. Nevertheless, it is confirmed that in the week before the abortive coup, Major General S. Parman, the army's intelligence chief, and one of the generals to be murdered, received fresh reports of impending Communist action, but discounted them.

Thus in this incredibly contradictory atmosphere of both tension and complacency began the night of September 30.

2. Treachery at Halim

It was all tension that evening at Halim air base, on the southern outskirts of Djakarta. A rambling complex of gaunt gray hangars, maintenance shops, barracks, and air force houses, Halim had been chosen as the command post and starting point for the coup.

For weeks the plotters had been planning their murderous business. Now Halim was a-bustle with their last preparations. The point of no return was fast approaching.

In one hangar just off the main air base taxiway stood President Sukarno's personal aircraft, a big, gleaming Lockheed Jet-Star that had cost the country $2,000,000. Secured for the moment, it was nevertheless ready, as always, to fly at short notice. And as always, it was kept here at Halim, under the guard of the Indonesian Air Force, rather than at Djakarta's commercial airport, Kemayoran.

In the clear moonlight the main runway, free of aircraft, cut a silver-gray swath through the surrounding darkness out to the air base perimeter. But silhouetted eerily against the blue blur of the landing lights were the bulky figures of armed troops assembling, and the square, squat shapes of their trucks.

At about 10 P.M. a final column of trucks, full of troops, rolled in from Djakarta. There was the clink of metal and weapons, the subdued bark of urgent orders, the confused expletives as officers sought their rendezvous points in the dark on an air base strange to most of them.

A little after this, a tan military jeep with a canvas roof came skidding down the road from Djakarta and onto the air base. It brought the two main figures in the actual carrying out of the coup, Lieutenant Colonel Untung and Brigadier General Mustafa Sjarif Supardjo.

Untung was a chunky man, well-built for an Indonesian, with a square face and bushy brows. He commanded the honor battalion of the Tjakrabirawa, the elite presidential guard to which even an ordinary soldier could only be appointed after proven toughness and actual combat experience. Born in Central Java, he was brought up in humble circumstances in Tegal, a town on the shores of the Java Sea.

Untung was a longtime professional soldier, with only one serious blotch on his record. According to his military colleagues, he had fought briefly with the Communists when they staged an abortive revolt in the East Javanese town of Madiun back in 1948. But in the years following he had proved himself an officer of courage and apparent loyalty.

He was the first officer parachuted into the tangled green jungles of West New Guinea when Sukarno launched a military campaign in 1962 to wrest it from the Dutch. Something of a hero as a result, he was boosted from captain to lieutenant colonel, to the disgruntlement of some of his envious fellow officers. Appointed to the presidential guard in Djakarta, a duty with which went all kind of perquisites, Untung soon acquired a house on a fashionable street in the capital's diplomatic quarter and, according to acquaintances, began to enjoy some of the affluence denied him in his youth.

As a military man, Untung was well known to a number of senior officers. General Yani, who would be killed by Untung's own men later that night, had been Untung's commanding officer when they served in a tough raider unit. Brigadier General (then Colonel) Sarwo Edhy, commander of the crack RPKAD (Resimen Pasukan Komando Angkatan Darat) para-commando regiment, which played a key role in crushing the coup, had earlier been responsible for Untung's training as a paratrooper. Brigadier General Kemal Idris, who moved swiftly to smash the coup in northern Sumatra, was at Untung's wedding. Of the three, the two surviving generals remember Untung as a good soldier and good commander.

A battalion commander of the palace guard, Untung had been given an additional assignment. He was in charge of arrangements for the big Armed Forces Day parade scheduled for October 5. This year was the army's 20th anniversary, and Sukarno had ordered that it be celebrated with a special show. Hence the movement to Djakarta of units from Central and East Java to make up a full infantry combat brigade for the parade—three battalions of infantry, one of tanks, one of armored cars, a mortar battalion, an antiaircraft battalion, and an engineers' unit.

Some of the unit commanders are said to have queried the line of march proposed by Untung. They are said to have protested because Untung planned to space palace guard units at regular intervals between army units throughout the length of the column. It is possible, as some observers suggest, that there were sinister motives behind such placing. For the Tjakrabirawa, or palace guard, units would in each case be able to cover with their weapons the army units ahead of them. One Indonesian Army source, however, believes that the army commanders were unhappy with Untung's proposed lineup for much more mundane reasons. Some of their men had only recently returned from service in remote Kalimantan and the pocket border war still going on at that time with Malaysia. They were well primed on jungle warfare techniques, but ragged in their marching and rusty on their parade-ground drill. Their commanders were anxious lest their jungle veterans make a sorry spectacle alongside the snappy palace guards, who had ample time for drill and spit-and-polish.

After the coup, when he was captured and brought to trial, Untung denied that he had been a member of the Communist Party and persisted in his story that he had acted on his own initiative. Now, so long after the event, there are a few of his military colleagues who claim they suspected Untung of Communist leanings. But again, it is difficult to know how prescient they really were at the time, and how much of their suspicion developed later, with hindsight. There is, of course, the question of his involvement at Madiun. There are acquaintances of his who say he displayed leftist views. Nobody can be sure what contacts he may have had over the years with Communists and the party itself. But if Untung was a clandestine member of the Indonesian Communist Party, he kept the secret well.

There is far less mystery about the political views of the second man who arrived with Untung by jeep at Halim that evening—Brigadier General Supardjo. A former regimental commander of the Siliwangi division, stationed in West Java, Supardjo had been in trouble with his commanders for pro-Communist sympathies and actions. So he had been sent off to Kalimantan, far from the capital and the levers of power, to take part in operations against British and Malaysian troops along the Borneo border between Malaysian and Indonesian territory. Based at Menggaian, in west Kalimantan, he was in charge of the Fourth Combat Command of KOSTRAD, the army's strategic reserve. It was there at his post in Borneo, a savagely beautiful land of endless, forested jungle, laced by rivers that come down ten feet high in angry, chocolate flood in the time of the monsoon, that General Supardjo should have been on September 30.

Instead, he had left his post and flown to Djakarta on September 28. The KOSTRAD commander, General Suharto, had no knowledge of this. Ostensibly, Supardjo returned to the capital because his child was ill. He had indeed received a cable to this effect from his wife, advising him to come home. But at Supardjo's trial in 1967, an ex-Communist official testified that the contents of the cable were in fact a code agreed upon earlier between Supardjo and Communist participants in the coup. The real reason for his return was that he was to play a commanding role in the plot.

Besides his apparent enthusiasm for the Communists, Supardjo may have held a personal grudge against army commander Yani, one of the plotters' principal victims. Some of Supardjo's military colleagues say he was resentful over the slow pace of his promotion. He probably bridled over his assignment to the jungles of Kalimantan. There is one story that has General Yani, on an inspection tour of Kalimantan, dressing down Supardjo angrily over troop conditions and unit finances, the quarrel ending with Yani slapping Supardjo's face. But this may be merely a fanciful, if colorful, story.

What is a fact, however, is that Supardjo tried to get units of General Sarwo Edhy's tough RPKAD para-commandos, renowned for their opposition to the Communists, shipped away from the Djakarta area at just about the time the coup was to take place. General Sarwo Edhy told me later that Supardjo asked in August for RPKAD reinforcements to be sent to Kalimantan. The date for their departure was set: October 1, the day the plotters launched their coup. As soon as Sarwo Edhy got word of the coup attempt, he canceled his men's sailing orders. They never did go to Kalimantan.

Months before the coup, Supardjo had talked to Omar Dhani, commander of the Indonesian Air Force, about restlessness in the army's officer corps. Supardjo had suggested that he might have to lead some action against the army's top generals.

Now when he flew into Djakarta on September 28, Supardjo went into a secret huddle with Dhani. It is difficult to believe that Supardjo did not brief Dhani on the broad outline, if not the details, of the coup action shortly to take place.

At nine o'clock the following morning, September 29, Dhani bustled along to the presidential palace and saw Sukarno in his bedroom. According to his own version, Dhani expressed concern about the concentration of some 20,000 troops in the capital for the upcoming Armed Forces Day celebration on October 5. He said he was fearful for Sukarno's safety. Sukarno, said Dhani at his own trial later, took it all quietly. He seemed to "know all about the subject." He told Dhani to report to him again on October 3, bringing Supardjo with him. The reporting time was to be 10 A.M., the place the presidential weekend palace at Bogor, 40 miles away from Djakarta.

General Suharto, the KOSTRAD commander soon to be catapulted into prominence, gave his own account long after the coup of this conversation between Dhani and Sukarno, based on the army's investigation. The Suharto account agrees substantially with Dhani's, but adds one item, namely, that Dhani informed the President that Supardjo's men were discontented with the army leadership and could no longer be controlled.

In either case, however, Sukarno was well aware of Supardjo's presence in Djakarta, even though it had been kept secret from General Suharto. And though there is contradictory information about this, there is a suggestion that Supardjo himself saw Sukarno on September 29.

In Dhani the coup plotters found an invaluable ally. Slim, handsome, sporting a clipped mustache, wearing his cap at a dashing angle, Dhani looked more the matinée idol than air force chief. He was also vain, ambitious, pliable. He had joined the air force in 1950, at the age of 20, after several years' work on a plantation, at the government radio station, in the ministry of information, and then in a bank. When Sukarno induced the Soviets to give him jet fighters and bombers, Dhani prospered with the rapid expansion of the air force.

Susceptible to flattery, he did not lack for it from the Communists. There are grounds for believing some of them encouraged Dhani in a Walter Mitty-like dream of succeeding Sukarno after the latter's death. It was an impossible dream, which the Communists, of course, had no intention of letting come true. But it made of Dhani a highly co-operative figure. At the air force staff and command college he introduced Marxism as a subject for study. Then he brought in top Communist Party officials to lecture on it.

Increasingly the air force became infected by the Communist virus.

When the Communists sought secretly to train a force of their own shock troops, a sort of forerunner to the "fifth force" peasant militia for which they were agitating, the air base at Halim was an obvious training site for them.

The trainees were drawn from the Pemuda Rakjat, the Communist youth organization, and Gerwani, the Communist women's organization. Their training was under the direct command of Major Sujono, commander of the air base security regiment, and an enthusiastic collaborator with the Communists. For a training area he selected a swampy region out on the air base's extended perimeter, a couple of miles from the runways and control tower. It was soon to become notorious. Its name was Lubang Buaja—Crocodile Hole.

There the Communists set up their tented training camp. There air force officers gave them weapons training and drill. There by their own instructors they were given political indoctrination. One Communist leader captured later, Njono, the Djakarta area party chief, admitted in his testimony that he had ordered Sukatno, the Pemuda Rakjat general secretary, to assemble 10,000 trained members of the youth organization at Lubang Buaja for military action against the "Council of Generals." Certainly, from interviews I held later with captured Pemuda Rakjat and Gerwani members, it is clear that they had been undergoing military training at Lubang Buaja, in rotating batches, at least since July of 1965.

At his own trial later, Dhani displayed a convenient vagueness about the training. He said he thought it had all been part of the air base defense program. He admitted he had heard that mainly Communists were undergoing training, but he said he had issued orders for the training to be balanced between Communists and other nationalist and religious groups.

In fact, it was not. Under Major Sujono's watchful eye, what went on was a program to teach Communist youths and women how to kill, with unquestioning obedience to their Communist superiors.

If Dhani did not know exactly what was in the wind, he must have been incredibly obtuse. Long before, Supardjo had confided to him his intentions. Now Supardjo had secretly left his post in Kalimantan and was in Djakarta. Dhani himself had had an anxious consultation with President Sukarno.

But by four o'clock on the afternoon of September 30, Dhani had been given the full story. His intelligence chief, Lieutenant Colonel Heru Atmodjo, reported to him that the Supardjo group would stage its action the following day. One piece of information was missing—the exact hour when the coup would begin.

Pent-up and excited, Dhani summoned his senior air force officers to a briefing that evening at his home in the Djakarta suburb of Kebajoran. Now Heru had the final details and reported them: who would move, against whom, and when. From Major Sujono, Heru brought a request for authority to use air force weapons and vehicles. After consultation, the meeting decided the request "could not be prevented." Thus the air force leaders were privy to the coup plan and gave their tacit agreement for the use of air force weapons and equipment. For safety's sake, Dhani decided not to sleep at his own house. About midnight he left, in a small Japanese car, for Halim. Dhani himself took the wheel; his driver sat in the back, his adjutant at his side.

During the weeks when Supardjo had been in Kalimantan, anxiously awaiting the signal to come to Djakarta, Untung had been engaged in a series of meetings, organizing the details of their coup. According to army interrogation reports and evidence emerging at the trials of the various participants later, the plotters met at intervals of two or three days throughout the month of September. The group was a tight little one, usually four or five in number, occasionally expanded to seven. Regularly in attendance were Untung and Colonel A. Latief, commander of the First Infantry

Brigade of the Djakarta garrison, who was deep in the plot. Also present were Major Sujono, the air force officer from Halim, and two representatives from the Communist Party, Supono and "Sjam."

The mysterious "Sjam," it is now believed, was actually Tjugito, a member of the central committee of the Indonesian Communist Party. Certainly, according to the interrogation reports, he purported to speak with authority for the Communist party.

Some of the first meetings were held at the house of a Captain Wahjudi on Djalan [street] Sindanglaja. Later the plotters moved to Colonel Latief's house, and later still to a house selected by Sjam on Djalan Djati Buntu.

To a neighbour or innocent bystander it must have seemed ordinary enough—four or five friends, several of them military men, gathering of an evening to chat and sip Java tea, perhaps behind doors carefully closed to keep out the insects and mosquitoes. But behind those doors the plotters were agreed from the beginning on one thing: the murder of the army's leading generals.

In their interrogation statements after capture, Untung and Latief persisted in saying that they feared a putsch by the "Council of Generals" and their action was designed to forestall it. Besides neutralizing the generals, they realized, they had to seize vital installations in the capital.

Initially the forces available to them seemed slender enough. Untung had his battalion of palace guards, and Latief could promise some units from the Djakarta garrison. Early in September, Sujono reported that between 3,000 and 4,000 Communist volunteers had been trained at Lubang Buaja, but he would need another week or ten days before they could be ready for action.

But there was anxious discussion about the strength of forces loyal to the army leadership, and in the Djakarta area. Latief calculated that with the RPKAD para-commandos stationed some miles outside the city, and KOSTRAD units, and other forces, there would be some 60,000 troops around or within relatively easy reach of the capital.

However, by mid-September, Sjam reported good news for the plotters: two Communist-infiltrated battalions from Central and East Java—the 454th Paratroop Battalion from the Diponegoro division, and the 530th from the Brawidjaja division—would be coming to the capital for the big Armed Forces Day parade October 5. Their officers could be counted on to pledge their battalions to the coup movement.

There was also talk about the availability of a cavalry unit of 30 tanks and armored cars, from the headquarters of the Siliwangi division at Bandung, some four hours' drive from Djakarta. Untung immediately sensed the importance of those tanks. His concern that they should be definitely committed to the coup forces ran like a thread through later meetings. Again and again he pressed for news of them and a pledge that he could count on them.

By September 23, the plotters had word that Supardjo would soon be arriving from Kalimantan. By September 25, the commanders of the subverted battalions from Central and East Java were in town. If Untung's interrogation report is to be believed, Sjam was by this stage pressing for the coup to begin on September 29. Untung himself was more hesitant; still he worried about those vital tanks from Bandung. But time was running out, and clearly the plotters would have to make their move while the two Java battalions available to them were in the capital for Armed Forces Day.

On September 29, Untung met emissaries from the two visiting Java battalions and with them checked preparations at Lubang Buaja itself. Late that night, the plotters gathered for a final meeting. This time it was the largest gathering they had held—there were nine people present, including two women, presumably representatives of Gerwani (the Communist women's organization).

And this time General Supardjo joined the group.

Now the decision was taken. D-day would be October 1. H-hour: 4 A.M.

So it was that when Untung and Supardjo roared down the road to Halim in their jeep, late on the night of September 30, they had at their disposal Untung's battalion of palace guards, the 454th and 530th Paratroop Battalions in town from Central and East Java (each about 1,000 men strong), some units of air force troops provided by Major Sujono, and several thousand Pemuda Rakjat members trained and armed by the air force. The vital tank unit never did appear.

The air force and Pemuda Rakjat units were already at Halim. The Tjakrabirawa and army battalions had rumbled in for assembly shortly before Untung and Supardjo themselves arrived.

Now, as midnight neared, officers ran through the final checklists in an atmosphere of nervous tension. The troops were divided into three sections. The sections were given code names derived from characters in the *wayang*, or traditional Indonesian shadow play.

First there was the Pasupati force, made up of Untung's Tjakrabirawa palace guards and Pemuda Rakjat trainees. Theirs was the grimmest assignment: the seizing of the army's top generals. The Pasupati force was under the command of one of Untung's Tjakrabirawa officers, Lieutenant Dul Arief.

Next was the Bimasakti force, mainly the two visiting battalions from Central and East Java. These troops were assigned to surround the presidential palace on Merdeka Square and seize and hold the radio station, on another side of the square, and the telecommunications building, on yet a third side of the square.

Finally came a reserve force, called Gatot Katja, under the command of an air force captain called Captain Gatot. This, made up of air force units and Pemuda Rakjat battalions, was to be held in reserve at Halim.

As the time for action neared, officers were briefed on a system of passwords and code signals. The password was to be "Ampera," the "people's burden." The rejoinder was to be "Takari," the word coined by President Sukarno to describe his August 17 speech that year titled "A Year of Self-Reliance." By car, the nighttime challenge would be headlights flicked three times; the reply, headlights flicked four times. In daylight, the driver of a car or truck involved in the coup would sound his hooter twice, and the response would be three hoots.

On foot, coup soldiers would check the allegiance of approaching troops with a signal raising the left arm over the head, weapon clasped in the hand. The correct replying signal would be a right arm raised above the head, with weapon.

The crux of the operation would be the successful action against the army generals by the Pasupati force. Its leader, Lieutenant Arief, had earlier been given photographs of eight generals he was to capture, dead or alive. The main target was the minister of defense, General Abdul Haris Nasution, with the army commander, Lieutenant General Achmad Yani, almost as important. Others on the original list were Major General S. Parman, the army's intelligence chief, Major General Suprapto, Major General Harjono, Brigadier General Pandjaitan, Brigadier General Sutojo Siswomihardjo, and Brigadier General Achmed Sukendro. (The name of Major General Suharto, the KOSTRAD commander, was not on the list.) When Lieutenant Arief came to his final briefing, he was confused to find that General Sukendro's name had been removed from his list of victims. Undoubtedly this was because Sukendro was out of the country and in Peking at the time with the big Indonesian delegation to Communist China's national day celebrations. So Arief was left with seven victims. He divided his force appropriately into seven squads. Some of the victims were given code names. Nasution was 'Nurdin.' Yani was 'Jonson.' Pandjaitan was 'Singer.' Sutojo was 'Toyota.'

There was a final hitch, which apparently angered Arief, when a promised platoon of air force shock troops failed to report, but finally his force was properly divided and ready. At a signal his men climbed into their trucks, weapons clanking. At 1:30 A.M., October 1, the killer squads rumbled out of Halim on their grisly mission.

3. Murder in the Night

H-hour was 4 A.M. By that time the seven squads were in position outside the homes of the generals they were to take.

Lieutenant Arief himself led the squad assigned to seize General Nasution. Promptly at 4 a.m. his team, traveling in four trucks and two military cars, cruised slowly down Djalan Teuku Umar, a quiet residential street of two lanes divided by a trim, grassy center island. At that hour the street was deserted, except for a guard tucked away in the darkness of his sentry box outside No. 40, a modest, single-story house set back from the road. This was the home of General Nasution.

The guard in the sentry box saw the trucks coming and watched them curiously as they drove by, then pulled up a little past him. Identifying the men on the trucks as soldiers of the palace guard, he was therefore unsuspicious. He felt no need to call out to his superior, Sergeant Iskaq, who was in command of the army detail guarding General Nasution's house that night. The sergeant was in a guardroom, built in the garden, with a half-dozen men, some of them sleeping. Another guard was asleep in the front garden, and one more was on duty at the back of the house. In a separate little guest cottage, or pavilion (which is common to Djakarta residences) slept two of General Nasution's aides, a young army lieutenant named Pierre Tendean, and assistant police commissioner Hamdan Mansjur.

Before the sentry could give the alarm, the raiders had jumped from their trucks and rushed to his sentry box and the guardroom, overpowering the bewildered and sleepy guards. Other Tjakrabirawa and Pemuda Rakjat soldiers slipped around the side of the house and covered it from the rear. Then about fifteen of the gang broke into the house.

Bothered by mosquitoes that night, both General Nasution and his wife were awake, but neither of them heard the commotion outside as the guards were overpowered. Now Mrs. Nasution heard a door in the house being forced. She got up, opened the bedroom door, and saw a man in Tjakrabirawa uniform outside, with a weapon, ready to shoot. With remarkably rapid reflex under the circumstances she slammed the door shut, locked it, and screamed out a warning to her husband. The General insisted on taking a look himself. As he opened the door, the man outside fired at him, the General flung himself to the floor, and his wife once again slammed and locked the door. Now the men outside the door started smashing it down, meanwhile firing a volley into the bedroom. Mrs. Nasution grabbed her husband, pushed him out of another door and down a corridor to a side entrance of the house. From there he made a dash in the darkness across his own garden to the wall separating his property from that of his neighbor, the Iraqi Ambassador. As he ran, he was spotted. The soldiers surrounding the house sent a flurry of shots after him, but missed him. However, as he leaped for the wall, scrambled over it, and dropped into the Ambassador's garden, he broke his ankle. Painfully he dragged himself into hiding in the bushes. Nobody pursued him.

Behind him the whole household had been wakened and frightened by the shooting. Living in the house were the General's mother and sister, both of whom rushed to his bedroom. His sister, Mardiah, swept the Nasutions' five-year-old daughter, Irma, from the bed in which she was sleeping and tried to run for safety, cradling the child protectively in her arms. But as she ran, a corporal of the palace guard fired a burst at her through a door. She herself was hit in the hand and arm, but not seriously. Three bullets hit Irma in the spine. The child died in the hospital five days later.

Meanwhile, the Nasutions' eldest daughter, 13-year-old Janti, and her nurse, Alfiah, had jumped through a window and run to the pavilion housing the General's aides. There they were hidden under a bed.

Lieutenant Tendean, after hastily loading his carbine, made for the garden, but was seized before he had gone more than a few yards from the pavilion. Though a much younger man than Nasution, Tendean did bear a slight resemblance to him. In the dark, some of the attackers mistook him for the General and held him at gunpoint.

In the meantime Mrs. Nasution, after thrusting her husband out into the garden to escape, had run back into the house and picked up her wounded child. As she sought desperately to telephone for a doctor, the Tjakrabirawa men harried her, demanding to know her husband's whereabouts. At one stage she apparently had a brief and angry exchange with Lieutenant Arief himself, in which she told him Nasution had been out of town for two days.

But then a whistle blew from outside, and the men in the house left on the run. They bundled Lieutenant Tendean onto one of the trucks, and roared away. The whole affair. though it must have seemed to the Nasutions like an age, had lasted just about nine minutes.

There was one further tragic side incident. Another neighbor of Nasution's was Johannes Lemeina, one of Indonesia's three deputy premiers. Lemeina had a policeman on guard at his house that night, who walked down the street when he heard shooting at Nasution's house to find out what all the trouble was about. In the melee he was shot and killed. The killing generated stories that circulated for some time that the plotters of the coup had Lemeina on their list, too, and that their men had attacked his house. This was not true. The killing of Lemeina's guard was unplanned.

As soon as the raiders left, Mrs. Nasution rushed her wounded daughter to the central military hospital, and the guards sounded the alarm. Summoned by a call on a special military line, the Djakarta garrison commander, Major General Umar, sped to the

Nasution house himself. But this was not to be his only call that morning as the first slivers of dawn light splintered the night sky. By now the reports were beginning to trickle in of other generals abducted and murdered.

About the same time that Lieutenant Arief launched his action against General Nasution, another squad, estimated at about two hundred men, quietly surrounded the residence of General Yani. This was a long, low house, on a corner site, commanding some open green space.

Although the army commander brushed off any ostentatious guard as he traveled about the city, there was usually a guard of eleven men on his home. A week before, according to his wife, the guard had been strengthened by an additional six men. These were men from the command of Colonel Latief, who, unknown to Yani, was deep in the plot against him. According to the General's wife, they mysteriously failed to report for duty at the Yanis' house that night.

As the rebel squad moved in and disarmed the guard before it could resist, Yani himself and his children were asleep in the house. Mrs. Yani was not there, for October 1 was her birthday, and as she explained it to me later, she had left to celebrate it "Eastern fashion," by staying up all night with a small group of relatives and friends.

Yani's own absence from the celebration is not explained. However, there had been a crisis in the family over his decision to take a new young second wife after long years of happy marriage with his first. This, under Moslem law, he was perfectly entitled to do. But it was a custom frowned on by educated Indonesian women in general, and by the first Mrs. Yani in particular. Sources close to the family say Mrs. Yani was extremely bitter toward Sukarno over the whole affair, believing that Sukarno had presented her husband with the girl and encouraged him.

At any rate, she drove shortly after 11 P.M. on September 30 to the army commander's official residence used for ceremonial occasions. Formerly the property of an American oil company, it stood directly across a grassy square from the residence of the American Ambassador.

She recalls that as she drove away from her own house, she saw someone sitting in the shadows across the street, as though keeping the house under observation. At that particular moment she thought little of it. Now, however, she wonders.

Another unexplained incident, mildly irritating at the time, was the fact that from about 9 P.M. the telephone kept ringing at intervals. When anybody in the house answered, either there was silence, or a voice would ask what the time was. The calls continued, after Mrs. Yani had left, until about 1 A.M. They were answered by her teenage daughter recently returned from Bandung and duty with a student regiment there. Now Mrs. Yani wonders whether it was a prankster or someone checking on the family's presence in the house.

Mrs. Yani says she had a premonition something was wrong that night. But she continued on her way and spent the night with her brothers, General Yani's aide, and a few close friends, playing favorite records, some of them songs sung by Yani himself when he was on the campaign trail as a guerrilla fighter against the Dutch years before.

Yani, meanwhile, following the pattern of many Indonesian officials, spent the evening with official callers. He had worked the morning of September 30 at his office, lunched with his family at home about 2 P.M., then spent the afternoon on the golf course while his wife played tennis. He had met with his family again around 6 P.M. for tea—"He loved Indonesian tea," says Mrs. Yani. Over tea he told one of his daughters to order flowers for her mother's birthday on the morrow.

At 7 P.M. he received briefly a colonel from KOTI, the Supreme Operations Command. Then arrived Major General Basuchi

Rachmat, the military commander in East Java, from his divisional headquarters at Surabaya. Basuchi Rachmat had been troubled by a series of increasingly provocative incidents in his area staged by the Communists. After a Communist-organized demonstration at the office of the governor, also a military man, Basuchi Rachmat requested permission to fly to Djakarta and report personally to Yani. Yani agreed and told him to get there September 30, as he planned to leave shortly thereafter for an inspection tour of Sumatra. Now Basuchi Rachmat told Yani the whole story.

After some discussion, Yani sat down and wrote out a cable of commendation and support for the governor in Surabaya. Then he told Basuchi Rachmat to be back at seven o'clock the next morning. Yani said he had an appointment with the President at 8 A.M., and he wanted Basuchi Rachmat to go along, to tell Sukarno the story of Communist subversion in East Java.

Basuchi Rachmat left, and before going to sleep in his own quarters elsewhere in the city, he watched on television the beginning of the meeting at Senajan addressed by Sukarno.

Mrs. Yani says her husband told his aide earlier that he had been summoned to see the President next day at the weekend palace in Bogor. This is possible, for it is not more than an hour's drive, and Yani could still have left home with Basuchi Rachmat at 7 A.M. and been at the palace at Bogor by 8 A.M. Yet if Mrs. Yani's story is correct, it is an odd little fact. For the following day was Friday, and though the President usually did travel to Bogor on Fridays, his routine was to leave in the middle of the day. He would not ordinarily have been at Bogor so early on a Friday. Nor, in the light of his actual movements that night, does it appear he had laid any plans to be at Bogor by 8 A.M., rather than at the Merdeka palace in Djakarta as usual.

Mrs. Yani was not, as has already been explained, in the house when her husband was seized, but months later she re-enacted for

me the drama, of which she was clearly well aware. Still bitter—
"See, the birthday present they gave me, the murder of my
husband"—she showed me how the intruders entered, where her
husband was shot down, over which route he was dragged away. She
and her children were by this time no longer living in the house in
which General Yani had been killed; in fact, Mrs. Yani was helping
to prepare it as a national museum in memory of her husband. As
such, it was kept as nearly as possible just as it had been during his
life. The furniture was the same. On General Yani's bed, his pajamas
were laid out; his slippers were at the bedside. In glass cases along
the walls were mementoes and personal possessions: the General's
medals, and pens and wallet; his Fort Leavenworth ring, of which,
says Mrs. Yani, he was particularly proud following his attendance
at an officers' training course there. And there were more macabre
exhibits—the bloodstained shirt in which he died, the stubby gray
automatic weapon with which he was killed, and which was
recovered later, and the bent, smashed bullets.

As she explained all the exhibits, it was clear that though Mrs.
Yani had not been there when her husband died, she had relived the
tragic scene many times.

"As the Tjakra [palace guards] surrounded the house," she tells,
"the noise woke up our youngest son, Ady [then eight years old]. He
came out into the front room. The soldiers were already in there—
we never locked our doors. They asked the boy where his father was.
They told him the President wanted to see his father.

"The boy didn't suspect. He told them his father was asleep in
his bedroom. Then they held him. They wouldn't let him go to
his father."

By now Yani himself was awake. He came storming out into the
room where the soldiers were. They repeated their story that he was
wanted, urgently, by the President.

Mrs. Yani explains, "General Yani said that in that case he must change, he must get into uniform. The palace guards said he didn't have to, that he must hurry, that there was a toilet at the palace where he could change. At that, my husband got angry. He hit a guard, for he was a general and he couldn't excuse rudeness, not from a sergeant."

In fact, Yani was so furious that the guard he lashed out at with his forearm was knocked unconscious. Then, perhaps insistent that he change, he swung back into the living quarter of the house, flinging shut a glass door behind him. Instantly, one of the palace guards fired a burst through the door, hitting Yani several times in the back, and sending him sprawling in a shower of shattered glass.

The shots woke up several other children and they all came running to the spot, crying for their father. Yani must still have been alive, for he tried to embrace his eldest son, an 11-year-old. But his murderers would have none of it. They grabbed his legs, dragged him across the floor, and flung him onto a truck waiting outside.

After they had driven off, Yani's own disarmed guards ran to alert a military police post. The alarm was flashed to the Djakarta garrison commander, General Umar, already heading for Nasution's house. Before Umar could come on to the Yani's house, however, Mrs. Yani had returned home about 5 A.M., less than an hour after the raid began.

Her children ran screaming to her and dragged her to the spot where Yani had been shot. She saw the blood on the floor, fainted, came to, fainted again. Then, told the details of what had happened, she called all her children to her. They knelt around the blood, and she told them to pray—to "pray to God that he [Yani] does not have to suffer too long"—for she had little hope for his survival.

Of the seven generals marked down for seizure that night, only Generals Nasution and Yani seem to have had guards on their homes. At the house of General Parman, the intelligence chief who had been warned anew just a day or so before that the Communists were planning a move, not a single sentry stood guard that night.

Ironically, one of General Parman's brothers, Sakirman, was a top Communist leader, a member of the politburo, and the party's leading economic expert. He was in Central Java at the time his brother was captured and killed. Despite the blood relationship, the two must obviously have been at political loggerheads. Another general, who knew them both, told me Sakirman once asked him, "How is my brother, the reactionary general?" Then, he said, Sakirman called Parman a "traitor." Meanwhile, Mrs. Parman points out that the family had widely diverse political connections. While her husband was an anti-Communist general and his brother was a Communist Party leader, other brothers were members of the Partai Nasional Indonesia (PNI) and the Nahdatul Ulama (Moslem Teachers' Party).

As Mrs. Parman told me the story of what happened during the early hours of October 1, it was evident that although she herself had apprehensions, General Parman himself either was unsuspecting until the last few minutes before leaving his house, or alternatively, tried to hide his suspicions from his wife.

"About ten past four in the morning," Mrs. Parman recalls, "there was the noise of a lot of people at the side of our house, next to the bedroom where my husband and I were sleeping. He got up and put on his dressing gown and went to the front door.

"About twenty people burst into the living room. They were all wearing brownish uniforms. They were from the Tjakrabirawa. General Parman came back into the bedroom and told me, 'Bapak [the President] wants to see me. They say something very interesting has happened.'"

At this stage Mrs. Parman got up. She could see there were people in the front garden and two trucks standing in the short driveway inside the gate.

"About ten men went into the bedroom with General Parman

while he dressed," she says. "He said that if he were going to see the President, he had to put on his uniform. They stood over him while he dressed, while he pulled on his trousers. He splashed some water over his face to freshen up. He almost forgot his cigarettes, but came back for the case."

Mrs. Parman was apparently much more suspicious. She went into the living room and demanded of the men there, "If the President wants to see my husband, you must have a letter from him. One of the men standing by the door said, *"Ibu* [mother], please. We have the letter." He patted his pocket, but did not show her any letter.

Then Mrs. Parman appealed to her husband, "Do you know these people?" "Yes, yes," he replied, "they are from the palace, from the Tjakra."

As her husband was leaving with his captors, Mrs. Parman tried to follow. "Some of the men," she remembers, "stood across the door and stopped me. They had rifles, with bayonets on them, pointing at the floor.

"They said I must phone General Yani. I went to the phone [in a room off the living room], but one of them cut the wire. They wanted me to open up the door of General Parman's study, but I said I could not. They left about twenty past four. I shut the door and started to pray. I am a Moslem."

A few minutes later a distraught Mrs. Harjono, wife of Major General Harjono, arrived by car. At her house the scene had been much more violent, and her husband had been shot.

As the Tjakrabirawa broke into the Harjonos' residence, the noise woke up Mrs. Harjono. She got up, left the bedroom and went through the living room, to the front of the house. There she saw a Tjakrabirawa soldier in uniform and glimpsed others with weapons around the house. "The General is sleeping," she told the men, "what do you want?" Again there was the same story: the

General was instructed by the President to come immediately.

Mrs. Harjono went back to the bedroom, locking the door behind her, and explained quickly to her husband what was happening. She told him not to go, to tell the guards to come back at eight o'clock in the morning. But the General himself apparently had no illusions about it all. He switched off the lights and tersely told his wife to move with the children to an adjoining room.

By now the Tjakrabirawa were at the door. Through it they fired a burst. Harjono flung himself to the floor, unhit. Now, in the dark, he waited. Through the bedroom door, carrying a burning newspaper for light, came the first of his attackers. Harjono jumped him, apparently in a desperate bid to get his hands on a weapon. But he failed, ran out of the door in the confusion, and was shot down with a burst from a Sten gun. Then he was dragged through his garden, and his body was thrown onto one of the waiting trucks.

At the house of General Pandjaitan, meanwhile, there had been a full-scale fire fight. Of all the generals' houses involved, this was the only two-story one. Pandjaitan slept upstairs, had a machine gun with him, and used it to try and fight off his attackers.

The squad detailed to seize him apparently tried to shoot its way into the house through a side—garden—door. Pandjaitan fired back from an upstairs window, and his attackers in turn sent a shower of bullets up at his room. Smashing their way into the ground floor, firing as they went, they hit two of Pandjaitan's teenage nephews, who had been sleeping downstairs, and one of whom had tried to hold them off with a revolver. A third nephew, who remained quiet on the upper tier of a bunk-type bed, went unnoticed.

Then there followed some angry shouting up and down the stairs between Pandjaitan and the Tjakrabirawa. The soldiers told the General they would kill his whole family unless he surrendered. He came down, in full uniform, and was roughly bundled out into the garden. There he must have resisted again. From behind, someone fired a burst at him, shattering his skull and killing him instantly. His body was thrown onto a truck.

General Suprapto had spent a restless night wandering about his house. He had been having work done on his teeth, and they were hurting him. So part of the night he had spent dabbling with a picture he was painting, which was almost finished.

Suddenly his dogs started barking. He went to the front door and found the Tjakrabirawa there. They refused to let him dress—took him away in his pajamas. Meanwhile his wife, awakened by the dogs' barking, came out into the living room but was forced back into the bedroom by her husband's captors. She was forbidden to use the telephone. When the soldiers left, and she rushed to it, she found it was cut, anyway. Quickly she scribbled a note to send to the Parmans' house, sounding the alarm. She could not know that General Parman himself had also been seized.

Meanwhile, for Mrs. Sutojo, wife of General Sutojo, her husband's seizure that morning would be doubly tragic. This was her second marriage, and her first husband, also an army officer, had been killed by the Communists as he fought against them during their uprising at Madiun, in East Java, in 1948.

Ironically, the Sutojos were neighbors of a palace guard officer called Untung. It was the same Untung even now awaiting a report from the murder squads he had dispatched against the generals—his own neighbor among them. But Untung was obviously not at home. He was at Halim busily helping direct coup operations.

General Sutojo apparently answered the 4 A.M. knock on his door himself. Again the story was the same—that he was summoned to see the President. But there was also some sort of scuffle as another party of soldiers ran through the garage to the back of the house, there found an aide and threatened him with a bayonet to get the keys.

The noise woke up Mrs. Sutojo, who had not been well that day. There was more noise to come, because before the soldiers left with General Sutojo, they smashed up the living room and cut the telephone line. As soon as they had gone, Mrs. Sutojo ran to a neighbor's house and phoned the house of another general. As she was halfway through her story, the phone was cut—probably at the same time that coup forces downtown seized the telephone exchange and cut off all telephone communication in the capital.

Thus, of the seven generals listed for arrest that night, the most important one, General Nasution, got away, although with injuries to his ankle. Three more, Generals Yani, Harjono, and Pandjaitan, were killed when they resisted. Three others, Generals Parman, Suprapto, and Sutojo, were taken alive.

4. Orgy at Crocodile Hole

Back to Halim air force base the trucks raced, carrying the bodies of the three dead generals, the three generals still alive, and Nasution's unfortunate aide, Lieutenant Pierre Tendean. Whether the rebels still thought, at this stage, that they had Nasution is not clear, but at any rate, Tendean was to face the fate that would have been Nasution's had he been captured.

By now the three surviving generals, squatting amid the Tjakrabirawa and Pemuda Rakjat men who had seized them, can have been under no illusions that they were still being summoned before the President on official business. At least one of them was blindfolded. At least one other was bound with rope. Yet it is difficult to believe they could have envisaged the grim scene yet to come.

Onto the base area the trucks bounced, then out to the training camp of the Pemuda Rakjat and Gerwani at Lubang Buaja. Awaiting them were the rest of the Pemuda Rakjat trainees who had been assembled there, and the girls and women of Gerwani who had been studying with Communist thoroughness and dedication the most efficient ways to kill.

Now the captives were hustled into an open space, not far from the camp's field kitchen. There their bodies were beaten with rifle butts, hacked at with knives, and finally riddled with bullets. Then their remains, together with the bodies of the generals killed earlier, were thrown down a well. The well was sealed, the top was filled in, and it was covered over to avoid discovery.

The details of the deaths do not make for pleasant reading, but they are important for political reasons. When the bodies were found the following week, and for weeks thereafter, stories about the extent of their mutilation flashed throughout the capital city and all of Indonesia.

It was whispered that the bodies had been dismembered, that

limbs had been torn off, noses and ears slashed away, sexual organs removed.

In my possession I have a number of photographs taken at the time the bodies were exhumed four days after being thrown into the well. They make for gruesome viewing. Pictures of a similar kind were circulated among the army, and they undoubtedly inflamed the fury of the army's crackdown on the Communists, but the photographs do not indicate dismemberment.

General Sugandhi, one of the officers actually present when the bodies were removed from the well, says there was evidence of torture, of many wounds, and many bullet holes. But the bodies were not dismembered, nor does he believe that sexual and other major organs of the bodies had been interfered with. He does say some of the generals had had their eyes gouged out.

The photographs do seem to bear out this charge. But the decomposition process, which had set in before the bodies were discovered, makes it difficult to determine what damage was inflicted by the generals' tormentors and how much by confinement in the well.

A medical inspection of the bodies was made by an Indonesian doctor, but his report is kept secret. President Sukarno is reported to have told confidants that he had a copy of a medical report indicating there was no mutilation of the bodies. There are other suggestions that Sukarno tried to tone down the atrocity stories. One of his most bitter critics, Major General Sutjipto, who then held a senior position in KOTI (the Supreme Operations Command), claims he was shocked by a conversation he had with Sukarno two weeks after the coup. According to Sutjipto, Sukarno complained about exaggerated press coverage of the generals' murders. Then Sukarno said that the three generals still alive when they reached Lubang Buaja were executed "in an orderly and graceful manner," by the decision of a kind of "people's court."

They were blindfolded before being shot, and their executioners "apologized first" before killing them. Sutjipto says he is prepared to testify under oath to the conversation.

The people who know what really happened that morning at Lubang Buaja when darkness was giving way to dawn are those who murdered the generals.

More than a year after the event, I asked military and police authorities to let me interview some of the women Communists trained at Lubang Buaja who had supposedly played such a central role in the killing of the generals, and who had been captured and were being held in prison.

After some negotiation, the authorities agreed. They placed no restrictions on what questions I might ask, or what I could write about the interviews. They did, for reasons of security, reserve the right to decide where the interviews would be held. In fact, the prisoners were transported from jail to defense and security staff headquarters, and it was there the interviews took place. The other condition was that I would use an interpreter provided by the military.

At the first session the authorities presented four women. Three of them, they said, had either been witnesses of the generals' killings or had taken part in them. Two of them were 17 years old, the third 16. A fourth woman, 38 years old, had not been at Lubang Buaja that night, they said, but was a fairly high official in Gerwani who had been in contact with top Communist leaders and was thus informed about Communist plans and intentions.

The authorities placed no restrictions on use of the women's names. I do not know whether the women will ever be brought to formal trial, but at the time I saw them they had not, and so I will leave them unidentified.

The interviews began one sunny Saturday morning in the comfortable conference area of a general's office borrowed for the occasion. There was a guard on the door, but none in the room.

However, as I talked with the women, one at a time, there was the military interpreter by my side. Some distance away, but still within earshot, sat a police official and an army officer.

I asked to see the older woman first. As with each of the prisoners I talked with, I told her I was an American journalist writing a book about recent events in Indonesia, and that I was in no way connected with the authorities. I said that there would be no official record of the interview, that nothing said could be used in any trial proceedings. I do not know how many, if any, of the women believed what I told them.

This first woman readily admitted she was not only a Gerwani member, but a local staff organizer in Djakarta. But she stoutly denied she knew anything of military training at Lubang Buaja, or of any coup plans. She declared she herself had been mainly involved in a campaign to lower food prices. She told me her husband had been a labor organizer for SOBSI (the Communist trade union organization). He had, she said, become ill before the events of October 1, had gone to Communist China for medical treatment, and was still there.

It seemed clear that both she and her husband were professional Communists, paid employees of the party, that she had said what she was going to say, and that she would say no more.

Now, one at a time, came the three younger girls. But to the glum consternation of the officers present, two denied being present at Lubang Buaja the morning of October 1, while the other went into a sullen, handkerchief-biting withdrawal in which she refused to answer any questions at all, or look anybody in the eye.

The two talkative ones admitted they had undergone military training at Lubang Buaja, one of them in July, the other in September. They had been taught how to strip small arms and been given some military drill. But they thought, they said, it was all part of the preparation for action against Malaysia.

What, I asked them, about interrogation reports the army said it had, and which they had signed, in which they supposedly admitted being present when the generals were killed at Lubang Buaja? Yes, they said, they admitted they had said all that, months before, but that was because they were frightened.

After much conversation back and forth, we came to the end of an exhausting session.

Then, but only then, I read the dossiers the authorities had brought along on each woman. They included lengthy, signed "confessions" of involvement at Lubang Buaja on October 1. They were statements in great detail, listing incidents and aspects of the affair difficult, one might think, to invent. The girls agreed they had made the statements and signed them, but now they denied they had been present when the events they described took place.

A week later we tried again, this time with some of the girls I had interviewed before and with some new ones. Now the authorities produced, for "psychological reasons," the original interrogators who had taken the statements. These turned out to be two pert and pretty women Indonesian Army officers. Also observing was a navy psychologist.

Again we went through the same ritual of the week before. Again the initial reaction was denial of any involvement at Lubang Buaja on October 1. But then the mood changed, as the women interrogators went back and forth over the ground, probing for an admission. Slowly, with tears and hesitancy, at times almost inaudible, it came from the girl who had been silent and withdrawn a week before.

Yes, she had been at Lubang Buaja, directed to go there on September 30 by an official in her village. Others had been similarly sent. She had been there for ten days on a previous occasion, learning how to strip and assemble pistols and the "Tjung [Chinese] rifle."

Now, during the night of September 30/October 1, she and other girls in her tent were awakened. They were told "some mangoes" were expected. She didn't know what that meant at the time, but the "mangoes" turned out to be the generals.

Haltingly she went on, "I saw a number of people in uniform, and they had some people with them. They were the 'capitalist bureaucrats.' They were partly dressed. One had his pajamas on. One was in shorts. One had his eyes covered. They were tied up. They were brought into an open field. All the people gathered, pointing to the men. There were a lot of people—Gerwani, Pemuda Rakjat—singing and shouting. There was dancing and shouting, too. They sang Pemuda Rakjat songs. There were three generals, sitting on the ground.

"Someone shouted 'Kill the capitalist bureaucrats!' They were beaten first, then smashed with rifle butts. Our platoon leader [one of the other girls interviewed, who persistently denied being at Lubang Buaja] gave us razor blades. We slashed at the bodies. Our platoon leader then told them to gouge out the eyes. The women did that. I don't know anything about the sex organs. The generals cried out in pain. Then they were taken closer to the well. They were shot afterwards. The women did the shooting."

Last week, I pointed out, she had refused to talk. Was she now telling the truth? She nodded her head affirmatively. Had anybody pressured her, threatened her, ill-treated her, since I last saw her? She shook her head in the negative.

Another girl I had not met before, 17 years old, told her story without much prodding. She, too, had been directed by a local village official to assemble with other Gerwani and Pemuda Rakjat members at Lubang Buaja. She, too, had received weapons training there earlier, in July.

On September 30 she had arrived about 3 A.M. after a truck ride. With others, she had been given weapons training in the morning and political indoctrination by a Pemuda Rakjat lecturer in the afternoon. Then she had gone to sleep in her tent with about thirty other girls.

"Near sunrise," she said, "men in trucks came. I didn't recognize them. But there were Tjakrabirawa there. I saw one man dead. Others were carried in straw mats. Then I saw two generals, one in a dressing gown, one in a sarong (traditional Indonesian dress). Both were fat. They were not tied up. They were taken into different tents. Then I saw two more men dead and another alive. The live ones were taken out and slashed and beaten. The Tjakrabirawa used their rifle butts. The generals weren't interfered with sexually. Afterwards they were thrown into the well."

Thus went the stories: of the generals' arrival; of their being clubbed by rifle butts in the midst of a shouting, screaming, apparently near-hysterical Communist mob; of their being slashed with knives and possibly razor blades; then of their being riddled with volleys of gunfire and thrown down the well.

How much credence should be given these stories? Obviously, the interviews were conducted under conditions controlled by the authorities. It may be argued the women could have been either threatened, or paid, to say what they did. If they were, they would of course have denied any pressure when I put my routine question to them about such cajolement.

Yet the fact that they had at first balked, and denied any involvement at Lubang Buaja, lends a certain veracity to their ultimate admissions. If the women were specially chosen and coached to play out a confessional scene for me, it could hardly have gone more awry than it did at the first sessions.

It may be argued that the ultimate confessions, with the original interrogators present and a psychologist silently observing, were hardly conducted under conditions of ideal objectivity, and this is true. Yet from the demeanor of the women involved, from other information, and from the evidence as best it can be gathered about injuries to the generals' bodies, I believe that their version of what happened at Lubang Buaja as they finally told it to me is substantially correct.

Some observers have suggested that the generals' killers at Lubang Buaja were drugged, or had been given "pep pills." Others have stories of lurid sex orgies both at the time of the killings and earlier, when the young Communist youths and girls were training together. All this may have happened. But I did not find the evidence of it.

Perhaps the generals were more badly tortured than the confessions of the Gerwani and Pemuda Rakjat members I talked to indicate. But if even only those admissions are true—as I believe they basically are—then it is clear that the victims put to death at Lubang Buaja were murdered in a scene of savage, revolting, and bloody frenzy.

Meanwhile, for President Sukarno the night had begun with a pattern no different from that of hundreds of others. He was scheduled to address a meeting at Senajan, a favorite spot for rallies and big political meetings, because it was the site of the huge sports complex built for Indonesia by the Soviet Union. Besides an international-size swimming pool and tennis courts and playing fields, the complex included a spectacular open arena and also a covered stadium which, though smaller, could still hold many thousands of people. Both were ideal for Sukarno-dominated rallies. On this particular night the indoor arena was to be used. The occasion was a conference of technicians.

The script for such events was standard. Long before the President's arrival, the crowds would be in their places in the rows of seats banked up steeply on each side of the square, center floor area. Probably there would be a warm-up, with political cheerleaders coaching various sections of the audience in slogan-shouting, cheering, and singing. Then, faintly and from a distance, would come the sounds of sirens as the presidential convoy sped on its way. The sirens would scream nearer and nearer, then come to a shrieking halt outside the main entrance to the stadium. The President would emerge from his big black limousine and stroll through an avenue of pretty girls, specially chosen and in national costume, who would strew a carpet of flower petals in front of him as he walked.

Inside the stadium, aides and bodyguards at his heels, he would take his place in a special reserved area about halfway up one side of the banked arena. Before him on a table would be his favourite brand of American cigarettes, a plate or two of cookies and sweet cakes, and always three glasses of liquid—reputedly tea, some soft drink, and perhaps a medicinal mixture—covered with silver lids. High in the eaves, the elite presidential guards would dart their eyes suspiciously over the assembled throng.

There would be some preliminary speakers, in whom the President would indicate interest or disdainful disinterest as the mood took him.

Then would come the moment for Sukarno himself to speak. Down the stairs he would pad to a dais on the floor of the arena, a stocky little man, always in a well-cut uniform gilded with medals and decorations, and always with the traditional black *pitji*, or Indonesian hat, on his head.

With a roar the thousands would surge to their feet. The bright revolutionary banners floating from the walls would flutter a little in the sudden breeze. The air, it almost seemed, would crackle a little with electric excitement.

Unsmiling, impassive, Sukarno would nod his head across the banked thousands, turning from one side of the arena to the other. For a few moments he would stand before the cluster of microphones on the dais, then flick a couple of them to make sure they were working. When he raised one finger briefly, perfunctorily, the crowd would instantly become silent.

He would begin to speak. Slowly, at first, in a hoarse, caressing, mesmeric whisper. Then faster. And louder. And faster and louder still. Until he had the crowd in ecstatic fervor.

Sometimes he would take them on flights of mystic fancy, as with words such as these: "How great is God, who gave that sense of struggle to me, when I as a youth, physically sitting on a grass mat under the flickering rays of a rushlight, conducted a mental dialogue in the metaphysical world with the great strugglers of many different nations, with the thinkers of all nations who steered the course of history"

But then seconds later he would thunder and roll his eyes with: "I am a dynamic man. I don't like tranquillity, which is frozen and dead. I don't like sluggishness. What I like is dynamism, vitality, militancy, activity, a revolutionary spirit. I prefer the painting of an ocean with boisterous waves, rather than a painting of rice fields full of calmness and tranquillity. If it is a painting of rice fields, I would choose one where the paddy sways and the wind blows. If I am to choose a portrait, I choose one with fire, power, vitality."

But always he was the superb entertainer, performer, manipulator.

So it went on the night of September 30 as he addressed the conference of technicians. There was one incident of note. At one stage he left the meeting and was away from the arena for perhaps five or ten minutes. Some observers say he seemed to falter. This stirred speculation that he had gone into a private room to get an injection, or medicine from his accompanying doctor. This in turn generated stories that news of this sudden deterioration in his health was flashed to the Communists, who hastily decided to move that night.

In the light of later evidence, this theory does not stand up. For the coup preparations were already too far advanced at that hour to have been triggered by some presidential faltering around

10 P.M. What is possible is that Sukarno was called out to be given some message about the night's coming events, or to be asked for instructions. The presumption behind this theory is that he was privy to the plotters' plans.

With no more incident, the meeting ended, and Sukarno sped away with his cavalcade. He intended spending the night at the villa of his Japanese wife, Dewi. Aloof beyond high screening walls in the suburb of Slipi, this was a small palace with its own swimming pool, of course—decorated with rugs and paintings and so on to the expensive taste of Madame Dewi.

But Dewi was still at the nightclub atop the Hotel Indonesia, celebrating with the party from the diplomatic wedding that had taken place earlier. So the President went there. While Sukarno waited in his car, an aide hurried in to fetch Dewi. But as those at the party recall it, Dewi dallied. The aide had to call her a second time, with a diplomatic indication that the President, waiting below, was restless.

According to testimony from Sukarno's aides and security officials later at the trial of air force chief Omar Dhani, the President and Dewi left the hotel about midnight and went to Dewi's house. The President is then supposed to have wakened about 6 A.M., been told of trouble and shooting at Nasution's house, and to have headed downtown for Merdeka palace. Almost there, according to the evidence, his car ran into a traffic jam. Meanwhile, a colonel in charge of security at the palace radioed the presidential escort that the palace was surrounded by unknown troops. Thus alerted, the President's party swung back and sped to the home of another of Sukarno's wives, Haryati, who presided over a complex of low, modern buildings set beyond lush green rice paddies on the outskirts of the capital.

There, as the story goes, aides discussed with Sukarno four alternative courses to preserve his security. One was to move him to a "well-situated house" in the suburb of Kebajoran. The second was to take him to Halim air base, where the presidential Jet-Star stood by. A third suggestion was to get him—somehow—to a warship of the Indonesian Navy and out to sea. A fourth idea was that he should travel overland to some refuge by armored car.

The President himself decided to go to Halim.

It was a decision that was later to provide Sukarno's critics with some of their handiest ammunition.

Halim was, after all, the command post of the plotters who had just murdered the army's leading generals and illegally seized key installations throughout the city. It was the place where some of the generals had been done to gruesome death.

Months later, as the mystery of what went on at Halim that night was unraveled bit by bit, Sukarno's critics challenged the presidential version of his movements. Deeply suspicious, they suggested he might have arrived at Halim earlier than 9:30 in the morning of October 1, as recounted by his aides. They implied that he even might have been present at Halim when the generals were being mutilated and buried in the well.

This is unlikely. The President's presence on such an occasion would have been almost impossible to hide later, despite a good cover story by his aides. And Sukarno himself has no strong stomach for bloodshed.

Alternatively, his critics suggested that the choice of Halim as a presidential retreat was no coincidence, and that in fact it had been planned in advance that he should go there. If this is so, the implication is clear—namely that Sukarno knew in advance of the plot and knew, too, that Halim was the rebels' headquarters.

However, the story as told by his aides is that Sukarno was driven in a small, inconspicuous Volkswagen from Haryati's house to Halim, arriving at the air base about 9:30 A.M. The President went straight to the "Koops" (Operations Command) building and there conferred with his air force chief, Omar Dhani. Dhani had slept in the building that night. Before the President's arrival, Dhani had listened at about 7:15 A.M. to a broadcast over Djakarta radio that indicated it was in the hands of Untung's men. The radio declared they had moved against a so-called "Council of Generals," which was a subversive movement sponsored by the American Central Intelligence Agency, and that they had other vital installations in their control. Untung's movement announced itself as the September 30th Movement and declared President Sukarno was "safe under its protection."

The latter seems an overly confident statement for the movement to have made at that time. For if the presidential party's version of events is accepted, Sukarno was still being shuttled around between Dewi's house and Haryati's house at this hour. The September 30th Movement had not even made contact with him, let alone put him "safe under its protection."

General Supardjo, one of the main plotters, had apparently gone early to Merdeka palace to report to Sukarno. Supardjo had discovered he was not there and had been whisked back to Halim, in an air force helicopter provided by Dhani.

There is one other contradiction in the official version of events that morning. In a statement carried by Antara, the official Indonesian news agency, two weeks after the abortive coup, the "leadership of the Tjakrabirawa regiment" gave its own version. Early in the morning of October 1, went the statement, the Tjakrabirawa leadership detected army units encircling the palace. "The Tjakrabirawa leadership," the statement goes on, "did not know the purpose behind the placement of these units. Since there were other suspicious signs, at about 6 A.M. Tjakrabirawa units immediately took the rapid and firm decision to take the President out of the palace and bring him to safety in a place they considered secure."

According to the President's personal aides, he was of course never in the palace that morning. He spent the night at Dewi's house, headed for the palace, was diverted before reaching it, and went to Haryati's house.

However, the Tjakrabirawa statement does agree with the testimony of the President's aides in pinpointing Sukarno's arrival at Halim at about 9:30 A.M.

After conferring with Dhani in the Operations Command building, Sukarno then saw Supardjo. This meeting holds the key to many unanswered questions about the coup. Supardjo reported to the President on the events of the night, but only he, Sukarno, and possibly Dhani, know how that report was phrased and what was Sukarno's reaction to it. Witnesses from a distance say Sukarno "patted" Supardjo on the back. But was that, as Sukarno's critics say, a congratulatory pat for a job done to the President's satisfaction? Or was it, as Sukarno's defenders maintain, a warning gesture that there must be no more bloodshed?

Supardjo, at his trial later, said that after he reported to Sukarno on the events of the morning, the President "clapped him on the shoulder." Then, according to Supardjo, the President said, "That sort of thing will happen in a revolution," and ordered him to stop further violence. According to Dhani, the President after listening to Supardjo's report said something like this: This is an incident in the revolution, especially in a big revolution, which with its ups and downs sometimes becomes bloody; but a revolution must not become stagnated; and now we must have no more bloodshed.

If this is anything like what the President actually said, it is a remarkably mild response to the news that the army's top generals had been kidnapped. It also indicates that Sukarno either suspected, or had been told, at this early stage that all the captured generals had been killed. At any rate, he gave no orders that a search be launched for them. Nor did he take any disciplinary action against

Supardjo. He did ask Supardjo, according to Dhani, whether he had any documentary proof that a "Council of Generals" existed, with subversive intent. Supardjo allegedly said he had and would produce it. But he never did.

Soon after this, the President left the Operations Command building and set up his own headquarters in the house of a senior air force officer not far away.

5. Enter Suharto

In the first few minutes of their coup operation, the plotters had made two blunders that were to prove catastrophic for them.

They had bungled the capture of General Nasution, the army's leader, and he had escaped. They had neglected to include General Suharto, the KOSTRAD commander, on the priority list of generals to be neutralized first, and he was at liberty.

For two men now catapulted into crucial roles, both generals were oddly self-effacing and retiring.

Nasution, 47 years old at the time of the coup, was born in north Sumatra and began his working career as a schoolteacher. He soon switched to the military life and after officer training was commissioned in the Royal Netherlands Indies Army. (The Dutch, of course, still ruled Indonesia at that time.)

Then came World War II, and like many Indonesian military men, Nasution was at first imprisoned by the occupying Japanese, then later worked for them. At the war's end, Nasution plunged enthusiastically into the fight for independence against the returning Dutch. A skillful guerrilla leader, he was a major general at 28 and commander of the Siliwangi division of the Indonesian Army.

Interestingly enough, seventeen years before Communists and rebel soldiers tried to murder him in their coup of October 1965, Nasution had played a key role in a drama with striking similarities. In 1948, in the East Javanese town of Madiun, troops under the command of Communist-sympathizing officers rebelled. Nasution was operations chief at nearby Jogjakarta. Swiftly he ordered the Siliwangi division into action, and quickly it smashed the Communist revolt.

Madiun, more than anything, may have been the event that stirred mounting suspicion of the Indonesian Communist Party in

Nasution over the years. However, it is all too simple to suggest, as some Western correspondents have, that Nasution was 'pro-Western' as a result. Most of the time, he has taken a strong nationalist line. In answers to questions I submitted to him at the height of Indonesia's confrontation with Malaysia he was slashing in his criticism of Britain and adamant that British bases 'safeguarding British political and economic interests in Southeast Asia' must go.

True, Nasution has many Western military friends. At the time of President Kennedy's assassination, Nasution and his wife were visiting the United States and stayed as the official Indonesian representatives at the funeral.

Though Nasution may have been suspicious of the Communists at home, it was to the Soviet Union that Indonesia's military establishment turned for much of its equipment. There is no indication that the Christian West has influenced Nasution, a devout Moslem, any more than the irreligious world of Communism has.

Despite his elevation over the years to highest military rank, Nasution maintained a relatively simple home life with his wife and two daughters. In his spare time he played tennis and golf and turned out various military books, among them a manual on guerrilla warfare used as a standard reference in several countries.

But now the peacefulness of that life was shattered as he lay injured, and in hiding, in the garden of his next-door neighbor, his five-year-old daughter dying from bullet wounds.

Meanwhile, though many stories have been told about General Suharto's lucky evasion of the killer gangs that night, the fact is that he was not on their list. Neither was he at home. Born in Jogjakarta (in 1921), General Suharto shares with many Javanese a belief in the mystic. Sources close to him say that he had, that night, taken the advice of a seer to spend it at the "confluence of two waters." So he had taken his son fishing at a spot where a river surged down into the sea.

In the days succeeding the murder of his fellow generals, Suharto, as he stamped about in battle fatigues directing the crushing of the coup, looked like a man in icy, but controlled, rage. Normally, however, he is a calm and patient man, a smile not far from his round, good-natured face.

Of humble origin, he worked his way up through the officer corps first under Dutch colonial command, then under the occupying Japanese, and finally in independent Indonesia's own army.

In the revolutionary fight against the Dutch he rose from battalion commander to brigade commander. But the high point of his career came later, in 1962, when he was given command of operations against the Dutch in West New Guinea. A year later he was appointed commander of KOSTRAD, the army's strategic reserve.

Now, after his all-night fishing trip, he returned home early on the morning of October 1 to find his household in confusion. Aides had a jumbled account of the generals' kidnapping, of a Communist coup, and of Sukarno himself having been killed. There was excited talk of making for Bandung, headquarters of the Siliwangi division, four hours' drive away, to try and set up some administration.

Some sources say Suharto checked with the Sultan of Jogjakarta. Despite his feudal title, the Sultan had a record as a good nationalist, and his name had been one of several suggested as an ultimate successor to Sukarno. He maintained a house in Djakarta, not far from Suharto's. According to these sources, the Sultan advised against a precipitate move to Bandung. Instead he checked with Madame Dewi Sukarno, who declared that her husband was far from dead.

Whether or not this consultation with the Sultan actually took place, Suharto's movements from then on are fairly clear. It was still very early, and his driver had not reported for duty at the General's house, so Suharto himself took a jeep and raced to KOSTRAD headquarters, a tight little group of brick buildings around a gravel parade ground, all fronting on Merdeka Square.

It was now nearing seven o'clock, and Suharto's staff officers were beginning to assemble for the start of the working day. Suharto called them into hasty war council, but at this stage had no clear picture of what was happening in the city. He soon had a better idea when General Umar, the Djakarta garrison commander, reported in. General Umar had made a tour of the homes of the kidnapped generals, then gone straight to Merdeka palace to try to contact Sukarno. The President was not there, but Umar did note that General Supardjo was in the palace. Umar's report of this caused consternation at KOSTRAD headquarters. Supardjo should have been at his post in Kalimantan commanding KOSTRAD forces there. He had not informed KOSTRAD, or Suharto, his superior officer, that he was coming to the capital. As Suharto himself explained later, with delightful understatement, he was "rather startled to learn that General Supardjo had come to Djakarta at all, let alone that he was at the palace very early in the morning."

With the pattern becoming clearer, Suharto announced to Umar and the other officers present that he was taking over leadership of the army. They agreed. His first orders were to confine all troops to quarters until he could sort out friend from foe. Then he got in touch with the navy and police force. Each agreed to give Suharto authority to coordinate all moves by the various armed services. But with the air force, as he recounted later, he "had difficulty in making contact. It was only with the air force that there was some foot-dragging in setting up coordination that morning. The affair had still not developed to the point where we knew who was friend and who foe."

By 7:20 A.M., however, the first rebel broadcast was coming over the radio. It was issued in the name of the September 30th Movement, whose leader was announced as Lieutenant Colonel

Untung. The movement had acted to forestall, said the radio, a coup by a "Council of Generals" in the army sponsored by the American Central Intelligence Agency. The Council of Generals the broadcast went on, had been "very active lately, especially since President Sukarno was seriously ill in the first week of August of this year. Their hope that President Sukarno would die of his illness has not materialized.

"Therefore, in order to attain its goal, the Council of Generals had planned to conduct a show of force on Armed Forces Day, October 5 this year, by bringing troops from East, Central, and West Java. With this large concentration of military power the Council of Generals had even planned to carry out a counterrevolutionary coup prior to October 5.'

The broadcast went on to say that action already taken against the Council of Generals in Djakarta "will be followed by actions throughout Indonesia against agents and sympathisers of the Council of Generals in the regions."

The announcement added that as a "follow-up action, an Indonesian Revolution Council will be established in the capital, while in the regions, provincial, district, sub-district, and village, revolution councils will be established. Members of the Revolution Council will be composed of civilians and military personnel who fully support the September 30th Movement."

As a fascinated capital listened, the radio broadcast went on to explain that the Revolution Council would consistently carry out the ideological concepts of the Indonesian revolution and the decisions of both the parliament and the Provisional People's Consultative Congress (MPRS), supreme policymaking body— both Sukarno-appointed assemblies. There would be no change in Indonesian foreign policy. This would remain "free, active and anti-Necolim." ("Necolim" was then Indonesia's word for Western imperialists and neo-colonialists.)

Nor would there be any change in the confrontation policy against Malaysia.

In Untung's name the broadcast then called on all military men to eradicate completely the influence of the Council of Generals and its agents in the army. "Power-mad generals and officers who have neglected the lot of their men," said the broadcast, "and who above the accumulated sufferings of their men have lived in luxury, led a dissolute life, insulted our women and wasted government funds, must be kicked out of the army and punished accordingly. The army is not for generals, but is the possession of all soldiers of the army who are loyal to the ideals of the revolution."

Then, in a significant addition, Untung was quoted as having "thanked all troops of the armed forces outside the army for their assistance in the purging of the army, and hoped that purges also will be carried out in the other branches of the armed forces against agents and sympathizers of the Council of Generals."

Within a short time, the broadcast concluded, Untung would announce the first decree concerning the Indonesian Revolution Council. Other decrees would follow.

Now Suharto was beginning to find his way. He suspected the air force, but he believed he had the navy and the police under control. He knew that Untung had troops under his command and that they were around the palace and had taken certain vital installations. But he was not yet sure how many troops Untung had, nor exactly where they were deployed. To find this out was his next urgent task.

About 8 A.M. he got good news. Nasution was rescued and safe. Suharto decided to keep him hidden till he could be brought to KOSTRAD headquarters under heavy escort. The precaution was a wise one. For when the plotters realized they had failed to capture and kill Nasution, they apparently sent assassins throughout the city to try and find him. Colonel Latief, it later transpired, visited the central military hospital, where Nasution's daughter had been taken, between ten and eleven o'clock. Dressed in civilian clothes, he inquired of hospital officials whether General Nasution was present with his daughter. If Nasution had been there, Latief would presumably have tried to gun him down. In fact, Nasution was kept hidden throughout the day and arrived at KOSTRAD with an armored escort early in the evening of October 1. There both he and Suharto, sleeping on simple army cots in a pair of offices just across the corridor from each other, were to spend the next three months.

By now Suharto was beginning to get a good idea of Untung's forces. The troops around the palace were wearing green berets— headgear of the two battalions from Central and East Java that had been moved in for the Armed Forces Day parade October 5, but whose commanders had put them at the disposal of the coup leaders.

Meanwhile the commander of troops stationed at the Senajan sports complex in readiness for the parade a few days hence reported that he had mustered his men, but two battalions, the 454th from Central Java and the 530th from East Java, were missing. Ironically, Suharto himself had inspected the whole infantry brigade, which was due to take part in the parade, only the day before. He was scheduled to watch a parade rehearsal by these troops at the Senajan open-air stadium that very morning. Needless to say, it never took place.

Instead, it now became apparent that the two visiting battalions that were in revolt were holding positions on three sides of Merdeka Square. On one side of the square they had encircled the presidential palace. On another they had taken the radio station. On a third they were in control of the telecommunications building.

KOSTRAD, meanwhile, the headquarters of the loyalist forces, was on the fourth side of the square! Though the square is a huge grassy expanse, so that the various forces were separated by some distance, it obviously was a potentially explosive situation. Totting up the forces at his disposal in the capital area, Suharto figured he could count on the following: the 328th Battalion of the Siliwangi division (also in town for the forthcoming parade), a KOSTRAD brigade (comprising a battalion of cavalry [armor] and a battalion of artillery), and garrison troops from the Djakarta area who had remained loyal although their brigade commander, Colonel Latief, had proved a traitor.

The two battalions in revolt mustered about a thousand men apiece. Later, Suharto was to discover that about 3,000 armed Communist civilians from the Pemuda Rakjat were loose, as well, in the capital area, but for the moment, his main concern was those two disloyal battalions deployed around Merdeka Square. He decided to try to talk them into surrender.

To help him in the task he assembled various officers who had friends in the two battalions, or who had commanded them at one time or another. One of these was General Basuchi Rachmat, the East Java commander, who had spent the previous evening reporting to General Yani and who was supposed to report with Yani to Sukarno this very morning. However, Basuchi Rachmat had been telephoned and told of the generals' kidnapping, so he took off for a cruise around town by car to try to find out what was happening.

Approaching Merdeka Square, he was surprised to see in position there the 530th Battalion from his own East Java command. He was even more surprised to see them wearing shoulder ribbons he could not identify—the ribbons issued by the coup forces. His aide was nervous and warned him not to stop, so his car wheeled away. Then he got word Suharto wanted him at KOSTRAD to help the others try to talk the two disloyal battalions into giving up.

Were it not for the tragedy of the night's events, the developments of the next few hours would border on the comic.

The rebels held points on three sides of the square, while the headquarters of loyalist forces was on the fourth side. Emissaries and officers from KOSTRAD were sent shuttling over to the rebels, trying to contact their commanders. To their astonishment, the rebel troops around the palace snapped smartly to attention and saluted them each time they passed. This was an indication to Suharto that at least the ordinary soldiers in the 530th Battalion guarding the palace were confused, with no clear idea whom they were serving.

With all the coming and going, Suharto soon discovered that the commanders of the two battalions were inside the palace. He succeeded in getting the deputy commanders to report to him at KOSTRAD. They told him they had been assigned to guard Sukarno against a coup by the Council of Generals. Suharto assured them there was no generals' coup and declared that they themselves were supporting a coup.

As Suharto himself explained it later, "I told them 'You have been tricked into thinking you are guarding the President. But actually you have been manipulated into protecting the activities of this coup movement. You've been used good and proper. Now if you're really still loyal to the revolution and the soldier's oath, go and collect your men and come back here to report to me. If you don't, I'll be forced to take drastic action.'"

With the 454th Battalion, Suharto was unlucky. As the deputy commander passed on to his colleagues the story Suharto had told him, the battalion commander returned from the palace, resumed control, and kept his men working for the September 30th Movement.

With the 530th, there was more success. By four o'clock that afternoon, the battalion had left its positions around the palace and was moving into KOSTRAD headquarters. After screening and separation of those men who were clearly disloyal from those who were simply misled, the battalion was in fact used later by Suharto in mopping-up operations against the coup forces.

6. Plotters in Disarray

At Halim air force base, the initial mood was apparently one of optimism among the plotters.

They had, they thought, wiped out the army's top generals. Their troops held key installations. Sukarno himself was now among them, not particularly angry about the action they had taken, and certainly indicating no intention of arresting, restraining, or even reprimanding them.

Air force commander Dhani felt so sure things were going well that he issued an order of the day virtually throwing the air force's support behind the September 30th Movement. Although it was not, in fact, broadcast until the afternoon, Dhani signed it early that morning.

The order made four points. First was that the September 30th Movement's actions had been to safeguard the revolution and the President against "C.I.A. subversion." In this connection, it said, "the body of the army has already been purged of those elements who are manipulated by foreign subversives and who endanger the Indonesian revolution."

Second, the order warned that "foreign subversives and their henchmen will not remain idle and will very likely intensify their anti revolutionary movement."

Third, the order pledged that the Indonesian Air Force would "always and continuously support and uphold any progressive revolutionary movement," and conversely "combat any action which endangers the Indonesian revolution."

Last, the order called on all air force men to "maintain vigilance against provocation and harassment and intensify preparedness against all eventualities, internal as well as external."

But Sukarno himself, the wily old fox of Indonesian politics whose expert instincts had given him a remarkable record for political survival, was apparently far from certain which way things were going, particularly after he got the news that Nasution was at large.

Installed at the home of a senior air force officer, he chatted with the officer's wife, took an unhurried breakfast, and began to confer with aides and advisers. Incredibly, at one stage later in the morning, he even retired for a nap.

To Halim he summoned the chiefs of the navy and the police force and the attorney general. Of the three deputy premiers only one, Johannes Lemeina, whose guard had been killed during the attack on Nasution's house, was in town. He arrived later. (Chairul Saleh, another deputy premier, was in Peking with the big Indonesian delegation attending China's national day celebrations. The celebrations, interestingly enough, were taking place on the same day the coup had been launched, October 1.) Meanwhile, the senior deputy premier and Sukarno's right-hand man, Foreign Minister Subandrio, was away in north Sumatra on a speaking tour. From Halim went a cable telling him to come back, and the President's Jet-Star went flying up there to fetch him, but cannily, Subandrio decided to sit things out for another day before returning.

Another key figure, Communist leader Aidit, was also at Halim, tucked discreetly away in the home of an air force sergeant. The circumstances of Aidit's survival at the air base are not clear. Several people involved in the plot say he arrived about eleven o'clock the previous night and slept there.

Several times during the morning and early afternoon of October 1, General Supardjo conferred with Sukarno. He may have been seeking Sukarno's blessing for the revolutionary council the September 30th Movement had promised to announce. If so, he was disappointed. Sukarno was too skillful a maneuverer to put his name to that document.

What he did was appoint a caretaker commander of the army, Major General Pranoto Reksosamudro, then third assistant to the minister of the army. Air force chief Dhani, at his trial later, recalled that when the President raised the matter with senior officers assembled at Halim, other generals' names were mentioned, too— KOSTRAD commander Suharto, General Mursid, first deputy to the army commander, and Basuchi Rachmat, the East Java commander who had flown to the capital to report to Yani. Sukarno, according to Dhani, dismissed them all. Suharto, said the President, was "stubborn." Mursid was "always fighting." Basuchi Rachmat was "often sick." Sukarno himself chose Pranoto and signed an order of the day that was issued early in the afternoon.

The order declared that he, Sukarno, was safe and well and continued "to hold the leadership of the state and the revolution." It said that he had temporarily taken the leadership of the armed forces directly into his hands, and that General Pranoto had been "temporarily appointed to carry out the day-to-day tasks within the army."

The appointment by Sukarno of a caretaker army commander at this particular time was later made much of by Sukarno's critics. The bodies of the murdered generals were not found until Monday, and how, runs the argument, could Sukarno have been so sure, so early, of General Yani's fate? The criticism is a little naive. For Sukarno was at the very air base where the generals had been murdered not a few hours before. He was among, and being briefed by, the officers who had ordered the generals killed. He can have been under no illusions at that time of the generals' fate.

Now it was time for the September 30th Movement to unveil its revolutionary council. All over the city, people hunched by their radios to hear the proclamation. At Halim, an aide hurried in to Sukarno with a transistor radio. At KOSTRAD headquarters there was an excited buzz as officers detailed to monitor the radio signaled the beginning of the announcement.

It came at 2 P.M. It was issued in the name of the Command of the September 30th Movement (Commandant Untung, Deputy Commandant Supardjo). The decree said a purge had been carried out against a Council of Generals, which had planned a coup on the eve of Armed Forces Day, October 5. A number of generals had "been arrested."

The September 30th Movement, the decree went on, was entirely confined within the army, but it had been "assisted by armed units not belonging to the army."

To facilitate the "follow-up" of the purge, the movement was setting up an Indonesian Revolution Council whose members would "consist of civilian and military individuals who unreservedly support the September 30th Movement."

For the time being, pending general elections, the council would "constitute the source of all authority" in Indonesia. The cabinet "automatically assumes a decommissioned status," said the decree. "Until the formation of a new council of ministers," former ministers were duty bound to carry out routine tasks, but were "prohibited from taking actions which may have broad consequences."

As instruments of the Indonesian Revolution Council there would be established provincial revolution councils (with a maximum membership of 25), district revolution councils (with a maximum membership of 15), subdistrict revolution councils (with a maximum membership of 10), and village revolution councils (with a maximum membership of 7). All these would be composed of "civilian and military personnel who unreservedly support the September 30th Movement."

The radio announcement went on to say that Untung and Supardjo would together form the presidium of the Revolution Council, and their written approval would be necessary for the composition of the various provincial revolution councils. The provincial councils would then approve the district revolution councils, and so on down the line.

Then came a list of 45 names of people appointed to the central Revolution Council.

It was in a number of respects a strange list. Headed by Untung and Supardjo, it included a number of central figures in the plot— Heru, Sujono, Latief, and Colonel Suherman, who was busy organizing revolt in Central Java. It included air force chief Dhani, but also the heads of the navy and the police force. Of the three deputy premiers, it included Subandrio and Lemeina, but not Chairul Saleh. It included Tjugito, the Communist Party central committee member who almost certainly was "Sjam," one of the principal plotters, and Sukatno, the Pemuda Rakjat leader charged with assembling his thugs at Lubang Buaja. But it also included Generals Umar and Basuchi Rachmat, who even now were at KOSTRAD helping Suharto put down the coup.

It made no mention whatsoever of Sukarno.

After all this came an odd additional little announcement. It declared that as the commandant of the September 30th Movement was an officer with the rank of lieutenant colonel, all ranks above that were "herewith declared invalid." Henceforward lieutenant colonel would be the "highest rank in the armed forces" of Indonesia. However, all enlisted men and NCOs who supported the September 30th Movement would be "promoted one grade above those they occupied before September 30, 1965."

And all enlisted men and NCOs who "took a direct part in the purge against the members of the Council of Generals" would be promoted two grades above those they occupied before September 30.

They would not enjoy their elevated ranks—or, in the case of senior officers, their demotions—for long. At KOSTRAD headquarters, Suharto was now moving confidently against the coup forces. He listened to the announcement of the Revolution Council and noted the declaration that the cabinet was "demissionary," as he put it later. He noted, too, that there was no mention of Sukarno. "On our analysis of their announcements," he explained later, "we now understood the objective of the September 30th Movement as being none other than a coup. We could now separate who was friend and foe. The foe was first of all battalions 454 and 530, and the first Tjakrabirawa battalion, who were all involved at that point.

"After the announcement of a Revolution Council led by Untung, the air force leadership issued a statement [Dhani's order of the day] that the air forcefully supported the movement and the Revolution Council. Various indications I had already received, first the difficulty I had in coordinating the air force, second the fact that the top leadership had been 'taken to safety' before the affair broke out, and third, the statement of support—well, even a fool would have been able to tell that the air force must be classed with the foe that we had now to face."

But Suharto's main concern was to avoid bloodshed. He was successfully talking the 530th Battalion into giving up its positions around the presidential palace and turning itself in to KOSTRAD. He was still trying to do the same with the 454th Battalion, which held the radio station and the telecommunications building. Now he gave them an ultimatum: evacuate their positions by 8 P.M., or he would blast them out with his own guns and troops.

Explaining his tactics later, he said, "I gave top priority to avoiding bloodshed. I could have seized the radio station early in the morning. But this would have resulted in shooting, and at that time I still did not know the real background to the September 30th Movement. Once the announcement of the Revolution Council and its composition had been made, their real activities were unmasked, convincing us that we no longer need hesitate to take action against the September 30th Movement."

In fact, the rebel troops around Merdeka Square were in no mood to fight. The 530th Battalion, purged of its disloyal elements, allied itself to Suharto's cause. By 6 P.M. Suharto had his troops in offensive position. He had summoned up, from their base about fifteen miles outside Djakarta, the RPKAD para-commandos led by then Colonel Sarwo Edhy. Together with a battalion of Siliwangi division troops already in the capital for Armed Forces Day, they were assigned to assault the radio station and telecommunications building and dislodge the rebels. But the attack was not necessary, for the rebels quietly pulled out and withdrew by truck in the direction of Halim.

Shortly after 8 P.M., Suharto was in control of the whole area and the key installations around Merdeka Square. Soon after that, the radio station broadcast an announcement that it had been liberated from counterrevolutionary control by the armed forces, which had been constantly loyal to President Sukarno. Then came an official army notice, explaining that the September 30th Movement was counterrevolutionary, that it had kidnapped a number of high army officers, and that it had illegally occupied the radio station and telecommunications building.

The announcement went on to say that both Sukarno and Nasution were safe, and that Suharto had temporarily taken over leadership of the army. The "general situation," said the announcement, "is again under control, and security measures are being actively carried out. The general public is urged to remain calm and continue their respective tasks as usual."

So far, so good. But despite Suharto's confident reassurance that the "general situation" was "again under control," there was still the dangerous problem of Halim air base to deal with.

Suharto knew that Halim was the command post of the September 30th Movement. But as he said later, he also believed that "not everyone there was involved in the affair." He knew that Sukarno was at Halim, but he was not sure whether the President was "secure" or "secured." He also knew that Sukarno had asked for various high army officers to go to Halim, but Suharto forbade them to do so on grounds he "did not want to lose any more generals."

Now some of the rebel soldiers had withdrawn to Halim. And Suharto had been given grounds for deepened suspicion of the air force by another ironic incident in the near-comic saga of events around Merdeka Square that day.

After the 530th Paratroop Battalion had placed itself under his command, he sent it off to secure the National Front building, the old vice-presidential residence, near the telecommunications building. Now arrived truckloads of Pemuda Rakjat trainees from Halim, unaware that the rebel army units previously in the area had themselves evacuated to Halim. The Pemuda Rakjat troops confidently called out the password "Ampera." But instead of the counterword "Takari," they got pointed weapons and were taken swiftly under arrest. Under interrogation they admitted that the air force had issued weapons to about 3,000 of them and that these armed members of the Communist youth group were at large in the city.

To Suharto this news was highly disturbing. "There seemed good reason to believe," he explained later, "that the early morning of October 2 would witness even more violent events, possibly a general attack, or an attempt to take back the area around the palace. As a soldier, I knew one should always anticipate the enemy. I decided we must take control of Halim that very night."

He was plagued by another fear, that the air force might launch an air attack on the capital, and specifically on his forces. KOSTRAD headquarters were in fact evacuated that night, for fear of such an attack, and temporary headquarters were established at the Senajan sports stadium on the outskirts of the city. Suharto and his staff moved back to their normal headquarters the next day, after Halim had been taken.

But for the moment Suharto was busy planning his assault on

Halim. Again, his concern was to avoid bloodshed if possible. To spearhead the attack he selected the RPKAD para-commandos, ordering them to infiltrate under cover of darkness. Also ready was a company of tanks. "If we had trained all of them on Halim," he later explained, "we could have destroyed it completely. But the airplanes and buildings were our—Indonesia's—property. I did not want everything, especially the air force [aircraft] to be completely destroyed." Thus his orders were to avoid shooting, wherever his troops could do so.

Before the attack could begin, however, there was one problem Suharto had to resolve—Sukarno's presence at Halim. About 8 P.M., Suharto talked to one of the President's aides, and told him that he must somehow get the President clear of Halim before the attack began.

The problem was soon to be solved, for the early optimism at Halim had deteriorated steadily throughout the day. The hodgepodge composition of the Revolution Council may be an indication that even by early afternoon, when the council was announced, the organizers of the coup were trying to cover their tracks by including people who could not possibly have been involved in the September 30th Movement. By evening, the plotters were in a state of desperate gloom and making plans to flee.

Supardjo, his troops in retreat and disarray, made an anguished last-minute suggestion that he attack KOSTRAD headquarters, but he was outvoted. The game was up.

Sukarno himself was now as anxious as Suharto that he should leave Halim before Suharto's troops attacked. But he was apparently uncertain where he should go. His Japanese wife, Dewi, hurried into Halim by car, and the President talked with her for a while. Dhani and others urged him to fly to Madiun, in East Java, scene of the 1948 Communist uprising. Dhani was himself planning to go there. Although the coup had failed in

Djakarta, some of the plotters had the vain hope that they could regroup in Central Java. If they could get Sukarno to go with them, it might give their movement an aura of legitimacy.

Sukarno apparently seriously considered the idea, but was talked out of it, mainly by Deputy Premier Lemeina. Lemeina insisted that the President should disentangle himself from the coup organizers and head for the weekend palace at Bogor, 40 miles south of Djakarta, by car. This Sukarno did.

Supardjo, meanwhile, was pleading for a plane for Aidit, the Communist Party leader. Dhani ordered one up, and Aidit flew off to Jogjakarta, in Central Java, landing there about 2 A.M. the next day, October 2. The troops who had taken part in the coup were ordered to withdraw to Central Java. Some were evacuated by air force planes; others set off by road.

By midnight the central figures in the coup had fled Halim. Air force chief Dhani himself took to a Hercules aircraft and flew around for six hours before landing at Madiun. While he was in the air, he talked to various air force bases throughout the country, briefing them on the situation. Also, he radioed Suharto, warning him not to assault Halim because the air force would fight back. But Halim was already within Suharto's grasp.

Throughout the night the para-commandos had been quietly surrounding the air base and infiltrating its perimeter. With radar they monitored outgoing aircraft, trying to assess whether they were going for reinforcements. On an incoming plane they opened fire. This was the Jet-Star that had been sent up to north Sumatra to bring back Deputy Premier Subandrio. Subandrio had balked and stayed, and thus was not on the aircraft. The deputy air force commander, Sri Muljono Herlambang, who had been with the Subandrio party, was aboard; the plane was not hit and landed safely.

At dawn the paratroopers rushed the air base. Resistance was negligible. There was some shooting, but this was at an angry water buffalo, disturbed by the red berets of the para-commandos, which charged them and had to be killed. By 6:10 in the morning of October 2, Suharto had taken Halim without a casualty to his men. Though much mopping up remained to be done, in the capital at any rate the coup had been smashed little more than twenty-four hours after it was launched.

7. The PKI Story

There now occurred one of the most inexplicable developments in the whole affair. Although General Suharto had clearly smashed the September 30th Movement in Djakarta, the Communist Party newspaper, *Harian Rakjat*, went on the capital's streets early October 2 with an editorial supporting the movement. It was an act of incredible political stupidity by the Partai Kommunis Indonesia (PKI) which was to set the seal on the party's fate.

The explanation is probably that the editorial was written, and the paper set and printed, late the previous afternoon. This would be in accord with the paper's normal publishing routine. At the time, the newspaper's editors must have deduced that things were going fairly well for the coup forces, although by late afternoon the tide had in fact set in against them.

But, having printed the editorial, it is astonishing that the Communists did not go to all lengths next morning to prevent the paper's appearing on the streets at a time when the coup had obviously failed in Djakarta.

With the damning editorial placing the Communists squarely on the side of the losers went a crude cartoon at the bottom of *Harian Rakjat's* front page. It portrayed a mighty fist, labeled "September 30th Movement," smashing into the face of an Indonesian general. His pockets were stuffed with money bills, he had dollar signs for epaulettes, his shoulder badges showed him to be a member of the Council of Generals, and his cap was stamped with the letters "C.I.A.," obviously for Central Intelligence Agency.

Propping him up with a now broken general's baton was a particularly unpleasant-looking Uncle Sam. A second picture showed a pair of generals, with dollars and C.I.A. labels flying, being tossed onto a row of bayonets and sharpened stakes.

The *Harian Rakjat* editorial read as follows:

"It has happened that on the 30th of September measures were taken to safeguard President Sukarno and the Republic of Indonesia from a coup by a so-called Council of Generals. According to what has been announced by the September 30th Movement, which is headed by Lieutenant Colonel Untung of a Tjakrabirawa battalion, action taken to preserve President Sukarno and the Republic of Indonesia from the Council of Generals is patriotic and revolutionary.

"Whatever the justification that may have been used by the Council of Generals in its attempt, the staging of a coup is a condemnable and counterrevolutionary act.

"We the people fully comprehend what Lieutenant Colonel Untung has asserted in carrying out his patriotic movement.

"But however the case may be, this is an internal army affair. On the other hand, we the people, who are conscious of the policy and duties of the revolution, are convinced of the correctness of the action taken by the September 30th Movement to preserve the revolution and the people.

"The sympathy and support of the people is surely on the side of the September 30th Movement. We call on the people to intensify their vigilance and be prepared to confront all eventualities."

With these 202 ill-advised words, the newspaper gave the coup the Communist Party's public endorsement—and provided the documentary justification for the party's own obliteration.

Here a glimpse of the party's past history is useful. This was the third time that the Indonesian Communist Party, the oldest Communist party in Asia, had been involved in catastrophic revolts. The party was born in 1920, when the Russian revolution was only three years old, and long before Communism had begun to cast its spell upon China. The party blossomed from something called the Indies Social Democratic Association, founded by H. J. F. M.

Sneevliet, a Dutch radical socialist aflame with Marxist ideology.

Its first chairman was Tan Malaka, a young Sumatran, but he was swiftly exiled by the Dutch colonial government. Sneevliet had already been expelled from the country by his own government earlier.

Now there developed a serious policy split in the party. One faction was for armed revolt in a desperate bid to seize power from the colonial rulers. Tan Malaka, now the Comintern agent for Southeast Asia and Australia, operating from Manila, was against it, but the extremists won out. In the early hours of November 13, 1926, two hundred armed men assaulted the telephone and telegraph building in Batavia (as the capital then was called). Simultaneously there were sporadic uprisings in various parts of Java with some violence and murder, but from the people there was no support for the Communists. Within hours, the Dutch colonial army had retaken the telephone and telegraph building in the capital. Within a week the half-hearted revolt was completely crushed. Then the Dutch cracked down on the Communist Party so thoroughly that it would not emerge again until 1935.

In the intervening years, Tan Malaka virtually defected from the international Communist movement and set up his own rival Marxist-Leninist party, operating out of Bangkok. But in Moscow the Soviets had been carefully cultivating one of the leaders of the abortive 1926 revolt, Musso. In 1935, Stalin sent him back to Indonesia to revive secretly the Indonesian Communist Party on pro-Soviet lines.

Musso left his country the following year, but after a further absence of twelve years he popped up again in Indonesia in 1948 as Moscow's emissary. His line was a tough one, but before he could carefully lay the plans for a new Communist drive for power, he was overtaken by events. On September 18, 1948, Communist officers in army units at Madiun, in East Java, seized control there. Musso and other Communist Party leaders hastened to support the rebellion.

Once again, Indonesia was confronted by a Communist uprising.

This time it was the Indonesian army, not the Dutch, that struck back at the Communists. The Siliwangi division moved on Madiun, held by rebellious troops and Communist irregulars. In Jogjakarta, loyalist forces captured Communist documents that seemed to indicate the party had been preparing for a coup the following month, but that the Madiun Communists in the army had jumped the gun.

Within two weeks, Madiun had fallen to the loyalist forces. They entered the town on September 30. The date is particularly interesting, for seventeen years later, to the very day, the organizers of the 1965 coup launched their operation.

Mopping up of Communist guerrillas continued in Central Java. Musso was captured and killed. Full details of the incident were not made clear, but in reconstructing the sequence of the 1965 coup, I came upon the army officer who executed Musso with a .38 Colt revolver, and who had sworn his colleagues never to reveal his name, all those years before.

Once again the machinery of the Indonesian Communist Party was smashed, its members hounded into oblivion. Into the vacuum on the political left jumped Tan Malaka, who, though he had broken with the formal Communist movement, had formed the Marxist Murba party under a kind of nationalist-Communist banner.

Tan Malaka now mounted a guerrilla campaign against almost everybody—the Communist Party, the leaders of Indonesia who had proclaimed independence in 1945 but were still fighting the Dutch for it, the Dutch themselves, Washington, and even Moscow.

But in 1949, Tan Malaka was arrested and executed. As in 1926, Indonesia's Communists were again discredited and in disarray after an abortive rebellion.

One of the party members who succeeded in slipping out of the country after the Madiun affair was a young Sumatran named Dipa

Nusantara Aidit. Born in 1923, he was the son of a forest worker who had not been able to keep up the payments for his son's education at a commercial high school in the capital. Aidit took a part-time job as a tailor's assistant to help pay for his education. Drawn into one of the student youth organizations of the day, he soon showed a flair for politics, and soon thereafter for the politics of the Communist Party.

In 1950, after two years abroad in Communist and other countries, Aidit returned to his homeland. His flair for politics had clearly sharpened. Swiftly, he seized control of the Communist Party's politburo. Not long after, at the age of 31, he became the party's secretary-general. In Aidit, Indonesia's Communists had a leader to guide the party to brilliant success.

Within a few years he had made it the third largest Communist Party in the world, ranking only after the parties of the Soviet Union and China.

When I interviewed Aidit at Communist Party headquarters in Djakarta in December of 1964, he was clearly a man conscious both of his future and of the distance he had come. By this I do not mean that he was pompous, or immodest. But he had a realistic appreciation of how much influence he and his party had achieved, and of how much power there was yet to be gained.

A brisk little man, with dark, flying hair, he was hardly friendly. But he was much more relaxed than many another Communist leader under cross-examination by a Western correspondent. And from time to time he smiled readily, as when I asked him whether he was satisfied with his party's then legitimate but limited role in President Sukarno's government.

"What party," he countered, spreading his hands, "is ever satisfied? We think the strength of our party entitles us to a bigger say in government than we have now."

As we talked, in a rather bare little reception room in the

party's wooden headquarters building, workmen hammered away outside and swung steel girders up and down the multi-story structure adjacent, which was to be the party's new home. A model of it, in the room in which we talked, showed it to be an impressive building, a symbol of Aidit's confidence in his party's future. But less than a year later, the Communist Party was again discredited after an abortive coup, Aidit was dead, the wooden building in which we talked was burned to the ground by angry anti-Communists, and the big new concrete office block was turned over to the Indonesian maritime ministry for its use.

Our interview was brought to an end by the arrival of a big black Mercedes bearing diplomatic plates. "And now," said Aidit with a chuckle, "I must receive the Soviet Ambassador. Print in your newspaper that I receive the Soviet Ambassador." He did not tell me, as I was to discover later, that he was informing the Soviet Ambassador that the Indonesian party, because of its pro-Chinese line, would not be attending a conference of world Communist parties in Moscow.

Clearly he enjoyed the bustle and importance of his considerable role as leader of the largest Communist party in the non-Communist world. As I left I heard him explaining in English to the Soviet Ambassador, "I am being interviewed by *The Christian Science Monitor*."

At one point in our interview, Aidit turned the tables and asked me, "How do you find the political situation in Indonesia?" With complete honesty, I was able to reply without hesitation, "Confused."

Aidit smiled. "That," he said, "is because you're not looking at things the right way. Everything's simple here, if you see it from a Marxist-Leninist point of view."

Nevertheless, from a pure Marxist-Leninist point of view, the Indonesian Communist Party under Aidit's guidance achieved its success via some strangely unorthodox tactics.

When Aidit assumed the party's leadership he had, of course, a notable advantage over his predecessors. Whereas they were operating a clandestine party under surveillance by a colonial government, Aidit was master of a party that could work legally in the free and heady atmosphere of an independent Indonesia. He had much more room for maneuver, much more opportunity for organization. So well did Aidit organize it that its membership snowballed from around 8,000 in 1952 to the 3,000,000 claimed by Aidit in 1965. In addition to actual party strength, Aidit built a series of Communist front organizations that he claimed gave the party a further following of about 16,000,000 people.

These fronts included a Communist peasants' organization (BTI) of some 8,500,000, a Communist trade union organization (SOBSI) of 3,500,000, the youth organization (Pemuda Rakjat)of 2,000,000, and the women's organization (Gerwani) of 2,000,000.

To achieve such growth, however, Aidit embarked his party on a series of remarkable compromises. Aware when he took over that his discredited party had little immediate prospect of gaining power, Aidit proclaimed a disarming policy of non-interference in the affairs of other parties and of co-operation in some kind of national front. He seems to have decided that if the Communist Party could not beat the others, it would join them, though— Communists being Communists—he probably had one further step in mind after joining them, namely, to beat them when they were not looking.

Thus, publicly at any rate, the Indonesian Communist Party went respectable. Aidit subscribed to Sukarno's *Pantja Sila*, a series of five principles: belief in God, nationalism, humanism, democracy and social justice. For atheistic Communists, perhaps this admission of a divine Being was the most surprising, but the fact is that the party recruited many sturdy members who continued to be good, practicing Moslems. As Aidit himself put it, "There are more real

Moslems in the Communist Party than in small Moslem parties. If a party member wants to go to a mosque or church—be it Moslem, Buddhist, or Christian—we let them go. The only thing we require is that they must be patriots."

Explaining his cooperation with other political parties, Aidit had this to say, "The concrete practice of Marxism-Leninism is not the same in any country. In China, Mao Tse-tung fought against counterrevolutionaries, and won. In our country it is different. We have a parliamentary system—not so in China. We have broad national unity between Communists, nationalists, and religious parties. We have a common program accepted by all parties.

"The special, principal thing is *Pantja Sila* and Nasakom [another Sukarno-devised concept indicating the three main streams supporting the government: nationalist, religious, Communist. The idea of Nasakom has existed since 1927, when Sukarno analyzed the political situation in Indonesia. To smash imperialism, he said, three groups should unite, the Marxists, the nationalists, and the Moslems."

Aidit went on, "The nationalists, Sukarno said, are an important force, but they have shortcomings. They must eliminate chauvinism from their rank and file, and must co-operate with other groups. The Moslems are an important force, but must be modernized. The Marxists are important, but must fight sectarianism; they must unite to cooperate with all patriotic groups. According to me, his analysis was correct."

Thus confident of Sukarno's blessing for a legal role in government, the Communist Party campaigned vigorously in the 1955 general election, the last to be held before Sukarno froze further national elections. The Communists won more than 6,000,000 votes, some 16 percent of the total cast, ranking fourth in the list of parties.

It was in Central Java, however, that the Communists struck pay dirt. Java is lush, green, fertile. But two simple statistics are enough to explain the Communists' success with its people. Java is about one seventh of the total area of Indonesia. Into it are crammed about two thirds of Indonesia's 105,000,000 population. Nowhere is the overcrowding more evident than in Central Java, which is one of the most densely populated areas in the world. There are too many people for too little land. Thus on those ominously familiar problems of land hunger, poverty, and frustration, the Indonesian Communist Party throve.

In local elections two years after the 1965 general election, the party came not fourth, but first, in Central Java.

Land reform was the promise with which Aidit wooed the peasants. The promises came not from afar and on high. Party leaders got out into the country, muddy and knee-deep in the rice paddies. They mixed with the peasants, listened to their tales of hardship, sympathized, and promised a better deal under Communist auspices. Aidit himself led a research team that made a four-month-long agricultural survey in Java. It was not all empty words, for the party came through with help in many instances.

In Djakarta a leading anti-Communist politician got a message one day that his father in Central Java had joined the Communist Party. As soon as he could get away, he sped home to his father's fields to find out what had happened. This is the story his father told him:

"I was in my fields when a man stopped and started chatting about my problems. The problems are always the same at this time of year—how to get money for seed and planting. Usually I have to borrow, and by the time the moneylenders are through, it costs me fifty percent interest.

"A few days later my visitor returned. He lent me all I needed at five percent interest. He was the representative of the Communist Party, and the party lent me the money.

"All my life I have been in debt, and my father and grandfather before me. Now for the first time I am free, and the Communists have made it so. And you ask me why I have decided to support them?"

Of course, the Communists did not make such loans indiscriminately. The meeting with the Communist agent was almost certainly planned, however casual it might have seemed to the farmer. He was selected for the loan because he was influential in his community. Similarly, loans were directed to village chiefs and others from whom the Communists hoped to profit most by the investment.

With its grass-roots, or rather rice-roots, base in Central Java, and its skillful penetration of the organs of government in Djakarta, the Communist Party rolled onward to success and influence. Aidit had hitched his party, at least for the while, to Sukarno's star. Thus the Communists backed Sukarno's policies fervently. They supported, after some initial hesitation, his concept of "guided democracy" for Indonesia. They encouraged him in the campaign to wrest West New Guinea from the Dutch. They pandered to his extreme nationalism.

In return, they did not find him ungrateful. By the end of 1964, many factions and parties hindering the progress of the Communist Party had conveniently melted away. Came the climax with Sukarno's banning of the Body for the Preservation of Sukarnoism (BPS). This was a group organized by a former journalist and politician called Adam Malik to draw attention to the Communists' departure from basic nationalist and revolutionary tenets expounded by Sukarno. It was a clever ploy. The object of the party was to do battle with the Communists, and in choosing Sukarno's own platform and preachings on which to justify the fight, the BPS movement believed it might be safe. It was a vain hope. Sukarno banned it.

Now the Communist Party was hungry for power, or at least a

substantial share of it. Though it had followed Sukarno loyally, it had never penetrated the inner cabinet. In some respects, this had been advantageous. For although close to the seat of power, the Communist Party had never been publicly identified with the government. Thus it could quietly dissociate itself from the horrendous corruption, the negligence, and the inefficiency that were grinding the country's economy toward a halt.

One serious obstacle lay in the path of the party's ambitions— the army. After West New Guinea (or West Irian, as it became under Indonesian rule), the Communists quickly came to the support of Sukarno in his next external adventure. This was confrontation against Malaysia, a federation of various former British territories to Indonesia's north. Some observers say one of the reasons the Communists were so enthusiastic was that confrontation distracted the army from the home front and enmeshed many of its units in remote northern border areas, far from the Communist Party's main base of operations in Java.

Another reason may simply have been that the Indonesian Communist Party, like Communist parties elsewhere, seemed to thrive on ferment, whether economic disruption that worked to its advantage at home, or adventures abroad that extended and sapped the energies and resources of legitimate authority.

Certainly a man as intelligent as Aidit can have been under no illusions that little Malaysia posed any real threat to Indonesia. It was a convenient political gimmick, and he used it to best advantage.

Soon, of course, the Communists injected into the anti-British hysteria of the confrontation campaign a stream of anti-Americanism. The dosage was steadily increased until the United States became a bigger bogey than Britain.

But despite the "threat" of the Americans and the British, and any other diversions the Communists could manufacture, still there stood solidly in the way of the party's advancement to greater things the physical power of the army. The army's officer corps remained largely non-Communist or anti-Communist. For a party of greedy ambition, it must have been a gnawing frustration.

8. Revolution off the Rails

Despite its skillful leadership and energetic organization, the Indonesian Communist Party could not have reached such importance by 1965 without two other factors. The first of these was the country's increasingly desperate economic crisis. The second was President Sukarno's own political slide toward the left.

Whatever the merits and demerits of Dutch colonial rule, and Japanese occupation during World War II, when Indonesia seized its independence in 1945, its fledgling government inherited a treasure chest. The country had oil, minerals, metals, and other valuable natural resources making it potentially one of the richest countries in the world.

The catch, of course, was that the treasure chest remained locked. Most of this underground wealth had not been exploited. Often it was remote, in outlandish parts of Sumatra, or in the inaccessible wilds of Kalimantan. To extract it would require roads, railways, machinery, and massive infusions of development capital that it would be unrealistic to expect the new government to have readily at its command.

But if independent Indonesia had understandable problems in unlocking its treasure chest buried beneath the ground, far less excusable is the squandering and mismanagement of its resources above the ground. The country is incredibly fertile. "Poke a stick into the ground," says one agricultural expert, "and in a couple of months you've got a tree."

Despite the exaggeration, it is a country where something or other is always easy to grow. Even so, after two decades of independence, a country that the experts believe can grow all its own food had become an importer of foodstuffs for its own consumption. In 1964 and 1965 the country's own production of rice, the staple foodstuff, was ten percent less than its people needed. The balance had to be imported, costing between $120,000,000 and $150,000,000 a year in foreign currency, which Indonesia could ill afford to spend.

Before World War II, Indonesia was a major exporter of sugar, growing millions of tons. By 1965, production had slumped to a mere 100,000 tons a year.

Cotton mills were working at 20 percent of capacity for lack of cotton. Experts argued that Indonesia could itself have produced the 30,000 to 40,000 tons of cotton needed by the mills each year. Instead, the Indonesian crop totaled about 300 tons a year, plus some 3,000 tons used in home industries.

The blame for all this must largely be laid at the door of the man who assumed total, ultimate control in Indonesia—President Sukarno.

With many today, it is the fashion to find no good whatsoever in Sukarno, no achievement during his regime. But Sukarno's greatest accomplishment was the welding into one nation, under one language, of an extraordinary mixture of diverse regions and brilliant tropic islands flung in an arc across more than 3,000 miles of ocean.

To this nation he gave some of those intangibles particularly precious to peoples emerging from foreign rule—a sense of national identity and importance, racial pride, the end of inequality and second-class citizenship. For all this, Sukarno became revered as the father of the nation, submerged in grandiose titles like Great Leader of the Revolution and Mouthpiece of the Indonesian People. Over the Indonesian millions he cast his charismatic spell. Long after his reputation began to tarnish, Indonesians of the older generation would speak reverently of him, waving aside his misdeeds like the minor peccadilloes of an emperor too grand to do serious wrong.

Thus when Sukarno argued that Western-style liberal democracy had failed in Indonesia and thrust it aside for his own "guided democracy," the country concurred. When Sukarno canceled further elections and assumed dictatorial powers, Indonesia sat submissively by. Indonesia became a country where nothing very important happened without Sukarno's consent. Only those political parties and groupings existed that had his nod of endorsement. Politicians, journalists, and others who incurred his disapproval faded quietly away.

It was not Sukarno's fashion to execute them. They languished in jails or exile. Sometimes, after repentance, they were brought back to positions of minor authority.

But the country was run by presidential and prime ministerial fiat. And Sukarno was both President and Prime Minister.

In a country of credulous, ill-educated millions, his benevolent autocracy at first fared well. What he was doing, he was doing in the name of the people. He strutted about the country in awesome splendor, and even the resplendent self-designed uniforms, the grand palaces, the expensive cars, and the lovely ladies on his arm, all seemed to go down all right with the crowds. For in a sense he was they. In a daydream of curious transference, this was the ordinary, simple little Indonesian up there, the man who had been kicked around for so long, now demonstrating to the world he was as self-confident and commanding as anybody.

The people cheered when Sukarno built, with borrowed money, his grandiose monuments in Djakarta and when he played host to expensive conferences of delegates from the "New Emerging Forces," or NEFOS, as he called them. All this seemed the manifestation of their country's new importance. When Sukarno told them that Indonesia had now become a "nation which helps determine the history of mankind," they believed him. When he asserted confidently that Djakarta and Peking had now been added to Washington and Moscow as the capitals that decided the world's destiny, they believed that, too. For it all helped to wipe out the ugly insult once hurled at Indonesia by a Dutch official who called it a "coolie among nations."

When Sukarno railed against the OLDEFOS, his word for the "Old Established Forces," they cheered that, too. For a while they even cheered when he gave them guns instead of rice. To enhance Indonesia's prestige, Sukarno bought from the Soviet Union a navy costing hundreds of millions of dollars. It included an ageing cruiser the Soviets were happy to off-load. A high Indonesian official present at the bargaining between Khrushchev and Sukarno in Moscow told me that when Sukarno expressed interest in the warship, Khrushchev set a highly inflated price on it. Sukarno snapped it up. Khrushchev, according to the story, could barely hide his astonishment.

With the rest of it went twelve submarines. For a nation having trouble feeding itself, it was an expensive shopping expedition.

It is difficult to assess accurately the stage at which the spell of Sukarno's magic began to fade—when he began, as his Japanese wife put it in a remarkably frank interview later, to lose touch with the people.

Two factors contributed to the change in mood. One was the development of a new urbanized class, of rising expectations, but of expectations that were not being fulfilled. The other was the slowly dawning suspicion that much of Sukarno's posturing, play-acting, and spending on prestige projects was more for the aggrandisement of Sukarno than for that of the Indonesian revolution.

Sukarno of course was lucky. The soil was rich. The climate was benevolent. True there were food shortages. Some people died of hunger. Many more, who did not die, suffered from outright malnutrition. But throughout most of Indonesia there was usually something to gnaw upon. And in a tropical climate there is little need for either heavy clothing or substantial houses.

Thus, when he confined his gaze to the countryside, Sukarno

was able to scoff at his foreign critics. "I consider," he told them once, "your psychological warfare the barking of a dog. Tens of times you have claimed that Indonesia under Sukarno would flounder, would collapse, would be destroyed. But we are immune. You have predicted the Indonesian economy would collapse. But it did not."

In a sense, he was right. By every normal economic yardstick, Indonesia was bankrupt and on the point of economic collapse, but still, somehow, it teetered onward.

Foreign exchange was exhausted. In Bali, in 1964 and 1965, I saw a splendid modern textile mill standing idle for want of raw material. A canning factory laid off 300 workers because there was no tin. Throughout the country the story was the same: no money to buy spare parts and raw materials from abroad. Before it could buy anything, Indonesia had to find many millions of dollars a year for debt repayments, and interest on debts to foreign countries, run up by Sukarno.

Yet, though an Indonesian in the countryside would beg the shirt off a visitor's back to replace his own, tattered beyond repair, the people somehow managed to grub along.

In the cities, however, the problem was much more acute. For the office worker there was no handy banana tree, no plot where he could grow a little food for his family. The price of rice rocketed from week to week. The inflation graphs soared right up and off the economists' wall charts. But wages remained unmoved. In real money, senior officials were earning the equivalent of several dollars a month. A friend of mine with a responsible position in the foreign ministry earned the equivalent of $4.50 a month. University professors made the same.

To feed their families, such men had little choice. The honest ones looked for extra work, sometimes ending up with two or three jobs at the same time. The dishonest ones became corrupt, or took to petty racketeering.

Thus, working the night shift. as a desk clerk at the Hotel Indonesia was the man you had seen earlier in the day giving Indonesian language lessons at the American Embassy. An official in the finance ministry ran a small building contractor's firm after hours. Wives who were able baked cakes, or gave piano lessons, to help out. University professors became language tutors or assistants to foreign correspondents during their hours outside the classrooms.

Less scrupulous workers sold equipment and supplies owned by the government or their private employers. Others in positions to grant favors demanded kickbacks.

All this fragmentation of energy affected efficiency. Because of the heat, government officials end their office hours at 2 P.M. in Djakarta. But with the collapse of the public transport system they were already arriving late for work. With no money for spare parts, most of the buses were off the streets. Getting to work in the mornings was a long, exhausting, and wasteful business. With working hours already short, and employees chiseling time for other occupations, officials spent less and less time at their desks. The machinery of government ran ever slower.

An Indonesian businessman told me his sad story: "Nobody in business can stay honest in this country today. There's no foreign exchange, so if you're an importer you have no money to pay for what you bring in. You have to go to a great deal of trouble lining up a year's credit with the seller overseas. You've got to pay interest on this, as well as insurance charges.

"Now you've got to get an import permit from the government. For this you have to pay kickbacks to officials in half a dozen ministries. After you've finished paying the unofficial bribes, next come the official levies to help pay for national monuments, and so on. Now you're in business.

"Except that at the end of the year the government comes along and levies tax of, say, sixty percent on your profit. You protest, you plead you can't pay, and they negotiate. An official tells you he'll knock it down to forty percent—provided ten percent goes to him."

With the economic situation deteriorating so badly, even Sukarno could no longer ignore it. But he tried to put a bold front on it. After one tour around the capital, he inquired of foreign diplomats whether they had seen any of his countrymen "frying stones" to eat. They replied, of course, that they had not.

Sukarno urged his people to vary their diet. "I ask you," he said, "to make a sacrifice. Add maize, sweet potatoes, and the like to your menu of rice. Maize is wholesome food. Peanuts are wholesome. Cassava and its leaves are also wholesome. Vary your diet. I myself eat maize at least once a week. Let us make some sacrifice."

Some government officials urged more drastic action. Crops in Indonesia suffer from two main ravages—floods and rats. To combat the rats, the government launched in 1964 a campaign to rid the fields of them. The Communist Party was an active collaborator in a project that saw whole villages out thrashing and clubbing away at rat packs. Sukarno himself became Honorary Chairman of the Action to Combat Mice—"mice" in Indonesian covering rats, as well.

But instead of simply exterminating the rats, some government officials suggested they be used as an extra food supply. Not surprisingly, the idea never caught on.

Sukarno enjoyed good fortune in another respect. If he could not pay for all he wanted abroad, he nevertheless could count on handouts from a string of countries. Indonesia was genuinely important to a number of governments. It was big, potentially prosperous, and the fifth most populous country in the world. Strategically, it stretched more than 3,000 miles from the Malaysian mainland to the northern tip of Australia. It had a commanding position astride east-west sea routes. From the

Soviet Union it had acquired a navy, and jet bombers with an impressive range. Clearly, this was no country to dismiss.

Thus it was wooed and aided by many lands. But as Sukarno embarked on a more militant foreign policy, aid to Indonesia became more and more one-sided. For while the Communists could support these adventures, the major Western powers could not. After Sukarno launched his confrontation campaign against Malaysia, Indonesian mobs set fire to the British Embassy in Djakarta, using drums of gasoline that had conveniently and mysteriously been dumped nearby by the truckload. Obviously there could be little British aid to Indonesia until confrontation was ended.

The United States, though not directly involved, was seriously disturbed. Just before the embassy burning, officials of the U.S. aid mission had been discussing details of a pending American loan to Indonesia. From the top floor of the AID building they watched the smoke rolling into the air from the British Embassy fire. Then they walked back downstairs, closed their files on the loan agreement, and never again opened them. The canceled loan was but one casualty of Indonesia's, or rather Sukarno's, new foreign policy.

Of course, Foreign Minister Subandrio subscribed to it, but Subandrio had risen to high office by playing astute and loyal political handmaiden to Sukarno. Subandrio would not have espoused the confrontation cause unless he was sure it was what Sukarno himself wanted.

A slight, bespectacled Javanese, Subandrio was a qualified surgeon who had early been caught up in the excitement of politics. After Sukarno proclaimed Indonesia's independence in 1945, Subandrio quickly rallied to his cause. By 1950, Subandrio was Indonesian Ambassador to London. After a four-year assignment there, he moved on to the ambassadorship in Moscow, returned to Djakarta in 1956, and became foreign minister the following year.

He rapidly became more than foreign minister. He headed

Indonesia's intelligence agency, the BPI, and emerged as Sukarno's right-hand man. Backed by a highly ambitious wife, he also aspired to succeed Sukarno. The road to attainment of such a goal lay, in Subandrio's calculation, via careful and loyal implementation of Sukarno's own policies.

So when Sukarno on the occasion of Indonesia's independence anniversary on August 27, 1964, lashed out publicly for the first time against the United States, there was no contradictory whisper from Dr. Subandrio.

Communist China's foreign minister, Marshal Chen Yi, dropped in for earnest talks with Sukarno in Djakarta, and the anti-American trend set in. Prior to this, top American officials had carefully explained to Sukarno the purpose of American involvement in the mission to rescue various foreign nationals trapped by Congolese rebels in Stanleyville. Sukarno kept publicly quiet on the question. But after Chen Yi had captured his ear, Sukarno lashed out at American policy in the Congo, ridiculing the explanation that the Stanleyville expedition was mounted for humanitarian reasons.

The mobs eagerly picked up the message and now launched a series of anti-American demonstrations, ostensibly based on opposition to U.S. policy in the Congo. Instead of the "Gangyang [Crush] Malaysia" banners, the slogan now became "Gangyang America."

For neither Subandrio nor Aidit did this new turn to Sukarno's policies pose any problems of conscience or politics. They embraced the new line eagerly. All three could make capital from it. For Sukarno it was yet another splendid foreign issue to divert attention from the economic chaos at home. For Aidit it whipped up the ferment on which his Communist Party throve, and every setback for the United States in Indonesia was a step forward for the Communists. For Subandrio, whose opportunism probably outweighed his natural addiction to the political left, it looked like the right horse to back.

While Sukarno lived, Subandrio's best strategy was to support him in every twist and turn of his policy. When Sukarno went, Subandrio—a man with no political party or base of his own— would need powerful support to win the succession. Subandrio would have no qualms about fronting for the Communist Party. It was entirely possible that the Communists, at least for an initial period after Sukarno's death, might be prepared to work through Subandrio. By actively supporting the rough new anti-American line, Subandrio would be serving well both of the figures most useful to him in his campaign for the succession—Sukarno and Aidit.

As the relationship between Washington and Djakarta cooled, American aid to Indonesia, which had totaled $666,000,000 from 1949 to mid-1964, trickled to a virtual halt. Subandrio was quoted as saying that most U.S. aid was being used to blackmail the recipient countries, anyway.

In December of 1964 the balloon went up. The anti-American campaign exploded in ugly violence at the USIS cultural centre in Djakarta. Tipped that the U.S. Embassy was expecting a Congo demonstration, I had installed myself in the lobby of the embassy, a long, low, modern building fronting on Merdeka Square. The outer gates were locked, the courtyard cleared. Armed Indonesian police were on the alert, and husky U.S. marines stood watch at the main door of the embassy, a building set back from the street. Embassy officials had also requested protection for the USIS centre in a crowded downtown street about a mile away.

Their concern for USIS was warranted. For USIS, and not the embassy, was the real target of the rioters that day. Suddenly in the embassy a telephone rang. It was Jordan Tanner, the young chief of the USIS centre, the only American in that building, now trapped there with a dozen or so Indonesian employees. Above the sound of breaking glass and shouting, he reported, "They [the anti-American mob] are smashing the windows. They're breaking in. They're burning the books." He had little time for more.

The embassy was in understandable consternation. But not much could be done to help Tanner except to keep on the phone to police headquarters and the foreign ministry demanding protection—which finally showed up thirty minutes after the rioters had left. The embassy was reluctant to risk sending an official car over, into the mob. So an Indonesian photographer and I took a couple of *betjaks*, or bicycle-rickshaws, to the back of the USIS block, then tried to cut down a side lane leading to it. We had not planned, as we ran into the lane, to find the rioters, their job now finished, dancing and shouting their way out of it. Before we could stop, we were into them. As they spotted the white face, they whooped and pinned us between two parked cars, spitting, waving their fists and placards, and shouting anti-American slogans. Later, my photographer friend was to tell me that some of them shouted, "There's an American. Let's get him!"

But a screen of four or five Indonesians blocked the crowd off from us and moved them on. "How do you know," they asked the rioters, "that this man is an American? He might be a Russian. And even if he is American, there are good Americans and bad Americans."

However, this minor incident was nothing compared to the ordeal young Mr. Tanner had undergone. A few minutes later we found him in the smoking shambles of the USIS centre. It had been thoroughly sacked. There had been no warning. Suddenly a mob of three hundred had surrounded the building and started smashing the windows. One of the first rocks crashed through Tanner's window and onto his desk. He gathered his Indonesian employees in his office and told them to try to keep calm. None of them was in fact harmed.

But the rest of the centre was wrecked. After they had smashed all the windows, the rioters poured inside. They overturned bookcases, hurling the books out through the windows; some they piled into a bonfire and set alight. The rioters also tore down from a wall the seal of the United States Information Service and smashed it to pieces. They ripped down a picture of President Johnson and destroyed that too, along with advertisements for *Years of Lightning, Day of Drums*, the commemorative John F. Kennedy film.

Surging through the wrecked downstairs library they rushed the stairs and made for the flag of the United States, hanging from a second-floor flagstaff. They tore it to shreds, then burned the pieces on the flaring bonfire outside. One piece of the flag they saved, tying it to a corner of the red-and-white flag of Indonesia they had brought with them. Then they hoisted the Indonesian flag in place of the desecrated American one.

It was a thoroughly nasty, well-planned affair, designed to inflame American feelings and send Indonesian-American relations plunging. Known members of the Communist youth organization were identified in the rioters' ranks.

But it was a pattern to become all too familiar in the following months. Four days after the USIS centre in Djakarta was sacked, a thousand anti-American rioters hacked their way by night into the USIS library in Surabaya, Indonesia's second largest city and major port. They burned the books, ripped down the American flag, and raised the Indonesian, all in a scene almost identical with that which had just taken place in Djakarta. Thereafter the embassy of the United States, its consulates in outlying towns, and USIS libraries around the country were to become regular targets of leftist and Communist mobs. At the embassy in Djakarta, the door would be slammed shut with weary monotony, the gates of the courtyard locked. The embassy staff would be mustered on the top floor. The marine guards would break out their tear-gas masks and riot equipment, in case the mobs should batter down the glass doors. Soon workmen began building a huge grille across the whole front of the building.

In a country where Sukarno ruled all, it seemed clear that if he had not ordered the anti-American onslaught, he was at least allowing it to continue. U.S. Ambassador Howard Jones pressed his protests and demanded apologies. Yet Sukarno, despite his once warm relationship with Jones, conveyed not even an informal message of regret.

At loggerheads with the Americans, at war with the British, over his head in debt to the Soviets, Sukarno was fast running out of allies. But brighter and brighter on his horizon dawned the red star of China.

As 1964 slid into l965, Sukarno threw a tantrum over Malaysia's seating on the Security Council. Angrily he announced Indonesia's withdrawal from the United Nations, from which Indonesia over the years had garnered some $65,000,000 in aid. Most of the world deplored his action. But Peking applauded.

As the months of 1965 rolled by, there was more and more good news for Communist China from Sukarno's capital. American rubber and oil companies in Indonesia were placed under formal government control. With most of its libraries seized or sacked, the USIS decided to close up operations in Indonesia and go home. The Peace Corps left, too.

American movies were outlawed. Communist unions halted the supply of water and electricity to American homes. Telephones were cut off; mail was left undelivered. Along the main streets huge anti-American posters showed Uncle Sam getting a crude come-uppance— usually at the end of a sharpened bamboo stake. The shrinking American community found Indonesian friends less and less eager to talk or visit.

Ambassador Jones was coming to the end of his seven-year assignment. The new Ambassador, Marshall Green, was to implement the State Department's new hard line on Indonesia, went the gossip along embassy row. American newspaper editorials began to discuss the possibility of a complete diplomatic break between Indonesia and the United States.

Mr. Green himself arrived to a flurry of signs along the road from the airport inviting him to go home. There were demonstrations against him when he went to present his credentials, and the demonstrators were waiting for him at his embassy afterwards.

In these circumstances, Djakarta began to assume an air of international intrigue, as foreign governments and their agents tried to unravel the mystery of Indonesia's intentions. The Americans watched the Soviets, and the Soviets watched the Chinese. The British, burned out of their embassy, worked from the residence of their bearded ambassador and watched everybody. The West Germans, who had an embassy in Djakarta, watched the East Germans, who had a consulate. The West Germans were building a solid-looking new embassy building on the capital's main boulevard. They lived in permanent anguish lest the Indonesians should recognize East Germany just as the West German Embassy was completed.

Probably the most frustrated of all were the Soviets. They had given Indonesia massive military and other assistance. They had built the huge sports stadium at Senajan. Yet the Indonesians did not seem to have learned to play the game—at least, not the way the Soviets wanted it.

This time it was not the Americans thwarting Moscow's ambitions, but the Chinese Communists. The Chinese maintained their embassy—secretive, austere, but huge, far removed from everybody else's—down in the Glodok Chinese quarter of Djakarta. The gates were kept locked, there was barbed wire atop the high red walls, and the visitors least welcome were the Soviets.

So the Soviets fretted and fumed up in their embassy on exclusive diplomatic row. It was a pastel mansion, very bourgeois, with coloured fairy lights trimming the facade, and air conditioners grinding away in the windows. In the driveway was the Ambassador's gleaming Mercedes. Not far away was the Soviet diplomatic compound, with swimming pool and tennis courts, where the staff could work off their frustrations and ponder the fickleness of a nation that had gobbled up their aid, then allied itself with Peking.

As one Russian correspondent told me glumly over lunch, "Those Chinese are *everywhere*. But we can never find out what they are *doing*."

So Russians and Americans alike pondered the complexities of life as Garuda, the Indonesian airline, stuck up posters all over town advertising flights to China—right alongside the Soviet Aeroflot posters advertising: "Cheapest Flights to Europe—via Moscow."

In this permissive political atmosphere, and against a background of deepening economic chaos, the pro-Peking Indonesian Communist Party used its considerable talents to win a role of dangerous influence. Only the army now blocked its acquisition of weapons and ultimate power. Such were the background events that led up to the drama of October 1, 1965.

9. Who and Why

As the years go by, more facts will undoubtedly become available about the coup of October, 1965, and about the events leading up to it. But what deductions can be drawn from the facts as we know them today? Who planned the coup, and why?

The possibilities are several.

The first is that Lieutenant Colonel Untung was telling the truth when he said he moved to forestall a coup by the Council of Generals planned for the vicinity of Armed Forces Day, October 5.

It is difficult to believe that Indonesia's top generals did not in fact, have some plan laid to assume power. In the atmosphere of those days, they would have been remarkably naive if they had not made some preparations. The question is whether this was a routine contingency plan, designed to come into effect in the event of Sukarno's death, or in the event of a lunge for power by the Communists, or whether the generals were really intending to oust Sukarno and install a military regime.

If the latter was the case, and the generals were on the eve of action, no evidence of it has come to light.

First, for men supposedly up to their eyes in a dangerous plot to overthrow the government, they were remarkably lax about their own security.

General Yani's guard, it is true, had recently been reinforced, although the extra men mysteriously failed to report for duty on the night of his murder. General Nasution had his normal guard. On the homes of the other generals seized there were no guards at all. It can be argued that if the generals really were plotting, it might have looked suspicious if they had suddenly placed guards on their homes. Yet it is difficult to believe that generals about to embark on so hazardous an enterprise would not have taken some precautions.

Nevertheless General Parman, the army's own intelligence chief, who had been warned anew only a day or so before of a pending Communist threat to the generals, had not a single soldier at his house. All of the generals were at home and in their beds when the killer gangs came. Some were not even suspicious at first of men who came knocking in the middle of the night.

Again, if the generals, as Untung charged, were planning a coup with troops brought into the capital for the October 5 parade, they were extraordinarily inept in their selection. The two battalions from Central and East Java, the 454th and 530th, were Communist-infiltrated, and their officers had days before agreed secretly to throw them behind the September 30th Movement.

Since the coup, nobody has produced any proof that the generals were about to seize power. It can be argued that the army has had control of the communications media and could easily have stifled any such evidence. But it is an argument that does not stand up. Key figures in the coup like Untung, Dhani, and Supardjo stood trial and could have aired their evidence then. Though access to Untung's trial was limited, foreign newsmen and almost anybody with a legitimate interest could, and did, attend the trials of Dhani and Supardjo. These were broadcast live to the nation. It would have been in the interests of the coup leaders to produce evidence of a generals' plot if they had had it. It would have contributed to their defense by providing the justification for the actions they took. Yet none came forward with any meaningful information. General Supardjo told Sukarno at Halim on October 1 that he had proof of the generals' duplicity. He has never come to light with it, even though he was at large for more than fifteen months after the coup, during which he apparently had channels to Sukarno through which he could have funneled his information.

If the generals had really made up their minds to topple Sukarno, another puzzling factor is the behavior of the army's leaders since the coup. By the evening of October 1, the army had control of the situation. There was unmatched opportunity for finishing off Sukarno, if that had been the generals' intent. Nasution, supposedly the leader of the generals' plot, was alive, the army's hero, and if he had been hungry for power, this would have been the moment to carry his ambitions to fulfillment.

Instead, though he later demanded a tough crackdown on the Communists, he procrastinated for months on the question of Sukarno. He it was who counseled moderation when the students, disenchanted with Sukarno, demanded the President's dismissal. His failure to act against the President, in fact, cost him the political support of many students and others. Yet this is the man who was charged by the September 30th Movement with leading a generals' plot against the President.

Far from moving in on the President after the coup, the whole record of Nasution, Suharto, and the army's high command indicates that they dragged their feet, had to be prodded by the students, and finally ousted Sukarno only with reluctance, in the gentlest way they knew how.

If the generals had been about to launch a subversive plot, the leaders of the September 30th Movement who had pledged to thwart it reacted with incredible inefficiency. After they had seized the generals, for instance, they made no attempt to interrogate those who were still living when brought to Halim. There was no suggestion that the generals be brought before Sukarno to confess, and prove, their guilt. There was no grilling to find out who else was involved, or what other dangers might still lie in store for the nation. There was no attempt to extract an admission implicating the American C.I.A., which the September 30th Movement leaders charged was behind the generals. The generals' captors in fact betrayed an extraordinary lack of curiosity about the details of a plot that they said was designed to overthrow the legitimate government of the country. Instead, all they seemed interested in doing was killing the generals and getting them out of the way.

Then again, if the President's life was in danger from a generals' plot about to be launched at any hour, Untung was very casual, especially for an officer of the palace guard, about protecting Sukarno. Here he had evidence, or said he had, of a pending plot. He knew that there might be gunfire in the streets that night as his own men moved against the generals. Yet he allowed Sukarno to roam the city, albeit with an escort. In fact, if the evidence emerging at the trial of Omar Dhani is correct, Untung and his co-plotters had no idea where Sukarno really was in the early hours of October 1. They thought he was at Merdeka palace, but actually he was at the house of his Japanese wife Dewi, then scurrying to the house of another wife, Haryati, and later out to Halim. Toward the man they considered in mortal danger from the generals, it was strangely unsolicitous action on their part.

As for the charges of C.I.A. implication, they have been put under the microscope by many people. No evidence has emerged to corroborate them. If the C.I.A. was involved in this operation, it must be the most brilliantly disguised secret in the entire history of the agency.

If, then, no generals' coup was to be launched between October 1 and October 5, Untung must have mistakenly, but genuinely, believed such a coup was about to take place. Or he must have known there was no generals' plot at all, and must have used the whole story to cover his own coup attempt.

In either event, however, it is difficult to see Untung, for all his chairmanship of the revolutionary council, as anything but a pawn in the September 30th Movement. He moved troops about, but he was not a controlling figure at Halim on October 1 when the plotters were making their policy decisions. He himself issued no political directives, nor does he seem to have been much consulted.

He cut rather a forlorn character that day.

Somebody then must have influenced him, for him to make his initial drastic move against the generals. But who?

It is conceivable that the generals themselves fed him the intelligence about a Council of Generals, intending to provoke the Communist Party into action, which would provide the justification for a savage crackdown on it. Of such a trap, or the possibility of it, the Communists were aware. Since the catastrophe at Madiun in 1948, they had warned their members not to be drawn into a provocative situation that would give the army the excuse for a crushing campaign. Yet if the generals did lay a trap in this case, it sprang shut on them, too. For its success, they paid dearly with the loss of their own lives. Again, it is difficult to believe that generals about to spring such a trap could have been so lax about their personal security.

For Untung there were several other possible influences. His inspiration to act could have come from the Communist Party itself. According to his own interrogation report, Communist emissaries were present throughout the whole planning stage of his operation. It could have come from fellow officers like General Supardjo, or air force major Sujono, each with his own vested interest in a power play against the generals. Or it could have come from Sukarno himself. Untung was the commander of the palace guard honor battalion. He was close to Sukarno on many occasions. It is inconceivable, as was suggested by evidence at the Dhani trial, that Sukarno did not know Untung and had to ask at Halim who he was. Sukarno, with his fear of assassination, was ever sensitive to faces around him. It is beyond belief that he did not know the commander of his palace guard's lead battalion. From the tapes of Untung's interrogation following his capture later, it is evident that Untung at first refused to talk and would only repeatedly ask to be taken to the President.

If Untung was the pawn of the Communists, who really masterminded the coup launched in his name, the key question is why the party decided to move at that particular time. After all, the general course of events in Indonesia seemed to be running in the Communists' favor. They had built their party to remarkable strength. They seemed to have Sukarno's blessing for further advancement within the structure of government. Perhaps in a few months' time they would have those 100,000 small arms from the Chinese Communists that Sukarno had sent Omar Dhani to talk about in Peking. Why move at that particular time, risking the party's destruction by the army, when by holding on they might achieve their aims?

Communists being Communists, the party almost certainly had a plan to seize power. Like the generals, they would have been foolish in the atmosphere prevailing in those days if they had not. But again, as in the case of the generals, the question is whether the Communists' plan was a contingency one, to exploit Sukarno's sudden death or to foil an army takeover, or whether the Communists had planned long and carefully for the coup attempt of October 1.

On the basis of their performance, it is difficult to believe the Communists were really ready for October 1. For a party that prided itself on its organization, it reacted in a sadly disorganized way. Coordination between Djakarta and the rest of the country was almost completely lacking. Communist participation in the events of October 1 had an air of desperate urgency about it. If the party had been planning a coup, it acted on October 1 like a party that had been compelled prematurely to put its plan into action.

What pressures could have impelled the Communist Party to this course?

There was, of course, the question of Sukarno's health. Acupuncturists from Communist China had been treating him and had probably passed on to Aidit their findings. The President had had what seemed to be a bad turn early in August, but later this proved to be not as serious as many believed. Although the President's kidney trouble could turn serious at any time, he could also, as proved to be the case, go on living a normal and active life. Would such a verdict in itself be enough to propel the Communist Party to such drastic action as that of October 1?

Then there is the possibility that the Communists themselves really feared a move by the Council of Generals before October 5 and were simply trying to forestall it. But if so, they, like the other principals in the coup, have been unable to produce any evidence since then that the generals actually were plotting. While it may be argued that the Communist Party apparatus has been smashed, there are Communists enough still at large, and channels available, through which such disclosures might be made. .

Another suggestion is that the main thrust for the coup attempt came from the disloyal army men like Supardjo who were the real influence behind Untung. With the rebel officers determined to move, the Communist Party had to jump on the bandwagon. The disloyal battalions from East and Central Java were being brought to the capital, and this was the opportunity Supardjo and Untung needed to act. The Communist Party, according to this theory, might have been overtaken if it had refused to join in.

It is all possible, yet the available facts suggest that far from competing with each other, the military men and the Communists engaged in the coup attempt enjoyed close liaison. The Communists signaled Supardjo when to come to Djakarta. There are indications that Major Sujono, one of the key conspirators from the air force, had been deputed by the Communists to tutor Untung in their ideology. When the coup attempt failed, both Supardjo and Dhani were solicitous in the extreme about Communist leader Aidit, personally providing his escape plane.

A further theory is that Peking ordered the Indonesian Communist Party to move, and that Aidit was merely carrying out the instruction in a Chinese master plan.

This does not stand close examination. The Indonesian party was pro-Peking, but it was strong and independent, with its own policies. It did not dance mechanically to Peking's tune. There are some grounds for belief that Peking was informed in advance about the pending move against the generals Undoubtedly the Chinese encouraged it. But so far, there is no evidence that Peking's hand was directly involved. After the coup, stories circulated that crate-loads of Chinese weapons had been smuggled into Indonesia with Chinese equipment for the CONEFO project—Sukarno's rival United Nations, intended to house a grand Conference of the New Emerging Forces. Yet the most senior Indonesian military men I talked to admitted that they had looked for those weapons and been unable to find any trace of them. A few Chinese small arms were discovered—along with assorted weapons from every other arms-producing country in the world. If Sukarno's secret deal with the Chinese had gone through, arms undoubtedly would have arrived from China in quantity. That they had arrived prior to the coup seems doubtful.

There is one further possibility. This is that the pressure upon the Communist Party to move came from Sukarno himself. Was Sukarno himself moving far closer to the political left, and much faster, than most people realized? Although a master of flamboyance himself, he seemed genuinely impressed by the austere achievements of Communist China. His addiction to Marxism became more pronounced, so much so that he made a point of reiterating it publicly in the months after the coup when Marxism was one of Indonesia's particularly dirty words.

He had, it seemed, at last been compelled to face the realities of his country's economic mess. Frustrated by Indonesia's laggardly rate of economic advance, he gave the Communists high marks for getting out into the fields and trying to do something about it. He admired their discipline, their relative lack of corruption. Had he also decided that the techniques of Communism were the answer to Indonesia's complex ills? If so, it would of course have been a Communism that he could bend to his own will, for he had no intention of surrendering his power.

If all this is true, the Communist Party may have been obliged to run to keep up with Sukarno's own pace, and to have embarked unprepared on an action against the army generals so stubbornly blocking Sukarno's way.

Unfortunately for Sukarno, the actions of Untung and his fellow plotters become more credible against a background of presidential approval, if not authorization. Throughout their enterprise, the plotters acted as though confident the President would support them.

Prior to the coup, Sukarno knew that Supardjo was in town, apparently without permission to leave his post in Kalimantan. There is a possibility that Sukarno and Supardjo actually talked on September 29. After the generals were killed, it was to Sukarno that Supardjo hastened to report. Apparently at no time did Supardjo fear that Sukarno might order him arrested or punished for his action. Supardjo's confidence was justified, for the President's reaction was mild, perhaps even congratulatory, in that shoulder-patting incident, the significance of which has yet to be satisfactorily explained. After the coup, Supardjo represented himself as "Sukarno's man." He was hidden for more than fifteen months by people who claimed at his trial that he carried a letter from the President requesting protection for Supardjo. Also at the trial there was evidence that Sukarno and Supardjo exchanged letters after the coup, while Supardjo was in hiding.

Thus, to Supardjo, one of the ringleaders of the coup attempt,

Sukarno seemed protective. Another principal plotter, Lieutenant Colonel Untung, also apparently counted on the President's benevolent attitude toward him, for as we have noted, upon capture he pleaded only to be taken before Sukarno, in the belief that Sukarno would understand and forgive all. To Communist Party leader Aidit, too, the President sought to extend a sheltering wing after the coup. The army claims it intercepted letters between Aidit, hiding in Central Java, and Sukarno in which the President, far from chastising Aidit, sought to rescue him. Meanwhile, to air force chief Dhani, who feared the army's revenge after the coup, Sukarno extended the haven of the presidential palace.

There are other factors of which Sukarno's critics have made much. For instance, when he first got official word of the coup on the morning of October 1, it was to Halim air base that the President fled—the plotters' command post, and the execution and burial site of the six murdered generals.

When it was clear that the coup had failed, it was to Madiun that the President considered flying, in company with the leading plotters. Sukarno could hardly have forgotten the historical implications of Madiun, the scene of the 1948 Communist revolt that failed. Yet only with some difficulty was he apparently persuaded to change his mind, disengage from the coup leaders, and go to Bogor.

When he heard the announcement of Untung's revolutionary council, he seemed not in the least disturbed by the shunting aside of his own cabinet. Ordinarily, one would have expected the proud and dominating Sukarno to be enraged by such effrontery. Instead, he reacted hardly at all, almost like a man who knew it need not be taken seriously.

Similarly, Subandrio, who as Sukarno's right-hand man was usually privy to the President's innermost thoughts, reacted in leisurely fashion to the news from Djakarta of a coup and the installation of a revolutionary council that had taken over from the cabinet. A normal reaction might have been to rush back to the capital to find out what was happening, protect the President, save the government.

Instead, Subandrio dallied on his speaking tour of northern Sumatra, like a man with inside knowledge of what was happening and no fear for either the President or the government.

There is not much doubt that Sukarno did have advance warning of pending trouble. Subandrio when he came to trial later admitted that his intelligence organization had picked up rumors about the Communist plot. But he had never passed on the information to Sukarno, he said, because he was sure the President knew all about it.

If the President had missed the news, he nevertheless got warning on the very day before the coup from General Sugandhi, the same officer who had also warned General Yani that the Communists were about to strike. From the President, Sugandhi got much the same reaction as from Yani. Sukarno dismissed the story and said Sugandhi was suffering from anti-Communist phobia.

Sukarno had also, of course, listened to Omar Dhani's warning on September 29 about trouble from the direction of the army. As General Suharto put it later, the President "paid his fullest attention" to this report about an army coup, but "did not believe in the possibility of a coup from the side of the Communists."

This explanation by Suharto was given in the course of his address to the People's Consultative Congress gathered in showdown session in 1967 to oust Sukarno from the presidency. Suharto, it must be remembered, was playing politics at the time. He was attempting to head off harsh Congress action against Sukarno for fear it might spark civil war throughout the country. Thus he told the Congress delegates that Sukarno was not "the direct instigator, or the mastermind" behind the coup. However, he hedged by saying that this was the army's conclusion "unless there are indeed still facts we haven't been able to find until this very day."

Nevertheless, Suharto admitted there were "very many actions and attitudes of the President hard to understand," which gave rise to "suspicion, and distrust of the President, because the President seemed to defend or favor" the coup forces.

Coup figures like Dhani and Supardjo went to extreme lengths to keep Sukarno's name clean when they eventually came to trial. There was even evidence that Supardjo while still free had been in touch with Dhani, in prison awaiting trial, enjoining him to keep Sukarno out of it all.

Despite all this, and despite Suharto's exoneration of Sukarno as the mastermind behind the coup, it is difficult to exempt Sukarno from involvement in it. This is not to suggest that Sukarno wrote out an order for the generals' removal. It does not mean the plotters came to Sukarno, asked for his assent, and got it. In Indonesia, things are not done that way. And in any event, Sukarno had proved himself too wily and experienced a politician for that.

But Sukarno was surely also too wily a politician not to have guessed from Supardjo's presence in the capital, from his talk with Omar Dhani, and from the information of his own excellent intelligence system, what was in the wind.

With that remarkable Javanese capacity for evasion of direct issues, there would have been no need for Sukarno to signal in actual words his blessing for the arrest of the generals. But from the behavior of the plotters it seems clear they believed they had either received such blessing or would undoubtedly be given it.

There is no question, of course, that the Indonesian Communist Party was up to its neck in the coup attempt. But still open to debate is whether the Communists planned the whole thing and gave the actual signal to jump, or whether the Communists jumped at somebody else's beckoning.

My own belief is that several groups were party to the coup attempt for different reasons. The Communists, I believe, threw their weight behind it because they believed circumstances compelled them to. They must have had misgivings about its timing. They would have been better organized had they waited. But they gambled on the operation's success. Under Aidit, the party had achieved great success by riding close to Sukarno's coattails. In backing the coup they believed they were following out that policy. The disadvantage of being left behind, and having their party overtaken, must have seemed greater than the hazards of plunging forward into the coup.

The military men among the plotters were, I believe, motivated by various reasons. Untung was the unfortunate tool, though of whom is still not entirely clear. Some of the other military men, like air force Major Sujono, were straight Communists. Supardjo, it seems to me, was ideologically attuned to the Communists, but was also militarily ambitious and saw great advancement for himself in a successful outcome to the plot. Omar Dhani was a politically unsophisticated man whose vanity and opportunism led him down the road to disaster.

Sukarno himself, I believe, wanted his obstructive generals out of the way. He did not seek revolt, or the destruction of the army. Nor, in fact, did the plotters attempt to do other than remove the army's existing command. Sukarno wanted the army retained, but he wanted it led by generals pliable to his own will, rather than generals of stubborn independence like Nasution and Yani, who thwarted him.

Sukarno's involvement in the coup will be debated for years. But whether he authorized the generals' removal or not, the coup of October 1, 1965, was for him the crisis point. It marked the beginning of his decline and fall as a demigod.

President Sukarno at a palace ceremony, Djakarta.

The Indonesian Communist leader, D. N. Aidit, receiving Japanese visitors in the days before the coup.

General Suharto and President Sukarno in happier days.

Four of the army leaders murdered in the September 1965 coup: (clockwise from top left) Brigadier-General Sutojo, Lieutenant-General Yani, Major-General Harjono, and Brigadier-General Pandjaitan.

Diver about to descend the well at Crocodile Hole, where the bodies of murdered generals were found.

Sealing the generals' coffins at Crocodile Hole.

Para-commandos bury their generals.

General Nasution throws earth into the grave of his murdered five-year-old daughter.

The widow of General Yani receives a decoration from President Sukarno.

Part Two: The Purge

10. The Great Whitewash

On the day of the coup, October 1, 1965, I was in the Philippines doing an advance story on the upcoming presidential election. I had been outside the capital, Manila, most of the day and returned to catch the first excited radio bulletins on the sudden crisis in Indonesia.

At the Associated Press office the story was confused. Communications with Indonesia were cut, and what information we could get was coming from garbled announcements over the Indonesian radio, monitored in Singapore and other countries nearby. As I read through the disjointed cables, which suggested that Sukarno had been overthrown, the teleprinter bells heralded a new bulletin. Now Nasution was back in control of the situation, it said. The story was still far from clear, and obviously the only place to find out what was going on was Djakarta.

I had a valid visa. Now I needed a plane. The first one to Djakarta was not till Sunday, October 3. As I made my booking, the telephone jangled on the airline clerk's desk. 'It's somebody else wanting an urgent booking to Djakarta,' she said. The somebody else was Peter Kalisher, of the Columbia Broadcasting System, who also happened to be in Manila.

The Sunday plane we were booked on did not fly. General Suharto had put the Djakarta airport under curfew for most of the day, and our aircraft could not make it during the time the airport was open. The pilot was not going to risk arriving outside the authorized hours and being shot down by General Suharto's suspicious antiaircraft gunners.

On Monday, October 4, we did make it to Djakarta. But, as correspondents, Kalisher and I had no idea what sort of reception we might get. We had visas, but it seemed perfectly possible that under the troubled circumstances the Indonesian authorities might refuse us entry, anyway. We rated our chances fifty-fifty.

At the immigration counter all passports were collected, ours with the distinctive red "Wartawan" or "Correspondent" warning that Indonesian embassies around the world stamp over their visas issued to newsmen. We tried to look unconcerned. Kalisher read a book; I think for a time he even whistled. Then an immigration official stepped out from behind the counter and called my name. This, we thought, was it. But the official gave me a cheery greeting. Then he asked, "Mr. Hughes, will two weeks be long enough to cover the upheaval?" I could barely keep from stammering, but there was only one way to play it. "Well," I said, "supposing the upheaval lasts longer?" He smiled. "In that case," he said, "come back and see us, and we'll talk about it."

Kalisher had equally good fortune. And it was good fortune. We were the first two newsmen from outside Indonesia to be admitted after the coup, and immediately after we were in, the authorities clamped down. For a week afterwards our colleagues hammered at the doors of Indonesian embassies in Bangkok, Tokyo, and other Asian capitals for permission to enter Indonesia. Some even flew into Djakarta without visas, but were turned back at the airport. One of them, Arthur Cook of the London *Daily Mail*, reputedly made a grand speech in front of immigration officials proclaiming he was a personal friend of President Sukarno. But the immigration men must have heard that one before. It made no difference. They put him right back on the plane he had arrived on from Singapore.

Despite the cordiality attending our own reception at the airport, one did not need long in the capital to detect the underlying tension. Strongpoints and communications centers were encircled by barbed-wire barricades. At key crossroads, wiry Indonesian soldiers sat atop stubby tanks and armored cars. From Merdeka Square the barrels of antiaircraft guns ranged upward in pointed skepticism of the air force's loyalty.

Telephone and cable traffic to the outside world was cut off. Within the city, local telephones were "presently disconnected." To talk with anybody, you had to visit him. This you could do only during the hours of daylight, for the army had imposed a strict curfew from six at night till six in the morning. After night's descent with sudden tropical swiftness, the streets were left to the jeeps and loaded trucks of the army, scurrying about the capital on official business.

The army controlled all the apparatus of propaganda and communications. All newspapers had been banned except two published by the army; on the Monday I arrived, these triumphantly carried facsimiles of Saturday's Communist papers backing the September 30th Movement, which had already failed. The main source of information was the radio, broadcasting only the announcements the army wanted broadcast.

Three days after the coup, few people could, or would, reveal the whereabouts of the principal characters. General Nasution was clearly not living at his home. About General Suharto there was tight-lipped silence. Both, as it later turned out, were working and sleeping at KOSTRAD headquarters. About Sukarno there seemed even greater mystery. In the early hours of Sunday, October 3, the radio broadcast a taped message from him which it was clear from the context had been made the previous day.

In it he said he was "safe and well" and continued to "hold the top leadership of the state and of the government and the

Indonesian revolution."

He said that he had talked with all commanders of the armed forces, Deputy Premier Lemeina, and other officials, Saturday, "with the purpose of quickly settling the problem of the so-called September thirtieth affair." But he gave no indication of where he was, where those talks were held, or the circumstances under which he was speaking.

He called for calm and the avoidance of armed conflict. He said the leadership of the army was directly in his hands, but that he had appointed General Pranoto to "discharge day-to-day tasks within the army" and General Suharto to "carry out the restoration of security and order in connection with the September thirtieth affair."

Later that Sunday, just a few minutes before midnight, the radio broadcast a second message from Sukarno, also taped. This one was particularly interesting, for it clearly sought to exonerate the air force from complicity in the September 30th Movement. Sukarno said he was making the broadcast to clear up "a number of misunderstandings which can create conflicts among the armed forces." In it, he made three points:

1. "The charge against the Indonesian Air Force of involvement in the September thirtieth affair is not true."

2. "My going to the Halim air base early on the morning of October first was at my own desire, as I was of the opinion that the best place for me was a place near an airplane which could transport me at any moment to another place if something unexpected took place."

3. "We must remain vigilant and prevent the playing off against one another of the air force and the army to the advantage of Necolim and other groups."

Meanwhile air force chief Omar Dhani was also busy extricating the air force from its involvement in the September 30th Movement. On Sunday the radio broadcast a statement from him, apparently issued late the previous day, affirming that the air force was not involved in the September 30th Movement, that it did not "interfere in the internal affairs of other services," and that the air force had "no knowledge of the Indonesian Revolution Council or of the composition of its personnel."

There must have been an air of desperate urgency about this attempt to dissociate the air force from the murder of the army's leading generals. For Suharto had Halim air force base under his control, and his scouts were out, sniffing for clues as to the generals' whereabouts. By Sunday night they had discovered the well at Lubang Buaja. Monday morning, with Suharto himself in attendance, there began the grisly task of opening it up and exhuming the bodies.

"It looked," he said later, "as though the murderers really thought and believed that the bodies would not be discovered. Because the well was closed, and the hole at the top was filled in solid, so that nothing would show."

But frogmen went down into the blackness, roped up the corpses, and one by one the bodies of the six generals and Nasution's young aide were brought to the surface.

At the time, Suharto was shaken with rage and emotion, but he had to keep control of himself. He was under orders from the President not to let the army take bloody vengeance from the air force. "You can imagine," he explained later, "the fury of a soldier once he learned what had happened. Perhaps an officer could be controlled, but an ordinary soldier would be very hard to restrain."

His aim at the time, he said, "was to keep a tight rein on undisciplined acts by our own boys."

So immediately he issued a statement calling on the air force to carry out its own purge of air force officers involved in the September 30th Movement.

In a broadcast over the radio that night, Suharto told the

Indonesian public that he had himself that day witnessed the recovery of the generals' bodies. "It is possible," he told his listeners, "that there is truth in the statement by our beloved President that the air force is not involved in the affair. But it is impossible that there is no involvement in this affair of elements of the air force."

He hoped, he said, that air force "patriots" would purge any air force personnel involved in the "cruel killing of our innocent generals."

Afterwards he explained, "By explanations and briefings, in accordance with the President's wish that we be magnanimous, we managed to convince our men to be magnanimous, too, and abandon all desire for revenge. This was especially once we discovered that the air force as an organ of state was not involved, only some air force elements. These elements had to be hunted down, but we left this to the air force itself."

Despite this moderate public stand, Suharto, normally a quiet man, was privately raging. After his flight to Central Java on October 1, Dhani had returned to the President's palace at Bogor and sought refuge with Sukarno against army vengeance. At a confrontation after the discovery of the generals' mutilated bodies, Suharto ripped Dhani's epaulettes from his shoulders and slapped his face with them. Thereafter, Sukarno quietly shipped Dhani out of the country on some invented mission, and he was replaced as air force chief.

But if Suharto held back his soldiers from an onslaught on the air force, he had no intention of diminishing the savage wrong done to the army's leaders. Their bodies were exhumed on Monday, October 4. Tuesday was to have been the day of the big Armed Forces Day parade. Suharto canceled it and instead speedily organized the whole capital for a massive state funeral. He was determined, as the army carried its heroes to their graves in the Kalibata Heroes Cemetery, to burn the memory of it into the pages of Indonesia's history books.

First the bodies, sealed in their coffins, lay in state at army headquarters on Merdeka Square. Thousands of people clogged the approaches as perspiring policemen wrestled to let through cars bearing generals, ministers, foreign diplomats, and other officials come to pay their last respects. Inside the hall, the air was sweet and misty with the smoke from containers of incense-like powder. Shoulder to shoulder the official visitors shuffled past the coffins, each bearing a picture of a murdered general. The atmosphere was one of taut silence, broken now and then by sobbing from an alcove where the generals' wives and children sat, supported by aides and family friends and relatives.

At one point there was a stir as General Nasution appeared under heavy guard. Hobbling on sticks, he looked bemused and stunned by the tragedy that had taken his colleagues and his young aide, and as a result of which his daughter now lay dying in a hospital.

In the background, General Suharto stamped about. Dressed in battle fatigues, his normally placid face was heavy with anger. Although till now he had been scrupulous in trying to avoid bloodshed, he was today a man nobody should interfere with. The army's intended day of pomp had become its day of sorrow, yet Suharto was going to allow nothing to mar the tragic ceremonial.

Finally the coffins were strapped reverently on top of armored cars. The long procession began its slow parade through the streets of the capital and out to Kalibata Cemetery on the city's outskirts. Policemen and troops lined the route. Thousands and thousands pressed in behind them, many of the women openly sobbing. In the garden of every humble little house, it seemed, there was a pole with Indonesia's red-and-white flag flying upon it at half-mast.

At the cemetery, dozens of tanks lined the final approaches, their guns raised in a final salute of immaculate precision. The diplomatic corps, in formal attire, had been lined up for several hours in the broiling sun. The military attachés were perspiring in full dress uniform. Prominent in the front rank were United States Ambassador Marshall Green and British Ambassador Sir Andrew Gilchrist, representatives of two countries that had been most reviled in Indonesia in recent months. Pointedly absent were the diplomatic representatives of Communist China.

Whispered among those waiting had been the momentous question of the day: Would Sukarno himself be here, perhaps arriving by helicopter from wherever he was secluded? But now, as a whinny from one of the cavalry horses signaled the arrival of the funeral party, it was evident that he would not.

To the army's elite RPKAD para-commandos was given the honor of carrying the generals and Nasution's young aide to their final resting places. Grim-faced and workmanlike in their spotted camouflage suits, they bore the coffins in on their shoulders, their heavy jump boots clattering over the concrete steps onto the silence of the thick turf. Then the coffins were lowered into the open waiting graves.

Within hours, the mystery of Sukarno's whereabouts was to be solved. Early next morning, the word was passed; he was at Bogor and had summoned a cabinet meeting for that morning. To the palace at Bogor I raced. At the gate, the guards checked my press card, then asked me to remove my sunglasses—a familiar routine in Indonesia. It is based on the theory that guards can always detect the telltale glint of violence in the eyes of a would-be assassin.

Inside the grounds I waited with a flock of Indonesian newsmen, as well as the resident representatives of various foreign news organizations, as car after car pulled up, disgorging ministers in Sukarno's sizable, but submissive, cabinet.

Finally, when all were seated, we were allowed in, but only to one end of the cabinet room where the ministers were ranged behind two long tables. Sukarno was at the end of the room farthest away from us. Guards and aides kept us where we were.

The aim seemed clear. It was to allow pictures to be taken, and to let reporters see that the President was alive, walking, talking, and apparently unharmed. But there was to be no questioning, no discussion with him.

Sukarno himself, however, torpedoed the plan. Dressed in a short-sleeved brown uniform, his usual black *pitji* upon his head, he moved down the length of one table in our direction, shaking hands with ministers and smiling as he went.

Then he circled the end of the table, just a few yards in front of us. To the consternation of guards and aides restraining us, he motioned imperiously for us to follow as he strolled up the second table to take his place at a seat in the middle of it. I scurried up the opposite side of the table and found myself, as he sat down, directly opposite him. Just three feet across from me sat the man who could unravel many mysteries of the past few days.

Despite the ban on interviews, it was an opportunity too good to miss. There followed an exchange between Sukarno and me that turned out to be fatuous, since he was obviously determined to say nothing of import. It was, however, his first interview with a newspaperman since the coup attempt.

"Mr. President" I asked, "have you some words for the foreign press?"

"Just a smile," he replied, banteringly.

"We note the smile," I tried again, "but would prefer some words."

At this, both Sukarno and his cabinet broke into laughter.

"How long," he asked me, "have you been here?"

"A few days," I replied.

"Mainly in Djakarta," he went on, "or have you traveled?"

"Only in Djakarta," I answered, "but when, Mr. President, are you returning to Djakarta?"

At this, Sukarno and members of his cabinet nearby broke into more laughter.

He clucked and shook his head and said, "You are angling me [*sic*]. These correspondents have very many tricks, many difficult questions."

"Well," I said, "as you asked me about my travel plans, I thought I would ask you about yours." The cabinet thought this amusing. There was another ripple of laughter.

But Sukarno would not be drawn. "We are not answering questions today," he said. "It's my turn to ask you questions."

"Well," I said, "if you have anything to say, the world's press is at your disposal."

Sukarno shook his head. "Later. Not yet, not yet," he said, as aides broke up the session.

At Sukarno's right hand as we chatted was Foreign Minister Subandrio, back from Sumatra and apparently in confident mood. The leader of the Communist Party, D. N. Aidit, was not in attendance. He was hiding in Central Java, of course, after his flight from Halim air base the previous week. But the second and third men in the party hierarchy, M. H. Lukman and Njoto, were present in their capacity as cabinet ministers.

After the meeting, it was Subandrio who distilled the gist of it to the waiting newsmen. We were not permitted to see Sukarno again.

As Antara, the Communist-dominated official Indonesian news agency, reported Subandrio's remarks, the President had definitely disapproved of the murder of the generals and the formation of the Revolution Council by Untung.

But that was far from the tenor of Subandrio's explanation to the English-speaking correspondents. Subandrio told us that Sukarno had given his own analysis of the "happenings" to the cabinet. According to Subandrio, the President told his ministers that "these things could always happen in a revolution" and that he was not surprised. This would "not be the last incident in the revolution."

Now the important thing was to maintain unity "not only of the armed forces, but of the political organizations and trade unions which are always the main force in a revolution."

As Subandrio related it, after the President spoke, various representatives of the political parties, including nationalist groups, religious organizations, and the Communist Party, gave their own views. "Also," said Subandrio, "the military spoke. They of course were very much excited by the happenings, and their emotions may sometimes have been out of control. But they all, I think, are loyal to the President and what the President asked of them—to create first a calm atmosphere and leave the political solution to him."

Subandrio said he thought the military would not be influenced by emotion or indulge in accusations between one service and another, but had full confidence that "later on, the President will make the final political solution."

Was there, Subandrio was asked, any discussion of punishment for those involved in the September 30th Movement? "As the President said," he answered, "it is a political problem which he will deal with later on. He does not condone these murders. He does not condone the establishment of the Revolution Council."

Did, then, Subandrio know how his own name came to be included on the 45-man Revolution Council? "No," he replied, "I did not know my name was on that list."

Had the cabinet discussed the Communist Party newspaper editorial of Saturday, endorsing the coup? "Yes," said Subandrio, "but the Communist Party issued a statement yesterday which was read out at this meeting.

"They are not supporting this movement. They are asking their members to refrain, I think, from any participation and to withdraw if they are members of the Revolution Council. Most of them who have been asked said they did not know anything about it. If something happened on the thirtieth of September, according to the Communist Party it is an internal question of the army."

Had he or anybody else, Subandrio then was asked, demanded an explanation from the Communists present at the cabinet meeting of those editorials supporting the September 30th Movement? "No," he replied, "I did not ask them."

The statement to which Subandrio referred, as having been issued by the Communist Party, had been released the previous day in the name of the party's politburo. It said the party supported the message of the President (broadcast Sunday, October 3) on settling the "problem of the September 30th Movement."

With regard to this movement, the politburo "considers it to be an internal problem of the army, and the Indonesian Communist Party does not involve itself in it," said the statement.

Then it went on: "With regard to the names of members of the Communist Party included in the list of the Revolution Council, it can be stated as a consequence of questions put to the members concerned that these members were neither informed beforehand nor asked for their permission."

Then the politburo called on the people to "heighten their vigilance" in carrying out the principles of the Indonesian revolution and in crushing "the joint British-U.S. project Malaysia" and continuing the "anti-Necolim struggle in general."

To the correspondents who listened to Subandrio's bland summation, it sounded like the beginning of the Great Whitewash Campaign. Both Sukarno and Omar Dhani had been at pains to extricate the air force from a plot in which its most senior officers had obviously been deeply implicated. Now, if we were to believe the words so easily dropping from Subandrio's lips, Sukarno himself seemed to be accepting the Communists' assurance that they were uninvolved in the generals' murders and to be virtually absolving the Communist Party from blame.

11. The Great Crackdown

But if Sukarno and Subandrio had launched the Great Whitewash of the Communists, the army was having none of it. Indeed, the army was about to launch the Great Crackdown on the Communist Party.

In the days immediately succeeding the coup attempt, Suharto's soldiers had been picking up individual Communists and plotters. But it was for Sukarno's reaction to the September 30th Movement they had waited—a reaction that they felt sure would involve suitable punishment for the Communist Party.

Instead, Sukarno at his Bogor cabinet meeting had been astonishingly mild in his reaction to the army generals' murder. He had, as we have seen, joked and laughed with ministers and newsmen. In private session he had prevaricated, had given no commitment he would take action against the Communist Party, and had indeed seemed anxious to protect it. His Communist ministers had sat confidently in on the session, as though nothing untoward had happened in Indonesia just five days previously.

The army was astonished and enraged. Sukarno had not been present at the funeral of his generals. Though there may have been questions of security involved, his absence now was beginning to look more and more like a national scandal. Moreover, Sukarno now appeared to be trying to shelter the Communists the army was convinced were involved in the generals' murder.

Suharto had heeded the President's injunction to maintain peace and had prevented his men from assaulting the air force, but now his patience was sorely tested.

From Nasution there came no lead, for Nasution was plunged into his own personal trauma of grief and shock. Although he was defense minister, he had stayed away from the Bogor cabinet meeting. His daughter had died from her wounds that very day, and he seemed incapable of action.

Not so his colleagues. They had abundant evidence of Communist involvement in the September 30th Movement. With Sukarno's authorization or without it, they were now determined to grind the Communist Party into oblivion. With cold, relentless fury they set about the task.

At the funeral of Nasution's 5-year-old daughter Irma, navy chief Admiral Eddy Martadinata passed the word to anti-Communist Moslem student leaders. As he brushed by them, from the corner of his mouth he spat out a single word, "*Sikat.*" They had no difficulty in grasping his meaning. The word means "sweep." The message was that they could go out and clean up the Communists without any hindrance from the military. With relish they called out their followers, stuck their knives and pistols in their waistbands, swung their clubs over their shoulders, and embarked on the assignment for which they had long been hoping.

The morning after Irma Nasution's funeral, a week to the day after the murder of the six generals, Moslem demonstrators marched on Communist Party headquarters. As they went, they tore down pro-Communist signs and scribbled on walls and fences "Crush the PKI [Communist Party]," "Crush Aidit." At the building where less than a year ago I had chatted with Aidit about his ambitions for greater power, there was not much resistance. Angrily but methodically the demonstrators smashed its interior to pieces, then put it to the torch. It was a wooden building, and it went up fast. Three fire trucks were in attendance, but waited carefully till only the ashes were left before they went into action. Army units were nearby, having cordoned off the streets leading to Communist headquarters. They made no attempt to interfere.

As the Communist Party's hopes of early power in Indonesia went billowing up into the humid air with the smoke from its sacked headquarters, thousands of demonstrators shouted, "Kill Aidit!"

"Dissolve the PKI!" Then they marched to the headquarters of the government-sponsored National Front, stopping cars along the way and smothering their windshields with crude stickers demanding the Communist Party's dissolution. As army trucks passed, they cheered, stopped them, and shook hands with the soldiers aboard. Some of the demonstrators, themselves cruising about the city in trucks, rattled past the American Embassy and called out, "Long live America!"

It was a historic little moment. For more than a year the embassy of the United States had been the target of an increasing series of hostile demonstrations. If anything was burning in Djakarta, it was a good guess that it was something belonging to the Americans or the British. Now, for the first time in the world as far as anybody could remember, the headquarters of a major Communist party had gone up in smoke at the hands of anti-Communists. Nobody pretended that the political situation in Indonesia had suddenly turned full circle. But at least from a truck speeding by somebody could shout out a greeting to the Americans. A week before, it could not have happened.

For the Communists, the writing was now literally on the wall. Leading party officials slipped out of town. Crowds marched on the homes of Aidit, Lukman, and Njoto and dragged everything outside and burned it.

But the wrath of the anti-Communists was not only directed toward the Indonesian Communist Party. The Chinese Communists had been ostentatious by their absence at the funeral of the army's heroes. Now they refused to obey the army's order that all flags should be flown at half-mast in a period of mourning for the dead generals. I took a drive down to the Chinese Embassy to confirm that this was the case. Outside the embassy's locked gates was parked an Indonesian police jeep. Its registration number, I noted with a smile, was 007, meaning not that it belonged to James Bond, but that it came from the 7th police precinct in the capital area.

The policeman in the jeep watched me curiously as I ran my eye up the flagpole, set back in the embassy grounds. Sure enough, the flag of Communist China was flying defiantly at the top of the pole, in disregard of the Indonesian order. I looked back at the policeman. With never a word between us, he nodded in the direction of the embassy, thrust his arm out with thumb stuck pointedly downwards, then waggled it up and down a couple of times in a gesture of supreme contempt for the Chinese.

It was symbolic of the mounting antagonism toward the Chinese, soon to be expressed in demonstrations outside their diplomatic offices and residences. One anti-Communist and religious organization after another, now re-emerging with the apparent eclipse of the Communist Party, demanded a break in diplomatic relations with Peking.

In their cleanup campaign, troops of the Djakarta garrison stamped into the Chinese commercial counselor's office and searched it despite protests from Chinese Communist officials. Later came a formal note of protest from the Chinese government. According to this, the Indonesian soldiers "tried to break in by banging the gate with rifle butts, and loudly threatened to set fire to the buildings and kill all the personnel in the office."

As the Chinese told it, the troops "opened fire and barged in by force. They threatened the staff with bayonets, forbade them to move, and searched and questioned them one by one." They ripped open cupboards, ransacked suitcases and wardrobes, searched for documents, and did extensive damage, "even pushing and striking the commercial attaché."

The Chinese note said the officer commanding the troops read: "they were dispatched by the Djakarta military area headquarters and were performing duty upon order of the government." All this, said the Chinese, constituted a "brutal encroachment on diplomatic immunities and a gross violation of international law. Since October 1, lies and slanders about China and anti-Chinese clamors have continuously appeared in Indonesia, and all kinds of threats and intimidations have been made against the Chinese diplomatic missions. An anti-Chinese wave is starting in Indonesia, and if it is not checked, the consequences will be serious."

Peking's hopes were in vain. The anti-Chinese wave in Indonesia was not to be checked. As a gesture to the mounting body of opinion against the Chinese, Subandrio made one or two remarks mildly warning Peking that Indonesia would take a "firm attitude" toward China "if necessary." And in a curious little incident, Ganis Harsono, the foreign ministry spokesman, gave an interview to three foreign newsmen, one of them me, in which he was clearly anxious to convey the impression that Indonesia was reappraising its attitude toward China. The Djakarta-Peking axis would still stand, he said, but we must not forget that it had only existed as a "bulwark against Necolim [the West]." Indonesia and China, said Ganis Harsono, would continue to collaborate in the campaign against Necolim. But all other items would "have to be dealt with separately." Indonesia, he said, would have to "watch China carefully for the next few months to see what Peking wants of us."

It was fascinating stuff, but in retrospect it is quite clear it was also merely window-dressing. Sukarno and Subandrio were in fact striving desperately to maintain the relationship with China in the face of opposition from the public and the army.

In a speech three weeks after the coup attempt, Subandrio had this to say, "Don't say 'Long live America' just because there is some tension between Indonesia and China. We still cannot say the United States is our friend." The tension with China, he went on, should not let Indonesia be trapped by the imperialists and colonialists. The Indonesian people should not become rightist.

Subandrio was but echoing the views of his master. A few days later, Sukarno himself exploded. If Indonesia's revolution veered to the right, he said, it would be a "big disaster, bigger even than the September thirtieth affair." He charged that a campaign had been launched in Indonesia to "instigate hatred" against Communist China, and he made it clear he disapproved of this campaign. As if to underline the point, he invited to his palace the Chinese Ambassador, Yao Chung-ming, for a friendly chat. Afterwards he declared relations between the two countries would remain friendly "despite efforts to undermine them."

But Sukarno had reckoned without public opinion. The anti-Chinese campaign picked up steam, and the Chinese angrily cut off their military aid to Indonesia and halted trade. From Sukarno's ambitious CONEFO project they withdrew their technicians and called them back to China.

In little more than a month, the Chinese Embassy in Djakarta filed fourteen consecutive protest notes over various incidents of harassment. At a luncheon one day given by the American Ambassador for correspondents, several of us were suddenly given a tip that the Chinese Embassy was being burned. Hastily we excused ourselves. Peter Kalisher of CBS, I from *The Christian Science Monitor*, and Jerry King of *The New York Times* (finally admitted to Indonesia with other American correspondents) raced down the steps of the Ambassador's residence, then stopped and looked at each other blankly. For various reasons, none of us had a car there at that particular moment.

In our crisis, one of the military attachés good-naturedly offered us his. With a variety of exhortations we urged the Indonesian driver to greater speed. Catching the excitement, he finally brought us swirling up to the Chinese Embassy in grand style and swung in at the gates before we could stop him. Fortunately, the gates were locked. But there were some perplexed looks on the faces of several Communist officials in the grounds, as they pondered this sudden arrival of a car bearing the diplomatic plates of the United States, before we could get it backed out and parked in more discreet circumstances.

As it turned out, we had missed lunch for no good reason. Though it was to be attacked later, the Chinese Embassy was not on fire at that time. But such was the mood in Djakarta then that the initial report that it was in flames seemed perfectly credible.

Soon afterwards some two thousand anti-Communist demonstrators stormed the Chinese consulate in Medan, in northern Sumatra. According to the official Chinese protest note, the consulate was under siege for five and a half hours and was bombarded with bricks and stones that smashed through the windows and tiled roof. The demonstration against the consulate spilled over into rioting against local Chinese residents in the city. These were some of the two to three million people of Chinese origin living in various parts of Indonesia who by dint of their industry and capital had acquired a dominant role in the country's economic life. Resentment toward them lay never far from the surface, and in the months to come they were to be continually harried.

The Djakarta *Daily Mail* set the tone of Indonesia's post-coup foreign policy when it warned its readers in an editorial that there were really two C.I.A.s. Of the American one it was not, of course, particularly enamored. Nevertheless, the misdeeds of the American C.I.A. seemed to pale into insignificance for the paper as it revealed the existence of the "Chinese Intelligence Agency." The *Daily Mail* hinted that the Chinese C.I.A. had a lot of explaining to do about its role in the September 30th Movement.

If Indonesia's relations with Peking were in the deep freeze, however, the army was bent on ruthlessly dismantling the entire Communist Party organization at home. Few holds were barred. Gruesome photographs of the generals' bodies were quietly circulated throughout military ranks. Now a sinister new word—*Gestapu*—was cleverly coined from the initials of the September 30th Movement, *Gerekan September Tiga Puluh.*

Although Sukarno was still pondering his "political solution" to the affair, the army wrote its own orders. In Djakarta the garrison commander announced a "military ban" on the Communist Party. Commanders in other parts of the country followed suit. Operating under a "state of war" that made it answerable only to itself, the army scooped up thousands of Communists and suspects throughout the capital. Fifty-seven Communist members of the parliament were "suspended." More than a hundred members of the People's Consultative Congress (MPRS) were "banned" for suspected complicity in the Gestapu movement.

Communist mayors in a string of important towns in Java— Surabaya, Tjirebon, Solo, Magelang, Salatiga—were dismissed or imprisoned. Throughout government departments there began a purge of Communists. In the maritime ministry alone, 1,371 were fired.

Antara, the official Indonesian news agency, was put under military control. Scores of its reporters were taken off for questioning. The new military editors began to clean it up, remove its notorious pro-Communist bias.

After their success in razing Communist Party headquarters, the crowds were turned loose on other Communist organizations in Djakarta. One Sunday they spent sacking the Communist youth organization (Pemuda Rakjat) headquarters and the Communist trade union organization (SOBSI) building. At the SOBSI offices they smashed every piece of furniture they could lay hands on, then gutted filing cabinets and ripped to shreds whatever documents they found. They tore down portraits of Indonesian Communist leaders and trampled on them. At Pemuda Rakjat headquarters the pattern was much the same. There they burned the organization's signboard, too. Any Communist organization car or vehicle they discovered was wrecked with brutal efficiency.

As they worked, the demonstrators shouted such slogans as "Aidit to the gallows," "Dissolve the Communist Party," "Dissolve SOBSI," "Crush the Pemuda Rakjat." Their plans for Aidit took a little longer to fulfill, but the army was swift to oblige with banning orders against SOBSI and the other Communist front organizations.

Aidit was in Central Java, and the crowds had already ransacked his Djakarta house once. Not content, they returned to it again. As the army newspaper, the *Daily Mail*, reported it solemnly, "Perhaps they opined that the house of the great Communist Party leader must be demolished completely." Apparently they did so opine. For as the army paper recounted, "One by one the tiles of Aidit's house were taken off the roof. Others started breaking up the walls." According to the army newspaper, "the crowds as they broke up the house found a suitcase crammed with cash.

All this sacking and burning and demonstrating was nothing particularly novel in the political life of Djakarta. What was new was that now the Communists, instead of the Americans and the British, were on the receiving end of it all.

Some people in the American Establishment, however, must still have had doubts about the direction of events. For in mid-October, just two weeks after the Gestapu affair, the announcement came from the American Embassy that wives and children of embassy officials were to be evacuated. It was a decision that to many outsiders seemed incomprehensible. Many officials in the embassy privately spoke out militantly against it. For months, after all, the embassy had been the target of Communist mobs at a time when the Communists seemed in the ascendancy. The dependants had, with fortitude and courage, sat out this crisis in Djakarta. Now, with the Communists on the run and the Indonesian army in apparent control, somebody had decided to pull those dependants out. At the very least, it hardly looked like an American vote of confidence in the Indonesian military.

The decision caused a flurry in Djakarta's diplomatic corps. Within hours of its announcement, diplomats from two foreign embassies were knocking on my hotel room door seeking the "inside story" on the American decision. Elsewhere, non-American diplomats were similarly assigned to ferret out "what the Americans knew that they didn't."

Ambassador Marshall Green handled the flurry calmly. "Would you," he asked his questioners, "be prepared to take the responsibility for keeping those women and children here when the decision could mean the difference between their living or dying?" Whether it was Ambassador Green's own decision, or whether it was imposed from Washington, the embassy wives and children were flown out. They were not to return until after Christmas—in time for a fresh round of anti-American activity.

As the anti-Communist and anti-China movement rolled relentlessly onward, Sukarno called angrily but vainly for peace. He demanded that Indonesians call off their campaign of what he termed "racialism, slander, and vengeance." He blamed the newspapers, now all under army supervision, for not having given his instructions sufficient play. He said he wanted the anti Communist demonstrations halted to avoid "all actions which can ruin our national struggle. Our struggle is against Necolim." He warned he would order the army to "shoot to kill" anybody who violated his directives.

The army took Sukarno's outbursts calmly. As one leading general told me at the time, "We agree with the President that our struggle is against Necolim. The only thing is, he looks at Washington and London when he talks about Necolim. When we talk about Necolim, we're beginning to look much, much harder at Peking."

As for "shooting to kill," the army was ready to do that. But it had its own list of those marked down for elimination.Indonesia was about to be plunged into a blood bath, and whether Sukarno agreed or not, the blood to be shed was that of the Communists.

12. Last Stand in Java

While Djakarta was the focal point of the Gestapu operation, the plotters had also struck in various other parts of the country.

In the north of Sumatra, the Communists were fairly well organized. They had the support of a governor who was an undercover member of the party. But any plans they had laid to secure northern Sumatra for the Gestapu were foiled by the lightning impulse of Brigadier General Kemal Idris, who was then in the area with a division under his command.

Kemal Idris is a youngish, courtly general with the faintest trace of a lisp when he speaks in English. But he has a reputation for swift and decisive action. There was no hesitation on his part as he got the first news of the coup on the morning of October 1 at his base at Tebintinggi, some 60 miles southeast of Medan, Sumatra's biggest city.

Today he admits he moved without orders. "I told my men to seize members of the Communist Party before I had any authority to do so," he says. "Their initial orders were to clean up the Communists within a five-kilometer radius of their positions. But they completed the assignment so fast that they spread outwards, still farther afield.

"Some of our troops were disloyal. We had a brigade commander and a number of officers involved in Gestapu. But we moved so fast, they were unable to react."

With his troops already in action, Kemal Idris managed to contact General Suharto in Djakarta. Kemal Idris asked permission to take his division and move on Medan. At first, Suharto demurred. Though Kemal Idris did not himself tell me this story, Suharto apparently was concerned lest Malaysia take advantage of the situation in Indonesia to launch an attack across the Malacca

Strait on Sumatra. Incredible though this seems, Suharto at that moment apparently considered Malaysia capable of such action and did not want a whole division committed against the Communists in Medan.

Thus Kemal Idris moved out at the head of a battalion and into Medan. There, as eyewitnesses tell it, he burst into government offices with pistol in hand to find some army officers furiously typing away at Gestapu directives and propaganda. To the head of one of these officers he put his pistol; then he looked around and shouted the question, "Are you for or against Suharto?" Support for Suharto was suddenly a hundred percent. The Gestapu documents swiftly disappeared. Kemal Idris had Medan under his control.

Now he contacted Suharto again. This time he got permission to use his division to "clean up" Communists. Nobody needed to spell out what "cleaning up" meant. One reliable source close to Kemal Idris says that the army killed twenty percent of the rubber plantation workers in the Medan area in those days of bloody retaliation succeeding the coup attempt.

On Indonesia's outlying islands there were sporadic, but apparently ill-coordinated, Gestapu incidents. In Borneo, young Communists made a vain attempt to set fire to a Shell Oil Company refinery. On Timor, high officials were assembled with their wives for a special briefing outside Kupang, the main town, to last several days. They thought it odd that the only important group absent was the Communist Party. But if it was a plot to move against those officials so conveniently collected together, it failed, for local army units balked and refused to align themselves with Gestapu.

Meanwhile, on the island of Flores the chief of police stumbled on a rallying Gestapu force by extraordinary accident. Driving home, he absentmindedly overshot his own driveway and went on up the road round a bend to meet the hastily gathered Gestapu supporters coming the other way. He wheeled round and raced back to alert loyalist military units.

In the central region of Indonesia's major island of Java, however, the Gestapu made a formidable stand. Central Java was the stronghold of the Communist Party. It had too many people on too little land, and it was easy prey for the Communists with their heady promises of land reform. It was to this region that Aidit fled in the early hours of October 2 after the collapse of Gestapu in Djakarta. The plane provided by Omar Dhani landed him at Jogjakarta, and he was soon huddled in conference with Communist officials, local Communist mayors, and the pro-Communist acting governor of Central Java.

For Aidit the selection of Central Java as a place for retreat was obvious and sound. In addition to the party strength there, the Communists had successfully infiltrated the Diponegoro division of the army (so named after a 19th-century Javanese hero), which was stationed in Central Java. Four of the division's battalions had allied themselves to the Gestapu banner and were in revolt. For Suharto and his loyalist officers, Central Java was to present their most serious challenge outside Djakarta.

The divisional commander got the first news of the Gestapu operation by radio early in the morning of October 1. Brigadier General Surjo Sumpeno was sipping coffee with his wife in his quarters at the divisional headquarters of Semarang, a pretty town on the northern coast of Central Java, near the Java Sea.

As he recalls the story today, he "immediately had a feeling something was wrong." He knew, he says, "there was nothing to this Council of Generals."

His first action was to summon local officials and officers in his divisional command to a meeting. He urged them to stay calm until the situation was clarified. One of his officers at that meeting was Lieutenant Colonel Usman. Ordinarily, Usman never wore side arms, but General Sumpeno recalls noting with brief curiosity at the time that on this occasion Usman arrived wearing a revolver.

After the meeting, General Sumpeno issued a statement to the public asking them to be quiet, not to take any unusual action by themselves, and to await further orders. Then he set off, in his Russian-made jeep, for Magelang on the road leading south to Jogjakarta, the cultural center of Java and one-time seat of government during the early days of the Indonesian republic. At Magelang was the military academy, and the General wanted to brief his officers there on the situation. To kill two birds with one stone, he asked the regimental commander from Jogjakarta, Colonel Katamso, to drive in to Magelang and attend the same briefing.

By now, Suharto's forces in Djakarta were moving. Over the military radio network came a message for General Sumpeno clarifying the situation somewhat and indicating the source of opposition. To his Semarang headquarters Sumpeno therefore sent a top-priority message confining all troops to barracks until he could confirm their loyalty.

After the Magelang briefing, the general decided to make a detour on his way back to headquarters via the garrison town of Salatiga to brief his officers there. Bouncing along in his jeep, he accidentally switched on a transistor radio he had borrowed from his chief of staff and brought with him. The accident produced ominous news. Over the local radio station he heard the announcement that officers of his command sympathetic to Gestapu had seized control of his divisional headquarters.

They were urging fellow Gestapu supporters to set up revolutionary councils throughout Central Java. Who were the officers heading this disloyal movement? The same Lieutenant Colonel Usman who had come wearing a revolver to General Sumpeno's briefing earlier and Colonel Suherman, the division's intelligence chief. Ironically, Suherman had only recently returned from a training course at Fort Leavenworth, in the United States.

General Sumpeno decided to race on to Salatiga. What he did not know was that troops of his 73rd Regiment based there had already gone over to the Gestapu. After he entered a building in the military compound, Gestapu troops surrounded it. A captain confronted him and announced, 'General, I have to arrest you.'

But the captain must have been either nervous or remarkably slow-witted, for the general was able to bluff his way to escape. Some Indonesian newspapers later carried a story that had General Sumpeno announcing to the captain that under arrest, or not, he was thirsty and wanted some tea. According to this story, the captain obligingly left the room, and the general jumped out of the back window and got away.

Sumpeno himself, however, laughs off this story as newspaper exaggeration. What really took place, he says, was a brief battle of wits between himself and the young captain. "I looked at him firmly," he says, "and told him 'I know much more than you about what is happening. I know the whole situation about the Revolution Council. Don't you think that I, as a general, am in on everything and know what is going on? Now you are ordered to stay here with your troops. I must get on.'"

Apparently the confused captain assumed Sumpeno was in secret league with the plotters. At any rate, he let the general get away.

With this successful little confrontation, Sumpeno may have saved his own life. If he had been kept prisoner, he might well have suffered the same fate as his unfortunate regimental commander in Jogjakarta, the same Colonel Katamso he had earlier summoned to his briefing at Magelang. For even as that briefing was ending, disloyal troops of Katamso's 72nd Regiment seized control in Jogjakarta in the name of Gestapu. Their leader was a Major Muljono who ordered both Katamso and his chief of staff, Lieutenant Colonel Sugijono, arrested. Later they were put to violent death. According to trial evidence later, an army sergeant smashed Katamso's head in with a mortar barrel. His chief of staff was similarly attacked and finished off with a big stone. Three weeks later, their bodies were discovered by loyalist troops in shallow graves at an army installation not far from the city.

With their commander murdered, the mutinous troops in Jogjakarta issued weapons to civilian sympathizers. The Communist Party called out 25,000 members for a rally pledging support to Gestapu. But despite this initial show of strength, the morale of the Gestapu forces sagged badly as news began to flow in from Djakarta that Suharto was in complete control.

The Gestapu leaders in Jogjakarta fled, and the rank and file collapsed. By October 5 the city was back under the control of loyalist forces under the command of one of Sumpeno's officers, Colonel Widodo, who arrived at the head of a column of tanks.

Sumpeno himself had retaken his divisional headquarters at Semarang even earlier. After escaping from Gestapu clutches at Salatiga, he ordered up a tank battalion from Magelang. With the guns of his tanks to underline his authority, he made a confident reentry into Semarang in an Opel car on October 2. By midday the local radio station was canceling out all the announcements of Gestapu and broadcasting a message of loyalty to the President and orders to follow the commands of General Suharto.

Though forces loyal to Suharto had now retaken the divisional headquarters at Semarang, and Central Java's most important city of Jogjakarta, the Gestapu supporters were still putting up a fight in the string of Communist-dominated villages that lay between them. Central Java is dotted with growling volcanoes, and because land is so precious, the peasants' plots ramble up over their foothills despite the destruction and heartbreak that occasionally come roaring down from the craters above.

Now, as they retreated, the Gestapu leaders took to the villages on the slopes of Mount Merapi, the great blue, often cloud-girt, volcano that soars upward above the Central Javanese plain. Like giant reflecting pools, the flooded rice paddies mirror its looming bulk for miles around. In those days, wherever Mount Merapi's shadow fell could be counted safe territory for the Communists.

The most solidly Communist town of all in the area was Solo, also once known as Surakarta. With the support of the town's Communist mayor, Utomo Ramelan, Gestapu forces there had broadcast their support for the coup attempt. There followed confused skirmishing between army troops, air force units, police, and student military organizations, all of differing loyalties.

After his initial landing in Jogjakarta, Aidit criss-crossed safe Communist territory trying to coordinate his forces, but for his headquarters he chose a hiding place in Solo.

The Gestapu leaders in Semarang, Colonel Suherman and Lieutenant Colonel Usman, fled with other disloyal officers to the Mount Merapi area, but in December General Suharto announced they had been shot and killed in a fire fight with security forces.

Of the Djakarta ringleaders, General Supardjo managed to evade capture the longest. He was not arrested until early in 1967, in Djakarta itself. Colonel Latief was captured a few days after the coup on October 9. According to the Siliwangi troops who took him, he was in the bath at his wife's house in Djakarta when they surprised him. They say he resisted and they had to open fire, wounding him in the legs.

Lieutenant Colonel Untung was captured in a bizarre incident near his home town of Tegal, Central Java, on October 11. He had deserted other members of his Tjakrabirawa battalion as para-commandos closed in on them and was trying to make a getaway alone by bus. Apparently he was seeking refuge in Tegal itself, for he had asked the bus driver to stop there. But though the bus had its Indonesian nickname for "Lucky" painted on its side, it was unlucky for Untung, whose own name, by even stranger coincidence, is the Indonesian word for lucky. Despite his identity papers stating his name was Bambang and that he lived in a suburb of Djakarta, two soldiers traveling in the bus recognized him and kept him under surveillance. Untung must have sensed this, for he suddenly leaped out of the bus as it passed through a village at the approaches of Tegal. The soldiers leaned out of the window and yelled the Indonesian equivalent of "Stop, thief!" The villagers took after Untung and seized him, holding him until the bus could stop and the two soldiers could come panting up to arrest him.

They summoned help, and Untung was returned to Djakarta with an escort of tanks and armored cars. There he was placed under heavy guard, and his interrogation was begun. At first he would say nothing, only demand that he be taken to Sukarno. Later he began to make his statement. Upon his return to Djakarta, his face and one side of his head were badly bruised. According to his captors, he came by these injuries because he crashed into a telephone pole as he jumped from the moving bus just before his arrest at Tegal. The injuries were no longer visible by the time he stood trial.

Though some of the coup leaders had got away and were trying to rally their supporters in Central Java, they were soon to face the vengeance of the army's elite shock troops, the RPKAD para-commandos. For two weeks after the October 1 coup attempt, the para-commandos were busy in the Djakarta area. They had taken Halim for Suharto and been given various other key assignments in the anti-Gestapu cleanup.

But after Suharto had consolidated his hold on the capital, Colonel, now General, Sarwo Edhy, the RPKAD commander, went to him and asked that his red-bereted para-commandos be ordered to Central Java. Suharto agreed. On October 17, the regiment climbed into its trucks and rolled out of its base near Djakarta for an intentionally ostentatious parade through the countryside into

Central Java.

Next day they arrived in Semarang and set up headquarters. As if to celebrate their arrival, anti-Communist demonstrators promptly burned Communist Party headquarters in the town to the ground.

The para-commandos are the swashbuckling glamor boys of the Indonesian Army. Since the coup, they have become the heroes of the anti-Communist forces. Though since transferred to a broader command, Sarwo Edhy, their then commander, is a hero of the students.

Long after the event, picking his words carefully in English, he told me, "When I asked Suharto to send me to Central Java, I was not seeking glory. The idea behind the march was to raise the spirits of the people. We wanted to put up placards demanding the crushing of the Communist Party. We wanted to show the people they were supported against Gestapu. We wanted to tell them who was behind Gestapu." Then, with a smile, "We wanted to do this in terms of President Sukarno's words. He had said, 'Give me the facts, and I'll give you a political solution.' Well, we wanted to create in people the courage to fight Gestapu, and to gather the facts."

Months after the event, in the orderly atmosphere of General Sarwo Edhy's office, the words seemed reasonable enough. From time to time, as he went over the details of his Central Java campaign for me, the general would trace a route with his baton on a wall map, or pore over his diaries to check a date or a unit's movement.

Yet unspoken between us lay the knowledge that the real purpose of his assignment in Central Java had been the extermination, by whatever means might be necessary, of the core of the Communist Party there. It was a mission successfully accomplished.

In the green rice paddies around Mount Merapi the para-commandos gave little quarter. On one occasion, Sarwo Edhy himself was on the scene when an armored car heading a column was halted at the approaches to a village that was threatening to resist. Women members of the Communist Gerwani organization danced out into the road, turned around, and bared their posteriors to the troops in a gesture of insult. Sarwo Edhy did not hesitate. Tersely he ordered the gunner in the armored car, "Shoot them." The gunner obeyed the command. Then some of the villagers surged forward in protest. The gunner looked at his general for instructions. "Shoot them, too," was the command. After the guns had stopped chattering, Sarwo Edhy gave the villagers one hour to turn in their weapons. From the scene they had just witnessed, they knew he would deal ruthlessly with resistance. The weapons were handed over, the village did not fight, and the power of the Communist Party there was broken.

One of the first things Sarwo Edhy did in Central Java was to set his men hunting for the bodies of the Jogjakarta regimental commander and his chief of staff. "We wanted to find them for psychological reasons," explains Sarwo Edhy. "We had to produce the bodies and say to our people and troops, 'Here are your heroes. Here is the evidence of what the Gestapu has done.'"

When the bodies were found, in shallow graves not far from Jogjakarta, the army ordered a military funeral with all pomp and splendor. As many units as possible were to attend. Prominent would be the para-commandos, riding in a show of strength as well as demonstrating their respect.

But on October 22, as Sarwo Edhy was readying his men for the funeral, he was given an urgent message: there was trouble in the area of Bojolali and Klaten. Though the funeral of the murdered officers went on, the para-commandos were pulled out of the ceremonial parade. Instead, they tumbled into their trucks and went roaring off to action.

It was an action that proved to be the Communists' last major attempt at a comeback. In villages throughout the area the

Javanese drums had rapped out the order for a general offensive against the anti-Communists. Trees were felled and used to block roads; telephone lines were cut. Communist youth gangs attacked police stations and army compounds, presumably in a desperate bid to gain weapons, for they were often armed only with knives and sharpened bamboo stakes. Anti-Communists were kidnapped and killed, their homes set on fire. According to Sarwo Edhy, in the town of Solo itself, anti-Communists were killed by the hundreds, houses were burned, and there were many calls for help.

But the offensive was short-lived. The Communists themselves took many casualties. The para-commandos were quickly on the scene. They rumbled into Solo and secured key installations in the town. On October 23, the Gestapu forces surrendered.

In terms of large-scale, organized military resistance, the Communists were finished in Central Java. True, there were clashes for weeks to come. Even in November, army authorities were reporting kidnappings and killings by Pemuda Rakjat gangs of Communist youth. But these were isolated incidents and not part of a general Communist offensive.

Now the para-commandos embarked on their task of "cleaning out" the Communists. As Sarwo Edhy explains it, the area was too big and too crowded for him to distribute his forces effectively.

"We decided," he says, "to encourage the anti-Communist civilians to help with the job. In Solo we gathered together the youth, the nationalist groups, the religious [Moslem] organizations. We gave them two or three days' training, then sent them out to kill the Communists."

Thus began Indonesia's post-coup blood bath.

13. Punishment in the Paddies

On a hill overlooking Java's volcano-studded central plain stands the famous temple of Borobudur.

It is a monument of grandeur, its gray stone turned mellow green in many parts by centuries of tropical climate. From a base whose sides are more than a hundred yards long, it climbs regally upwards in a series of curved terraces to a central dome. This is surrounded by more than five hundred carved stone Buddhas, some of them set in niches, others protected by massive bell-like structures of latticed stone. Its terraces are faced with stone relief panels carved in exquisite detail.

Borobudur is not, perhaps, as splendid as Angkor, the ruins of the ancient capital of the Khmer empire in Cambodia, but dating from the late 8th or early 9th century, it is one of Asia's great relics and testimony enough to the great cultural history of the Javanese people.

Around Borobudur the countryside seems tranquil enough. As the young rice shoots up in the flooded paddies, there is vivid green as far as the eye can see. The land is overcrowded, but this garden of Java is clearly lush and fertile. In the little towns, pony carts clatter along with a tinkling of bells. Heavier loads, of rice and sugar cane and coconuts and swaying bamboo poles, are dragged by massive, serene, humped white cattle. And at the end of a day's plowing, the gray water buffaloes sink into some pool in an ecstasy of sucking, squelching, splashing muddiness.

There is a saying in Java that happiness is a home, a wife, and a singing bird. And so, outside the simple little houses of plaited bamboo strips, there is often a pole, atop which hangs a birdcage with a brilliantly colored bird in it trilling merrily away. With all the formality of a national flag being raised and lowered outside some building of state, the bird is hoisted by pulley to the top of its pole at dawn, then hauled down again at dusk when people start lighting up their flickering little coconut-oil lamps.

Then, too, come marching home in a flurry of clucking self-importance the fat white ducks, which have spent the day pecking away in the fields. They are not as clever as they think, for they are really the prisoners of an urchin who carries a stick with a piece of tattered white cloth tied to it. Like soldiers trained only to obey, they follow that little piece of white cloth all day. When their youthful keeper rams his stick into the muddy earth and leaves the cloth flying, they never stray beyond sight of it.

Yet for all the ancient estheticism of Borobudur, and the apparent tranquility of the surrounding countryside, this island of Java in the last months of 1965 was the scene of one of history's worst orgies of slashing, shooting, chopping violence. Thousands of Indonesians who were members of the Communist Party, or who supported it, or who were suspected of supporting it, or who were said by somebody to have supported it, were put ruthlessly to death. In the mayhem, people innocent of Communist affiliations were killed too, sometimes by mistake, sometimes because their old enemies were paying off grudges in the guise of an anti-Communist campaign.

Not many miles from Borobudur there took place a bloody massacre under the very walls of another religious shrine, the 9th-century temple of Loro Djonggrang (Slender Virgin) at Prambanan. Moslem youths were attacked there by Communist members of the Pemuda Rakjat. A number of Moslems were killed and quickly buried. When their friends and families came looking for the bodies to transfer them to another burial place with proper religious rites, the Pemuda Rakjat resisted. The Moslems called in the army to help, and the military say they killed fifty Communists in the battle that ensued, but a knowledgeable resident of the area says the retaliation did not stop there. For weeks afterwards, he says, the army ferreted out Communist supporters and seized them. Each night under the temple's moonlit walls about three hundred people were killed by the army's guns and buried in unmarked mass graves.

In Central Java the army seems to have exercised broad control over the blood bath, although many civilians were also recruited to kill Communists. In East Java, the mass execution of Communists was largely handed over to civilians, mainly the black-shirted Ansor youth of the Nahdatul Ulama (Moslem Teachers' Party), who killed with fanatical relish.

Thus in Central Java the prisons quickly filled up as the army went through the motions of arresting and screening Communist suspects. Schools and military compounds were turned into makeshift jails. Political prisoners were even jammed into the Jogjakarta building that had been used to house the Thomas Jefferson Library of the USIS until the Indonesian government closed it down at the height of the anti-American campaign.

No trials followed the mass arrests. Punishment was arbitrary and without appeal. Prisoners' names would be checked off against a seized Communist Party membership list, or against information supplied by informers. Those guilty of Communist affiliation were marked for execution. Usually at night, the army trucks would rumble up, and the doomed men would be marched into them at gunpoint. Then they would be driven a few miles out of town to some discreet spot chosen as the place of execution. Sometimes local villagers had already been ordered to dig big pits for the bodies. At other times, the prisoners themselves would be set to digging their graves.

Then they would be killed. If the army was in charge, death usually came with a volley of gunfire. But often the army would hand over batches of prisoners to anti-Communist groups. Then execution would be usually by knife or the broad-bladed sickles used by many Javanese for work in the fields. Many Communists were decapitated as they kneeled, thumbs tied behind their backs, on the brink of their graves.

One young Indonesian I know, invited to join the killer gangs, was asked, 'How will you kill, with knife or gun? Just choose your weapon, and we'll give you what you need.'

The execution of Communists, however, did not always follow this pattern of crude selection from suspect lists, even when the army was in control. As the troops swept through Central Java in their "weeding out" campaign, they would be led to villages and individuals by anti-Communist informers. In cases where informers pinpointed a village as being 100 percent Communist, everyone in it died, except the youngest children. Says one nauseated Indonesian professor at Jogjakarta's Gadjah Mada University, "The anti-Communists certainly had a grudge. But there was no need to kill children, too. In one family, women, children over six, everybody was killed. And they call themselves religious people. But they killed like pigs."

Within villages, anti-Communists were assigned to eliminate Communists. It was easy for them to pick out their targets, for in such tight little communities the political views of each man were well known. Sometimes anti-Communist villages were as signed to eliminate Communist villages. In these instances, brother might often be set against brother. Many handed the names of Communist members of their family to the army so that the soldiers, rather than they, would carry out the executions.

For the historian who may one day seek to record the events of these times, there is an accumulation of grisly lore. There is the story, for example, told by soldiers riding through one Central Javanese village in their open jeep. Laughing children who had been kicking a round bundle around in the dirt shouted and waved and tossed the package into the back of the jeep. When the soldiers opened it, they found its contents to be a human head.

Certainly there were instances where heads were impaled on stakes and publicly displayed as a deterrent to further Communist activity.

Yet now as the blood bath fades into history, there seems increasing reluctance on the part of many Indonesians to admit that they themselves took part in any killings. A year after the coup, I talked in the former Communist stronghold of Solo with a group of Moslem students who had been active in the anti-Communist campaign. In detail they told me how the Communists had initially held the town, of how the grip had been broken, and of how Communists were hounded down in later months. For my concluding question I asked them directly whether any of them had taken part in the executions. As I expected, there was an embarrassed silence, then a lengthy exchange in Indonesian between one of the young men and my interpreter. "No," said my interpreter, "they say they were not involved in the killings themselves."

Later my interpreter gave me the real gist of the exchange. The student who had done the talking had not wanted the visiting correspondent to know of his own part in the executions. But actually, he told my interpreter, he had drawn weapons with other students from the para-commandos. Under their instructions he himself had killed more than a dozen Communists.

Student was set against student, professor against professor, as well as villager against villager. Among the ranks of Gadjah Mada University's 24,000 students there were many gaps when the student body reassembled after the October coup and subsequent wave of killings. Nobody needed to ask what had happened to the missing young men, nor to the professors who so quietly disappeared during the anti-Communist purge.

Throughout Central Java the story was the same, of missing mayors and municipal councilors and headmen from villages and towns known for their Communist allegiance.

Some may have been dumped into the underground river at Wonosari, not far from Jogjakarta, which was used to dispose of many bodies, according to Moslem student leaders. Said one of them to me, "It's a big river, and fast-flowing. There was no problem about it clogging up. The bodies were just whisked away with the current underground. I suppose some were eaten by fishes. The rest would have been swept out to sea.'

While all this went on, the handful of foreigners in the region looked on aghast. The Japanese manager of the new, government-owned hotel in Jogjakarta was told by military authorities one day to stay in, behind closed doors, as there would be shooting in the area behind the hotel. There was, and thirteen of his employees were killed.

A little later the authorities made another request. Could the military borrow his big food truck, with its hotel driver, for a few days? The manager agreed, but within 48 hours the driver was back, shaken and determined to drive no more for the military. The truck, he revealed, was being used to transport dead bodies. The manager protested, and got his truck back. A little later he took delivery of some special refrigerator trucks, to be used to ship in frozen food from the port of Surabaya. Again the army asked whether the trucks could be borrowed. This time they got an emphatic refusal.

So many people were being killed that disposal of the bodies was a serious problem. In the little coastal town of Tjirebon, according to residents, the anti-Communists set up a guillotine that worked steadily throughout the day, day after day.

But the most savage slaughter in Java was in the island's eastern region where Moslem fanatics were turned loose on the Communists apparently with little military supervision.

In East Java there was no overcrowding problem in the prisons. Without the army to go through the formality of arrest, the Ansor youth dealt out instant and final punishment to their Communist enemies. Says one army general stationed in the area at the time, "There are about three thousand villages in East Java. Each of them had Communist Party members. I'd say each of them lost about ten to fifteen people as the Ansor people swept through. That means between thirty and forty-five thousand people were killed in East Java. But it could have been as high as a hundred thousand.'

In the beginning, known Communist officials were quickly put to death. Then began a systematic sweep through the villages. At night the killer patrols would check from house to house. Everybody was invited to identify himself and declare his politics. If he was not a member of any party, he had to prove it, and quickly. If he was a member of a nationalist or Moslem or some other non-Communist Party, he had to produce his membership card. If he turned out to be a member of the Communist Party, he was marched away to certain death, probably that very night.

In East Java the Moslem youth did not have the authority, as did the army in Central Java, to order villagers to dig mass graves, so those to be executed were often marched into the fields and there made to dig their own graves before falling to the knife and the sickle. Sometimes the execution site was the bed of a sandy river, where shallow pits could quickly be scooped out. There seems little doubt that in their haste the executioners sometimes buried some people who were still living.

But often there was neither time, opportunity, nor inclination to bury the dead. Then they were tossed into rivers. So many bodies came floating down the Brantas river that villagers downstream stopped eating fish from the river for fear some might contain a human finger or other portion of a decomposing body. One village lodged a formal protest with the authorities, claiming that the logjam of bodies posed a health hazard.

In the port city of Surabaya townsfolk were ordered to clear the bodies that washed up on the riverbanks. The British consul one morning found several bodies on the riverbank next to his garden. Still today, citizens point out a bridge, or a curve in the river, where they say the corpses were piled up in dozens.

Matter-of-factly, and unemotionally, one of the Ansor leaders long after the bloody events explained to me his organisation's viewpoint. "We were taking revenge," he said, "not only for the Communists' involvement in the coup, but for their activities against us over the years.

"At Madiun, in 1948, the Communists rebelled and were smashed. But they set about organising again. By 1963 they were very strong, and very active again, in Central and East Java. In the east they attacked Ansor, and it was a pretty one-sided action. The army had only three battalions of troops in East Java, two of infantry and one of cavalry [armor]. So we Ansor people had no protection. There was physical fighting. The Communist Party took our land. Tension was rising. This [the 1965 coup and the succeeding purge] was simply the climax."

According to this Ansor spokesman, when members of his organization first moved against the Communist Party in East Java, they discovered documents implicating the Communists in the abortive coup. "So from October to January," he continued, "we took our revenge. We knew who were Communists, and we would go to the villages and *kampongs* and kill them. The people just went wild against the Communists."

He had no hesitation about admitting his own part in some of the executions. "At Djombang, on November first, I was leader of an Ansor group," he explained. "The army handed over to us twenty Communists they had arrested. We knew what to do. We took them to another place where we killed them. They were not difficult to kill. They died like frightened birds.

"We'd already dug a hole for them. We killed them with knives. Guns would have been too noisy there. They would have panicked the local people. We keep quiet about where the graves are, otherwise the families might try to find them. In that particular case we dug the graves deep, so they could not be discovered."

Much of the time, he suggested, the Communists went quietly to their deaths. Sometimes, as he told it, they even co-operated. "There was an instance," he related, "where a Communist was kneeling to have his head cut off. The executioner told him, 'Lift up your head a little, so I can cut better.' The man about to die immediately lifted his head to help his executioner."

Did the Communists sometimes resist? "They did," he said, "fight back here and there, but much of the time they just seemed to crumple up and give in. There was one time, for example, where four Ansor youth came on fifteen Pemuda Rakjat boys who were armed. The Communists could have given our boys a bad time, but our boys called on them to surrender, to give up their arms. They did, and we got them."

Not all those involved in the orgy of killing could take it so quietly afterwards as this Ansor leader, however. One Indonesian acquaintance of mine has a friend who went insane because he had killed so many times. Another has violent nightmares each time he tries to sleep. A doctor in East Java tells of patients who see the faces of their victims in their sleep.

One place where the Communists did strike back was Banjuwangi, a town at the eastern tip of Java whence departs the ferry across the Bali Strait to the Indonesian island of Bali. There, a few days after the coup attempt in Djakarta, the Communists launched a full-scale attack on Ansor members. They were not armed with sophisticated weapons. According to Ansor, the Communists came at them wielding swords, knives, and sharpened stakes, but they killed 61 Ansor youths. Their leader, according to Ansor members, was an army surgeon. (This story does coincide with reports that the army medical corps was particularly effectively infiltrated by the Communist Party.) Though the army and Ansor later took control of the town, Communist subversion continued for some time.

East Java's worst slaughter took place in the Kediri district, where the military commander was a brother of General Sutojo, one of the six top generals murdered in Djakarta. Here thousands of Communist Party members were killed, mainly by Ansor squads, in a kind of holy war that had the blessing of the local Moslem leader, Hadji Makrus Ali. Explaining the killings as the "will of God," he said that the Communists got no more than they deserved.

The district is conveniently close to the Brantas river, and it was into this that the slashed bodies of the Communists were tumbled.

To keep the bodies from floating into irrigation channels leading off the river, the executioners protected the mouths of the channels with crude bamboo gates that let the water through, but deflected the corpses.

The killing in East Java was to leave a particularly bitter legacy. From this area were recruited many members of the Indonesian Marine Corps and Air Force. Many lost members of their familes in the anti-Communist purge. It was a grudge they would not easily forget.

14. Aidit's Hideout

One day as 1966 drew to a close, I set off from the Central Javanese town of Solo on an expedition of some minor drama. The aim was to find the last hiding place of Dipa Nusantara Aidit, leader of the Indonesian Communist Party (PKI), who had so brilliantly planned his ascent to major influence in Indonesia, and then—fortunately for Indonesia—seen it all shattered before influence could be translated into power.

After the collapse in Djakarta of the attempted coup on October 1, 1965, Aidit had fled Halim air base for Central Java in an air force plane provided by Omar Dhani. He landed at Jogjakarta in the early hours of October 2. He conferred with Communist officials, but must have left the city soon afterwards, certainly before it was retaken by loyalist forces on October 5. Thereafter he scurried about Central Java on Communist Party business and presumably played an organizing role in the last major act of Communist resistance in the Klaten-Bojolali area around October 2.

When Sarwo Edhy's para-commandos moved in and started sweeping the area, keeping a special lookout for him, Aidit must have found his movements increasingly restricted. But he managed to evade arrest until November 22, when he was captured in a little *kampong*, or village unit, on the outskirts of the town of Solo, long the Communist Party's principal base in Central Java.

Now, a little more than a year after the event, I wanted to find the place for myself.

With a driver, my interpreter, a local informant, and a map compiled with assistance from many sources, I set out. At first we drove westward from the town on a metalled road busy with buses and carts and pedestrians. Then we wound our way through side roads until we came to an earthen track just wide enough to take the car. Down it we bounced, disappearing in a green tunnel as the palms and other trees arched together overhead, blotting out the blue sky and bright sunshine.

Finally we could go no farther by car. Leaving the driver with it, the three of us—two Indonesians and a Westerner—went on by foot. We trudged along, and the path narrowed again, burrowing now between simple little huts at the approaches to the *kampong* of Samben. A small boy sitting beside the path said quietly to my interpreter in Indonesian, "Be careful, they're not friendly."

As we proceeded, there certainly was an unusual, unsmiling sullenness about these villagers in a land where a friendly gesture from a stranger almost automatically wins a broad smile in return.

Now we were winding our way along a footpath between shoulder-high hedges, and suddenly as it took a turn we were upon a typical Indonesian bungalow-type house. Its walls were white and wooden. It had a *genteng* roof of burnt-red Indonesian tile. In front it had a little stone veranda. It was the house for which we were looking. Here it was that Aidit had been captured, about nine o'clock in the evening of November 22, as Sarwo Edwy's para-commandos swooped suddenly on the *kampong* of Samben.

Aidit had chosen his hiding place well. As we knew from our own approach, anybody coming by vehicle could be spotted long before reaching the village. Yet someone who wished could slip out of the *kampong* at its rear, then by slithering down a riverbed and striking across country, be within easy reach of both a road and a railway without ever using the main approach track to the village.

It was across-country, obviously with detailed knowledge of the terrain, that the para-commandos had quietly come in the darkness of that November night before surrounding the house and bursting in.

The house belonged to a retired railway worker who lived there with his family. Against the wall of a living room stood a tall, double-doored wardrobe. The soldiers opened it, hammered at its back, found it solid. Then they shouldered the whole wardrobe away from the wall. Behind it they found a small opening, leading into a narrow, concealed space just big enough for a man to lie down in. From this wooden-walled hiding place, cleverly constructed between two rooms of the house, emerged the man they were hunting, Aidit.

As my interpreter and I circled the house a year later, it was clear the family living in it were in no mood to let us examine it closer. Nor, apparently, were we welcome in the *kampong*. Within seconds of our arrival, the villagers had begun to filter in around us. My interpreter, who in the past had proved himself a good judge of when trouble was real or only threatening, became increasingly nervous.

The area had, after all, been a Pemuda Rakjat training center. Even though the army presumably had cleaned it up, its people still were surly. Almost certainly, after Aidit's capture there, the village must have suffered bloody vengeance. Now, eyeing the quickly growing crowd, my interpreter muttered, "It's time to get out of here." Soon afterwards, we left.

That Aidit was seized in that little house in Samben, there is no doubt. Nor is there much doubt that within a day, possibly within hours, of his capture he was executed by the army. But about the details of his fate and last hours there is an official conspiracy of silence so complete that it can only have been imposed by the topmost military circles. One man who knows what happened is General Sarwo Edhy, whose men took Aidit; but he is not talking. Though he will discuss much else that happened during his Central Javanese campaign, about the manner of Aidit's dying he is silent.

The reason for this secrecy, as some generals privately explain it, is that the army wants no legend built around Aidit. After the Communist revolt at Madiun, in 1948, the Communist leader Musso was publicly cremated with thousands watching the ceremony. The army wanted no repetition of that event with Aidit's body. Nor indeed do they want his place of execution and burial to become a shrine in years to come for any Communist pilgrims who attempt to rebuild the party.

So Aidit's death is unrecorded in any official document available to the public. But when you ask individual generals about rumors that Aidit slipped away, perhaps to China, they reject them with the knowledge of certainty and tell you, "That Aidit is dead, there is no doubt whatsoever."

Why was Aidit killed and not brought to trial for complicity in the Gestapu movement? There is not much doubt about this. The army feared that if Aidit were returned to Djakarta for trial, Sukarno would protect him as he had protected others with links to Gestapu, perhaps even extricate Aidit from the army's grasp. The army had evidence that Aidit was in touch by letter with Sukarno, proffering suggestions as to how the political situation in the aftermath of the Gestapu affair should be handled. The army claims it also had evidence that Sukarno had sent a message of reply, explaining that he could not follow out all of Aidit's suggestions and urging Aidit to leave Solo for Djakarta because of "technical obstacles" in extracting him from Central Java.

There are, of course, strong moral and legal arguments why Aidit should have been brought to trial. To such criticism from abroad Indonesia's generals show themselves sensitive today. But in the heated atmosphere following the 1965 coup attempt, such arguments were thrust into the background by considerations of security and politics.

Even if the army could have guaranteed that Aidit would not somehow evade trial as a result of presidential intervention, the generals of the day could see little political advantage to it. There was no guarantee that Aidit might not go on the stand and deny any Communist Party involvement in Gestapu. Even if he confessed that the Communist Party had taken part, the army could afford to get along without this testimony discrediting the party. For with or without public opinion on its side, the army had already decided to demolish the Communist Party with ruthless efficiency. Aidit's testimony would have made no difference to the army's actions.

As must inevitably be the case when the details of such a happening are officially withheld, macabre stories circulate about the manner of Aidit's death. A member of an official commission assigned to investigate the extent of Indonesia's post-coup massacre told me that Aidit was shot and buried, but that the body was exhumed after five days and then burned. He also told me that there were 78 bullet holes in the body, but I do not believe this gentleman is a member of that relatively tight little circle that knows the facts about Aidit's death.

Some people say that General Suharto himself flew to Central Java to interrogate Aidit, or at least to view the body. It is true that on November 25, Suharto visited Sukarno in Djakarta just before leaving on a trip to Central and East Java ostensibly to attend a change-of-command ceremony in Surabaya. But by this time Aidit was probably dead and buried.

However, proof of Aidit's death was sent to General Suharto in the form of photographs accompanying an official military report on the Communist leader's arrest and execution. The photographs showed Aidit alive and in custody before his death, as well as after he had been killed. The report has, of course, never been published.

Probably Aidit's end was simple enough. Almost certainly he was driven some way out of Solo under heavy military escort, shot in some quiet place by an army officer, then buried in an unmarked grave.

Did Aidit talk before his death? Was he made to talk? And if so, what did he say? These are fascinating and important questions. One Indonesian journalist who was with Sarwo Edhy on the Central Java campaign claims Aidit babbled away, revealing all kinds of party secrets.

That is an account I find difficult to believe.

Another story is that Aidit spent the night after his capture dictating a 50-page confession to his military interrogators. This, too, in my opinion, should be treated with skepticism.

The truth, I believe, lies in the comment of one of Sarwo Edhy's closest aides. Pressed as far as he would go, he finally exclaimed, "Good Communists never confess." Aidit was a good, professional, die-hard, ruthless Communist. Unless he were put to the most excruciating torture, it seems extremely unlikely that he blurted out after his capture a lengthy confession incriminating both himself and his party up to their necks in the Gestapu plot. If so, for a man who built the Indonesian Communist Party into the third largest in the world, the largest outside the Communist countries, he crumpled up amazingly easily.

The only "evidence" of such a confession is an alleged partial text of Aidit's statement that was published by a leading Japanese newspaper, *Asahi Shimbun*, early in 1966. With the text were published three photographs of what certainly appeared to be Aidit in the custody of Indonesian soldiers. In one picture he was standing, dressed in white shirt and trousers, apparently with hands tied behind his back. In another he was similarly dressed, hands still tied behind his back, but sitting in an armchair. In a third photograph he now was wearing dark trousers and white shirt, had on spectacles, had his hands free, and was signing what purported to be his statement. In each of the pictures he appeared to be much thinner than when I had seen him last.

There are statements in the text published by *Asahi Shimbun* that do coincide with the facts as we know them. Certain of the dates of Aidit's movements are correct. Certain conversations cited, for example with air base commanders, actually took place. But all this information was available to anybody investigating the Gestapu affair. Many people other than Aidit could have written such a "confession" for him.

The key question is whether Aidit himself would have sat down and supplied a confession assuming the "highest responsibility" for Gestapu, "supported by other PKI [Communist Party] officials."

The *Asahi Shimbun* text was acquired by the newspaper's Djakarta correspondent, presumably from Indonesian military sources. Though the military have never confirmed the *Asahi Shimbun* version, it is to that that the generals refer inquirers about Aidit's final confession. Certainly, at the time it was published, before Sukarno's own involvement in the coup had been so publicly brought into question, it was the version the Indonesian military were happy to publicize.

Whether bogus or not, however, it is the only document that purports to be Aidit's record of events. As such, it is of historical interest. Underlining once again that its veracity is in serious question, I include it here, as published in the Tokyo newspaper:

"I was the one with the highest responsibility for the September 30 incident and was supported by other PKI officials and officials of the people's organizations under the PKI.

"Dissatisfaction with the existing system was the basic beginning of the idea for this coup. If a people's united front government could be established under the leadership of the PRI, the state could get back on its feet, the people's standard of living would improve and a fair society in which there would be no gap between the rich and the poor could be established.

"If the coup d'état had succeeded, my policy was to establish closer economic relations with Communist China.

"The PKI originally had set 1970 as its target year, but details of this plan leaked out, so that relations with the army became unstable. Consequently, the original plan was changed to carry out a coup as soon as possible.

"I drafted a plan to be carried out May 1, 1965, but Lukman, Njoto, Sakirman and Njono—all party officials—opposed the plan.

They argued it was dangerous, since preparations were not completed, and that the plan would undoubtedly fail.

"The discussions with Lieutenant Colonel Untung and others were held many times after June, 1965.

"From July, 1965, action corps of the Pemuda Rakjat, the People's Youth Front, and the Gerwani, the Indonesian women's movement, were gathered at Halim air base on the outskirts of Djakarta and were trained in the use of heavy and light weapons. Preparations were pushed.

"When returning from Algeria in early August, I stopped in Peking and discussed the health of President Sukarno with the Communist Chinese leaders.

"As soon as I returned to Djakarta in the middle of the same month, a secret meeting was held. The execution of the coup d'état was discussed with Lukman, Njoto, Brigadier General Supardjo and Lieutenant Colonel Untung.

"Since we had information that the army, under orders from Army Minister Yani, would search the Communist Party and related organizations on suspicion of illegal possession of weapons, the situation was such that we could not help but speed up the execution of the coup d'état.

"It was on September 25 that we chose the 30th as the date of the coup.

"There were proposals that the coup d'etat be carried out October 5, Army Day, but the date was moved up because details of our coup d'état plan were beginning to leak out.

"I ordered Second Vice-Chairman Njoto to Sumatra because I believed that he would be able to persuade the people of Sumatra to our way of thinking.

"Lieutenant Colonel Untung was made chairman of the Revolutionary Council only as a temporary measure. I did not name myself the man with the highest responsibility for the incident, except within the PKI, because of considerations concerning the possibility of success of the coup d'état.

"We asked President Sukarno to sign the bill establishing the Revolutionary Council and to broadcast this to the whole nation, but he refused.

"The position of the President was to have been maintained even after the coup d'état had succeeded, but we intended to criticize and revise his policies gradually.

"As for the five basic principles of Indonesia's political philosophy—religion, nationalism, humanism, democracy and socialism—we planned to gradually reduce their use and eventually make them nothing more than figureheads.

"Also, after the success of the coup d'état, we intended to form a 'fifth military force' apart from the existing four military forces centred around the People's Youth Front, BTI (Farmer's Front), SOBSI (Central Indonesian Federation of Labour Unions) and other organizations under the PKI.

"The coup d'état failed because it was premature and also because there were not a few—even among the top PKI officials— who were opposed. I recognize this fact.

"In the secret meeting of the PKI central committee, the coup d'état was originally scheduled for 1970.

"The second reason for the failure was the lack of support of Communist China and international Communism on which we had placed hopes.

"PKI power had infiltrated 25 percent of the Indonesian Army, but they did not act as we had expected them to. This was because the anti-Communist group within the army was too strong and because the army carried out mop-up operations so speedily.

"I was in Djakarta from September 30 to October 1, leading the coup try. At Halim air base, I informed President Sukarno of the existence of the Council of Generals and of the coup d'état plan, but he apparently did not believe me.

"Together with others, I showed him the bill for establishment of the Revolutionary Council and asked him to approve it, but the President refused.

"During this time, Army Minister Yani and five other generals were killed by armed members of our side in the vicinity of the air base.

"As a result of the Djakarta central broadcasting station having been taken away from us by forces commanded by General Suharto, an emergency meeting was held.

"The meeting was attended by Lieutenant Colonel Untung, Brigadier General Supardjo, PKI First Secretary Lukman, and Political Bureau member Njono.

"However, we recognized that the coup d'état in Djakarta had failed. I decided to fly to Central Java, establish a Revolutionary Council there and work to maintain and revive power.

"I left Halim air base at 1:30 A.M. on October 2 by plane and arrived at Jogjakarta base at 3 A.M. I told the commander of the air base, 'Since the situation in Djakarta is unstable, there is a possibility that President Sukarno will take refuge in Jogjakarta, so I came to make a prior check.'

"On October 2, I went from Jogjakarta to Semarang and from Semarang to Solo. At all these places, I instructed the government officials and army officers who were pro-PKI to establish revolutionary councils. I intended to have the council in Solo become the nucleus for revolutionary councils in Central Java.

"At 8:30 A.M. on October 3, I met the commander of the Solo air base and asked that he provide me with a plane to fly to Djakarta or Bali island, but he refused.

"As a result, I worked on the plan to collect Communist power in Central Java. I inspected the various areas around Solo and provided leadership until about October 21. Up to this time

I was comparatively safe.

"The uprising in Solo, decided as the central point in Central Java, was scheduled for October 23, and orders were sent out to all areas. Orders were issued to the PKI cells to cut down the trees alongside the roads leading into Surakarta (Solo) at 12:01 A.M. on October 23, to form barricades, carry out general strikes in the government offices, government railways and government firms, and arrest the leaders of rightist groups.

"However, early on the morning of October 23 the RPKAD [para-commandos] and KOSTRAD [strategic reserve] of the army advanced into Solo and grabbed power so that the uprising plan failed.

"To rebuild our power, I went around the outskirts of Solo and returned to Solo on foot, November 5.

"Army patrols were already rough, and it became harder day by day to contact PKI members in other areas. Not only that, but I myself was in danger.

"I was always guarded by about 20 members of the Pemuda Rakjat and kept changing my residence. I planned to escape from Solo, but the guard became stricter and finally I was unable to move.

"I was finally captured at 9 P.M., November 22, at the home of a PKI member in Samben village to the west of Solo."

15. Frenzy on Bali

Floating off the eastern tip of Java, Bali is one of the rarest and most exquisite gems in Indonesia's island chain.

Its beaches are white, riffled by gentle tropical breezes, and shaded by tall palm trees. For a few cents, perhaps even a smile, agile young Balinese boys will shin up these trees and lop off coconuts that come thudding down awash with cool, clear milk.

Inland the country sweeps up over terraced rice fields of brilliant green and incredible ingenuity to blue volcanoes whose deceptive innocence belies their occasional cruel explosions.

Bali is not as some fanciful foreigners in far-off lands believe. Everyone does not spend the day lolling around on the beach. All the men do not look like Rock Hudson in a sarong. The girls do not cavort semi-naked. True the climate is kind, and true the Balinese people are handsome and attractive. But bare-breasted maidens are the exception these days, and the people of Bali have a workaday routine in which they must labor long and industriously to extract a living from the soil of their over-populated island.

The rice must be planted, transplanted, tended, harvested, and hauled in great swaying golden sheaves back to the villages. There are long days in the waterlogged paddies, splashing about behind the strong gray working buffalos.

Pigs and ducks and chickens must be reared and hauled squealing and clucking off to market in rickety containers of latticed, plaited palm fronds.

For an island people, fishing is important. Some of the men stride out into the sea to fish chest-deep with rod and line. For others there is the deep water out beyond the reefs and sandbars. Out they go, cluttering the horizon with their brightly painted outriggers. Inshore, the women and children scoop up starfish and eels and water snakes. Thigh-deep in water, they plant their traps, marking them with stakes. Then, as the tide trickles out, they pick up their booty, emptying the traps and scavenging among the rocks and shells for whatever small sea creatures may have been left stranded.

What is true is that if Balinese have to work as hard as anybody in Indonesia, they can do so in surroundings that are idyllic, and where Eden creeps right up to their doorsteps. The air is balmy, and exotic with the scent of wild tropical blooms. The foliage is lush, the trees are hung with trailing vines, and green moss gives a mellow sheen to rocks and stone walls.

Thus even before man's touch, nature has given Bali a headstart on the road to Arcady. But the Balinese are themselves a people dedicated to the pursuit of beauty. When they build a wall, it rarely remains a wall. It becomes the canvas of an artist in stone, who carves a picture lovingly upon it, then probably crowns it with four or five statuettes and garlands the statues with living flowers.

The island is ablaze with painting, decorated with endless carvings in wood and stone. From its villages comes the sweet tinkling of temple bells, the melodic tympany of the *gamelan* orchestra's xylophones and gongs for innumerable festivals and exhibitions of gracious Balinese dance.

At dawn the visitor established in one of the simple beach houses is awakened by a gentle scuffling outside, which he at first has difficulty in identifying. It is the swish of bare Balinese feet over coral paths as servants armed with baskets of fresh-plucked flowers wander the grounds placing crimson hibiscus or white frangipani blooms behind the ears of every statue.

As Java erupted in violence and bloodshed throughout October and November of 1965, Bali continued its way of life, but the ominous rumbles of pending trouble were inescapable. Finally in December, after a clash between troops and Communists in the western part of the island, Bali erupted in a frenzy of savagery worse than Java's.

Whole villages, including children, took part in an island-wide witch-hunt for Communists, who were slashed and clubbed and chopped to death by communal consent.

Whole villages that had made the fatal mistake of embracing Communism were wiped out. Almost within view of the big new luxury hotel the government has built to woo tourists to Bali stand the charred and blackened ruins of one such village. For their Communist affiliations the menfolk were killed. The women and children fared better; they were driven screaming away. The village itself was put to the torch.

Night after night the sky flared red over Bali as villages went up in flames and thousands of Communists, or people said to be Communists, were hunted down and killed. Knowledgeable sources say 40,000 Balinese were killed in two weeks of butchery. Estimates have gone as high as 80,000. Nobody will ever know the exact toll. As one Balinese told me, "When people were killed in batches of less than ten, nobody even bothered to keep count."

Just why did these people of grace and charm embark on so frenzied a massacre? Obviously the catalyst was the sudden boiling over of resentment toward the Communists, who had been busy beneath the placid surface of Bali but had made the serious mistake of deriding and attempting to undermine not only the island's religious values, but its deep-seated cultural traditions, as well.

Some thoughtful Balinese believe the reasons for the orgy go much deeper, however, and are rooted in frustrations that have been simmering away for years in Bali, despite its superficial serenity.

According to this thesis, the action against the Communists may have been a mass self-purification process for the island. "This," says one Balinese, "may be difficult for the Westerner to understand. But what happened here was a sort of mystical cleansing of all the island's problems and ills. Things had not been going well for some years.

Balinese had to labor under the Dutch, and then under the Japanese who occupied the island in World War II. Then came the revolution to make Indonesia independent, which meant further upheaval. Some years ago we suffered tragic loss of life and land when our big volcano erupted. Then, after that, we got the Communists here stirring up trouble.

"In many people's minds, all these troubles blurred into one sense of discordancy. And by ridding the island of Communists, they believed that all the other problems would somehow be removed, too. It was a kind of purging of the land from evil."

Whether there is anything to this theory of long-standing frustration or not, Bali in the months preceding the 1965 coup certainly had descended to that same abject state of poverty existing in many other parts of Indonesia. Its schools were without books, and then without teachers because the state could not, or would not, afford to pay them. Its clinics were without medicines. Its few factories were closed down or working slender hours for want of raw materials and spare parts for neglected machinery.

Compounding this problem of government neglect was the stark fact of Bali's overpopulation. With 2,000,000 people on some 2,000 square miles of land, much of it unsuitable for agriculture, the soil was simply incapable of supporting them adequately.

Perhaps this explains in part how the harsh ideology of Marxism-Leninism made such inroads on a tropical island of deep Hindu belief, artistic bent, and ancient traditions.

The appeal of the Communists was simple. To the peasants the party promised land. But to the landlords the Communists also made undercover promises that their holdings would not suffer, come the revolution—provided support and substantial contributions to party funds were forthcoming now.

Thus the party recruited members in Bali who often were Communists of the most nominal kind, and sometimes not

Communists at all. During interrogation after the purge, some peasants who were party members were blank and uncomprehending when accused of Communist affiliations. Some protested that they had belonged only to "that party with the hammer and sickle on its flag which promised land reform."

But if the Communists found Bali a fruitful field for their propaganda, they seem to have been betrayed by their arrogance and overconfidence. In Java the Communists had sought a compromise with Islam. But in Hindu Bali they seemed to have no such flexibility. Buoyed by their success in recruiting simple peasants on the land-reform issue, the Communists showed scant respect for Bali's religious and cultural traditions.

They mocked religious observances and festivals. They obstructed the repair and building of shrines and temples. They ridiculed traditional Balinese dance and costume. They tried to smash the tight-knit *banjar* system, an arrangement of village wards, or cooperatives, whose members' allegiance to each other is strict and binding.

In the economic sphere the Communists often made their own laws. They boycotted community development plans and worked against the transmigration policy that would move Balinese emigrants to other islands where land was plentiful, but undeveloped. In one particularly flagrant violation of official policy, they encouraged peasants to chop down trees and clear forests for rice cultivation in areas where deforestation was specifically forbidden.

"It was almost," says one Balinese official today, "as though they wanted to sabotage the economy, wanted to destroy our social system, so that they could take our individuality away and build a Communist state out of the ruins."

In all their plans, the Communists enjoyed the protection of the island's openly pro-Communist governor, Sutedja. The Governor had near-absolute power. The military on Bali were subservient to him. Decrees from Djakarta on which he frowned were either held back completely or not fully implemented. At his elbow was his old friend and crony, Gde Puger, leader of the island's Communist Party.

Fifteen years before, both of them had been active in nationalist politics. But somewhere along the line they had been converted to Communism. Sutedja's home county of Djembrana, in the western part of the island, where his father was rajah, had become a Communist stronghold. Puger had acquired funds in plenty, which many Balinese believe came from Peking. Whatever Sutedja wanted—advice, money, girls—Puger was ready to supply.

With the Governor so solicitous for their welfare, the Communists on Bali were able to hold off until December the vengeance that overtook their colleagues in Java throughout October and November.

But an evil kind of tension was mounting. Hindu tolerance of other faiths was running out. "We're easygoing," says one Balinese official, "and we let the Communists practice their religion alongside ours for a good long time. Then we found out they were trying to destroy our religion."

The Communists' fatal mistake had been to try and impose an alien ideology crudely and harshly upon an island in a state of perpetual enchantment with its own mystique. In contrast to their successes in Central Java, they had failed to convince the Balinese that their brand of Communism was somehow "localised," springing from frustrations within rather than from foreign machinations without.

One further Communist mistake on Bali was that party officials showed their affluence. Puger had become a wealthy man, and the whole island knew it. The amount of cash found, or said to have been found, in his home after his death has now become legend. At lower levels, according to one Balinese, party officials "always had stone houses." On Bali a stone house signifies wealth.

As November drew to a close, some party members apparently could sense what was coming. They denounced Gestapu, renounced the Communist Party. But they were not to be saved. Youths of the Indonesian Nationalist Party, the Partai Nasional Indonesia (PNI), began stoning Communist houses, attacking individual Communists.

Then in early December the bubble burst, spewing savage violence across the breadth of the island. The incident that touched it off was a clash between Communist youth and an army unit in the western part of the island. One of the military men was killed. The local commander called his superior in Denpasar, the island's capital, and asked for instructions. "Behave as a commander should," was the reply. After weeks of frustration the officer needed no further prompting. His troops were unleashed against the Communists. The massacre had begun.

But military forces on Bali were slender, and as the death toll in the two ensuing weeks mounted through the thousands, it was civilians who were mainly killing Communists. In the forefront were black-shirted bands of PNI political shock troops called Tamins. Working in teams they went through village after village, checking off names against Communist Party lists, accepting the word of informers, and putting their victims to death. Usually the execution was by knife or sword. Men marked for death would either have their throats slit or be decapitated. Sometimes they would be run through with a sword. The executions were swift, with apparently no torture, when carried out by the Tamins. As one Balinese told me in an incredible conversation later, "There was no personal hatred about any of this. There was no torture. It was all very orderly and polite." This coincides with other reports that the executioners sometimes delivered little speeches before killing their victims, explaining that they felt they were only doing their duty.

But many people, too, were killed in wild orgies with mobs at their heels. Whole villages, children included, turned out against some Communists, chasing them across fields and finally stoning and slashing them to death.

The worst violence was in Governor Sutedja's own county of Djembrana, where crowds ran amok in the main town of Negara, killing several thousand people. Communist leader Puger was killed and his house sacked. The palace of Sutedja's father was destroyed and the family thereafter consigned to live in outbuildings.

Sometimes villages were specifically assigned to purge themselves of their Communists. Then took place communal executions as the village gathered its Communists together and clubbed or knifed them to death. Sometimes the army handed back to a village Communist Party members it had already arrested. The village as a whole was instructed to execute them. Almost every village on the island was affected by the purge. "In many villages," according to one official, "it was a point of honor to have executed Communists. A village was ashamed when it had not killed." And in several instances, whole villages with Communist affiliations were wiped out by neighboring non-Communist villagers.

After two weeks of slaughter, the situation was getting out of hand. Thousands had been killed and dumped into mass graves dug by themselves or their executioners. Proper burial rites are immensely important in Bali, but the bodies fell so fast there was no time for that. Though corpses were not flung into rivers as in Java, some were taken out to sea and dumped.

Now the executions were in danger of becoming indiscriminate. Chinese and Javanese merchants who were not Communists but had prospered on Bali were struck down, their stores looted.

Old grudges, debts, and feuds were being settled under the guise of the anti-Communist campaign. So Suharto ordered Sarwo Edhy's para-commandos to move into Bali from Central Java. The assignment was to restore order. This did not mean that Communists were no longer to be killed. It meant that the para-commandos were to halt looting, prevent anarchy, and see that innocent people were not harmed. But the execution of Communists was to go on in "orderly" fashion. As Sarwo Edhy remarked to one leading Balinese, "In Java we had to egg the people on to kill Communists. In Bali we have to restrain them, make sure they don't go too far."

But with the arrival of the para-commandos, the worst was over. One official explained, "From then on, the killing was coordinated. The military and police got together with civilian authorities and made sure the right people were being executed." People were still arrested and, usually, shot by the soldiers. But the mayhem in the villages was at an end. Responsible Balinese believe that 40,000 people had by then met their deaths in the purge.

Some Communists committed suicide rather than face the execution squads. Others died bravely at the hands of the black-shirted Tamins. Many more faced death calmly, even submissively, in one of the strangest aspects of this whole grisly affair. There is reliable evidence that some party members, knowing their fate, dressed in white ceremonial burial robes and marched calmly with policemen or village officials to their places of execution. Others who could have made some attempt at escape offered themselves to their executioners with composure.

As some Balinese intellectuals explain it, they were cooperating in the purging of the island. They had seen the mistake of their Communist affiliation and by dying would be helping cleanse both themselves and the island.

With their strong belief in reincarnation it certainly is true that death is not a particularly tragic concept for most Balinese. The traditional cremation ceremony is a joyful one, so celebrated because the departed is beginning a new life in a new role with new opportunities.

The Balinese have on earlier occasions carried to an end this mass joyful death-wish. In 1906 they marched in knowing self-sacrifice against the guns of a Dutch military expedition, being mowed down until their bodies piled up in a wall under the mouths of the cannons.

A small freighter shipwrecked on Bali had been looted by the islanders, and the Dutch were intent on a retaliatory show of force. They landed a military expedition, which marched on Denpasar flourishing its weapons.

The Balinese had only their krisses, or daggers, and spears. Opposition was futile. Yet, to the astonishment of the Dutch, the local rajah marshaled his puny force, his retinue, his advisers, his wives and children, and marched them out against the Dutch guns. In front was the rajah himself, his only protection a golden parasol, as he swayed regally upon the shoulders of his bearers.

Several times the Dutch commander called on the advancing Balinese to halt, but still they came on, fully knowing their fate. Eventually the Dutch opened fire, their guns chopping the Balinese to pieces, the bodies piling up in front of the Dutch positions. Some of the rajah's wives survived the gunfire, but stabbed themselves to death with their krisses.

Perhaps the sacrifice of many thousands of people in 1965, apparently with the compliance of some of them, was intended to exorcise Bali's evil spirits. It is a concept difficult for the Western mind to grasp, but it is not entirely fanciful, for Bali is steeped in mystical belief, and the Balinese are never far removed from their own private spirit world. When the Indonesian government built a soaring new Miami Beach-style hotel on Bali to attract the affluent tourist trade, construction could not proceed without a series of ceremonials to placate neighboring spirits. And though the hotel is under American management and serves chocolate malteds and Bali beefburgers with ketchup, the visitors will still find little offerings of food within the grounds placed there by hotel employees for various gods.

After a series of automobile accidents, the hotel's entire fleet of buses, station wagons, and taxis was lined up for a ceremony by Balinese priests to be cleansed of evil spirits.

What is all too tragically clear is that the decimation of the Communist Party has not, in fact, solved Bali's ills. The island is still overpopulated and poor. Bali is suspended between the uncertainties of the future and the horrors of its past.

16. Inquest on a Massacre

From the foregoing chapters it is clear that in the months of October, November, and December of 1965, Indonesia was swept by a massacre of staggering proportions. Though the blood has long since been washed away, many tens of thousands of corpses lie rotting beneath the country's tranquil-looking rice fields.

Just how many people were actually killed we will never know. As Foreign Minister Adam Malik puts it, "We'd never taken a census before the coup. We didn't take one after." There is absolutely no way in which the exact death toll can be computed.

Estimates vary widely. The London *Economist,* basing its calculation on information from a team of Indonesian university graduates, suggested a million people may have lost their lives in the slaughter. It set the figure for Java at about 800,000, plus 100,000 in Bali, almost as many in Sumatra, and a few thousand in outlying islands. This one-million estimate, however, is the highest made by anybody and has not gained wide acceptance.

The Washington Post talked of half a million people killed, *Life* magazine of 400,000, and *The New York Times* said, "Best informed sources estimate 150,000 to 400,000, but concede that the total could be far more than 500,000."

At the end of 1965, an official nine-man investigating commission reported to President Sukarno that 78,000 people had lost their lives in the massacre following the October coup attempt. But when Sukarno publicly announced the figures, he squinted through his spectacles, got the first two figures transposed, and declared that the toll was 87,000. Reporters present sent the 87,000 figure around the world.

Palace officials were embarrassed, but with the fatality figure already so high, anyway, a few thousand lives either way hardly seemed to them to matter. So because the President misread the figures, the total as publicized throughout the world was wrong by 9,000. What the commission had reported was 78,000.

What the commission had reported, however, was very different from what at least one of its members really believed.

This I was startled to discover when I talked with that particular commissioner a year later. Was he satisfied, I asked, with the accuracy of the 78,000 figure the commission had submitted?

He laughed merrily. "Oh, dear me, no," he said, "that was nowhere near the right figure."

What, then, did he believe to be the correct figure?

"My own view," he replied unblinkingly, "is that about ten times as many people as that were killed."

Taken aback, I asked him to spell that out again. Was he really saying that although the commission had reported 78,000 people killed, he himself believed the figure to be 780,000?

"Yes, that's right," he assured me. "You mustn't forget that when we talked to officials and village headmen after the coup, they were trying to downgrade the figures of people they'd killed. On Bali they gave us a death figure of 10,000. I believe it was nearer 100,000. There was covering up elsewhere, too. So I calculate that about ten times as many people were killed as we actually reported."

In view of this massive discrepancy between what the commission reported and what this commissioner believed, Sukarno's error of a mere 9,000 lives was scarcely significant.

Shaken, I asked the commissioner why he had permitted a report to go forward to the President setting the death toll at about ten percent of the figure he really believed to be accurate.

"Ah, well," he replied, with that cheerful Indonesian capacity for bemusing and confounding the Western mind, "you mustn't forget that all this was back in December of 1965. You must remember what the political atmosphere was then. The President was still in charge. We gave him the figures we thought he wanted to hear."

This commissioner's personal estimate cannot be entirely dismissed, for he did, after all, have access to official data; he talked to people who had carried out some of the killings; he toured the areas where they had taken place. Even so, 780,000 is still a very high figure, which would not find general acceptance among objective observers trying to assess the toll.

Since the coup, Indonesia's new leaders have shown mounting sensitivity to foreign press reports of the extent of the massacre and to criticism from international humanitarian and legal organizations. There is a tendency to try to sweep the whole ugly affair under the rug and to minimize the number of deaths.

Thus Mr. L. N. Pilar, now retired, but then Indonesia's Ambassador to Washington, told an American television audience a year after the coup that estimates of the death toll in his country had been exaggerated. His own view, he said, was that about 100,000 people had been killed.

Adam Malik, the Indonesian foreign minister, said sections of the foreign press had "grossly exaggerated" the number of killings. His own information, he said, indicated that between 100,000 and 200,000 people were killed. A few days later, he touched on the subject again, stating in an interview that he thought a "fair figure" for those killed would be about 160,000.

Both Mr. Pilar and Mr. Malik conceded that some non-Communists and innocent people had been killed.

Among foreign diplomats in Indonesia there is a school of thought which holds that initial reports of the number of killings were exaggerated by Indonesians themselves. One diplomat has even scaled down his own estimate of the total number of deaths to 60,000. But this seems as improbable, at one end of the scale, as the figure of a million, at the other end.

With no scientific method of calculation available, estimates must be based entirely on word-of-mouth reports. Obviously, reports vary in accordance with the reliability, objectivity, character, political persuasion, religious belief, and vested interest of the teller. An excitable and over-enthusiastic Moslem student leader may, in the midst of the killings, have tended to exaggerate his organization's "achievements" against the Communists. A conservative village headman might have downplayed the bloodshed in his area.

The foreign observer faces special problems in trying to establish an accurate figure. At the time of the massacres, his movements outside Djakarta were restricted. He had great difficulty in witnessing for himself what was going on in the villages. Now, when he can go over the ground, memories have often become genuinely blurred. Villagers think they saw things they did not see; sometimes they forget the details of events that did take place. Beyond this genuine lapse of human memory, a veil is often drawn across those bloody scenes of 1965 by people who will not talk, who will not remember, especially for foreigners prying into this violently intimate chapter of Indonesia's history.

Thus, estimates of Indonesia's death toll range from a low of 60,000 to a high of 1,000,000, neither of which extremes is likely to be correct. "Popular" estimates have polarized around the 400,000 figure.

It is indeed possible that something approaching half a million people were killed. If all these were Communists, which they were not, it would still only mean that some 15 or 16 percent of the 3,000,000 party members claimed by Aidit were executed.

Certainly great gaps have popped up in Indonesia's population since the killings. Over dinner one night the education minister mentioned that his major problem was a shortage of teachers. I asked him how many teachers he had, and the answer was 53,000. Then I asked him how many he should have, and the answer was 93,000. Some 40,000 had vanished since the coup. Not all, of course, had been killed. Some were in jails. Some had fled. But this was a striking indication of the impact of the Gestapu affair on a vital section of the community.

One factor some observers may have overlooked is that although the killings went on for three months, the tempo of executions varied from province to province within that period. The areas worst hit were East and Central Java and Bali. But on Bali the killings were mainly confined to a two-week period in December. Elsewhere, the graph on the death chart rose and then tapered off. There was not consistent slaughter throughout the country for three solid months.

By general agreement, the most savage massacre took place on Bali. There the troops had to call the people off, whereas elsewhere they egged them on to kill Communists. The most reliable estimate I have had of the death toll on Bali is 40,000.

After Bali, East Java was the region that embarked most energetically on the elimination of its Communists. One of Indonesia's generals best-informed about East Java says each of its 3,000 villages must have lost between 10 and 15 people—a total of 30,000 to 45,000. Although he concedes the figure might have gone as high as 100,000.

Then there was Central Java, although here the killing does not seem to have been as extensive as in East Java. In parts of Sumatra the killings were heavy, and there were purges of Communists throughout the outer islands. In north Sulawesi, the Communists' executioners were neither Moslems, nor Hindus, but Christians.

My own conclusion is that the death toll during the three last months of 1965 probably was in the region of the upper figure set by Foreign Minister Malik—about 200,000. Killing certainly continued into 1966, although on nothing like the scale of the months previous, so it is possible that the total number of lives lost in the whole purge may have reached 250,000. As in the case of all the estimates, this is guesswork. Any inquirer into this period of

Indonesia's history finds the facts few and slender to support deductions. Nobody can produce a figure whose accuracy can be argued with certainty.

In one sense, however, it is tragically academic whether 100,000 or 200,000 or 500,000 people lost their lives in the blood bath. For whichever of these figures is most nearly accurate, any one of them makes the Indonesian massacre one of the ghastliest and most concentrated bloodlettings of current times.

As the nation ran amok, most of those killed were Communists. Predictably, there has been an onslaught against Indonesia's new regime from various Communist capitals. Most violent has been Peking, which had captured the allegiance of the Indonesian Communist Party and thus had most to lose by its obliteration. Particularly embarrassed has been Moscow, for, on the one hand, Moscow was obliged to protest angrily against the massacre of Communists in Indonesia, whether their leadership was pro-Peking or not; but on the other hand, Moscow had made a major investment in Indonesia, in the shape of tremendous military and other assistance. To protect that investment, it could not afford to be too harshly critical when Indonesia's military leaders came to the fore, even though the blood of the local Communist Party was still fresh upon their hands.

Aside from the attacks of foreign Communists, Indonesia's army leaders have been severely criticized by non-Communist organizations and individuals around the world for permitting and encouraging wholesale slaughter declared illegal, immoral, inhuman.

The army's response and justification is a simple one: "It was the Communists or us. If we hadn't killed them, they would have killed us."

The generals are convinced that the Communists planned to wage open warfare after the October coup, disrupt the economy, and bring sabotage and terror to both cities and countryside. They charge that the Communists had long lists of anti-Communists, and military men, and foreigners, due for execution if the coup had been successful. They claim that the Communists had in various parts of the country been digging pits, and there is some evidence of this, though whether they were, as the army maintains, destined to receive the bodies of the Communists' intended victims is difficult to determine.

The army's reasons for charging the Communists with murderous intent are fairly substantial. The army had, after all, just had its high command slaughtered, and Communists had participated with eagerness and enthusiasm in those killings. Yet there remains a puzzling factor—the poor performance of a Communist Party whose strength had been its capacity for mass organization. If the Communists had really planned the nation-wide reign of terror after the coup that the army says they had, they made a dismal showing at it. There were some sporadic attempts at sabotage. There was some fighting in Central Java. But nowhere else did the Communists present any formidable military or terrorist opposition to the army.

If the Communist Party was propelled into the Gestapu affair by factors that developed suddenly in 1965, it may not have perfected the countrywide plan for upheaval the generals say it had.

But what is probably true is that if the Communists were not organized for mass reprisals against their opponents in October of 1965, they would have been organized for such action at some time still to come. A showdown was clearly looming between the army and the Communist Party. Once the Communists had got their hands on those 100,000 weapons being secretly negotiated for from Communist China, they obviously did not intend to use them for pigeon-shooting.

In talking with me, Aidit had frankly admitted his party's interest was power. I would not have believed him had he suggested otherwise, for power is the goal of any Communist party. But the obstacle to achieving that goal was the Indonesian Army. As such, the army—or at least that portion of it that could not be subverted to Communism's cause—was the Communist Party's sworn enemy.

In this sense, the generals are probably correct when they say that if they had not moved against the Communists, the Communists would ultimately have moved against the anti-Communists. And if the Communists could not achieve all their aims by political pressure and manipulation, there is no indication they would have been reluctant about turning to violence. Their participation in the murder of the generals rather starkly underlines this point.

So when the Communists presented the army with the opportunity for an anti-Communist crackdown, the army command seized it. Seventeen years before, the army had smashed a Communist revolt at Madiun, but then allowed the Communist Party to climb back to a position of dangerous influence. It was determined not to make the mistake a second time. The army had the guns and the military strength, and before the Communists got their guns, the army set out to smash them.

Although Aidit and his colleagues tried desperately to retrieve the situation, they knew the rules of the political game in Indonesia well and can have been in no doubt about their fate after the coup attempt failed. They had played for high stakes and lost. If they had won, they would have dealt out to their opponents the same ruthless treatment they themselves were now about to receive.

This acceptance of the situation may partly explain the stoic and unresisting manner in which many Communist Party members appear to have met their deaths. There are those eerie stories of party members in Bali donning white burial robes and marching calmly with their captors to execution. There is the story, confirmed by eyewitness, of the Communists who lined up for decapitation at a bridge in Sumatra; although under no guard or restraint, they shuffled along to the centre of the bridge, where perspiring executioners lopped heads from bodies and tumbled both into the swift-flowing river below.

In part, as in Bali, this may have been an act of repentance. Elsewhere, it seems to have been phlegmatic or fatalistic acceptance, difficult for the Westerner to understand, of the inevitable punishment for having played the Communist game and lost.

For many of the killers, the purge of the Communists took on all the aspects of a holy war. As they saw it, they were rooting out an unclean and impure ideology that threatened Islam's hold—this despite the very un-Communist concessions Aidit had made to religious observance by party members. Many Moslem leaders egged on their people against the Communists, justifying the killings as the "will of Allah." By executing Communists, they told their followers, they were serving both Islam and the state.

In its bloodletting, the army, along with civilian executioners, had the encouragement of General Nasution, himself a devout Moslem and a highly religious man. In the weeks immediately succeeding the coup, Nasution had been withdrawn, shaken and grief-stricken by the death of his small daughter and of his closest colleagues in the army's high command. By November, however, he had come out publicly fighting, intent on revenge. He told a student meeting that some of the principal characters in the Gestapu affair had turned out to be "prominent veterans" of the Communist revolt at Madiun in 1948.

Three times now, said Nasution, the Communists had tried to kill him. They had "savagely butchered" the army's generals and even tried to overthrow the state (by the Gestapu affair). Civilian victims lay "sprawled everywhere." For this reason, Nasution told the student gathering, "there must be no more hesitation against the executants, supporters, and especially the masterminds of the Gestapu. They should not and cannot be given any more opportunities, and their activities should no longer be protected by law. They must be immediately smashed. Since they have committed treason, they must be destroyed and quarantined from all activities in our fatherland."

If they were still permitted to enjoy freedom of movement, he went on, the safety of the state would "constantly be menaced." Indonesia must indeed be united, he said, "but must we, although this Communist group has committed murder, torture, terror and treason against our state and government, still embrace it?"

Later in the month he became even more specific. Addressing a marine corps parade, General Nasution said the army had come into possession of documents that indicated the coup had been prepared and led by the central committee of the Indonesian Communist Party. The key Gestapu figure, he charged, was Aidit, and Untung and his associates had been merely the "military executors" of the plot. He said information concerning the health of President Sukarno had impelled the Communist Party to act.

Within days of this statement, General Nasution charged publicly that the coup was "directly or indirectly assisted by a foreign country." Of the foreign country he had in mind there was no doubt. It was Communist China. Thus, along with Indonesia's slaughter of its own Communists, there went a frenzied campaign against Chinese residents of Indonesia, as well as against Communist China, which Sukarno was powerless to halt.

In those days of anti-Communist and anti-Chinese hysteria, all evils were attributed to Aidit or Peking. In October the three deputy premier—Subandrio, Lemeina, and Chairul Saleh—had to put out an official statement denying that former Premier Djuanda, who had died two years previously, was in fact the victim of poisoned wine from China. One Moslem newspaper had just made such a charge. In denying it, the deputy premiers solemnly declared that Dr. Djuanda had died from a heart attack and that two of them had been with him at the time. They all warned against sensational and untrue newspaper reporting.

Those were wild and dangerous days in Indonesia, when the atmosphere was highly charged with emotion. According to one excellent source, Nasution demanded that every Communist be killed. But Suharto, urging restraint, said, "Some Communists can be changed."

The army did not, of course, kill every Communist. Many more party members survived than lost their lives. Time will tell whether these have been changed in their political views. What Indonesia must cope with in the upcoming generation is many thousands of youngsters who will remember that their fathers, and perhaps their mothers, too, were done to death by the anti-Communists. This legacy of bitterness and hate is one whose removal presents the new leadership with one of its most formidable challenges.

Front page of the Communist newspaper Harian Rakjat *of October 2, 1965, proclaiming support for the September 30th Movement after the coup had already failed.*

Cartoons from the same paper ridiculing the Council of Generals, allegedly supported by the American CIA.

Slogans in Djakarta demanding the banning of the Communist Party, 1966.

Troops seize a student during anti-Sukarno demonstrations.

Lieutenant-Colonel Untung, ringleader of the coup attempt, is brought to trial. He was executed in September 1967.

Student placards assert Sukarno's implication in the Gestapu (September 30th Movement) affair (above) and demand that he be brought to stand trial (below).

General Suharto.

Victory parade in Djakarta after Sukarno handed authority to Suharto, March 11, 1966.

Part Three: The Fall

17. The Comeback Trail

As the army relentlessly pursued its extermination of the Communist Party, Sukarno wrung his hands in anguish and issued a string of commands to halt. The army paid no heed. In the days immediately after the October coup, the army had waited expectantly for Sukarno's order outlawing the Communists. It had not come. He procrastinated; he promised a political solution in due course. But the army could not wait for that; angry and impatient, it went out and imposed its own bloody solution to the problem.

As the killings went on into November and then December of 1965, Sukarno appealed again and again for an end to the "hating, beating, and slashing." Men should love their neighbors, he said, and it was not true that a revolutionary must inevitably use guns and dynamite in his revolutionary actions. "Jesus Christ," he told one gathering, "was an example in point. Jesus was one of the greatest revolutionaries in mankind's history. And yet he did not need weapons to drive home his revolutionary teachings and carry through his revolutionary acts."

The slaughter, he said, was endangering national unity and must stop.

But Sukarno did not confine himself to such broad appeals for unity and an end to bloodshed. To the Communists he was particularly protective. Vengeance against them, he told a Moslem student group, was a betrayal "not only of Islam, but also of our state."

He was reluctant to condemn them for their part in the coup, and he refused to proclaim the formal banning of the Communist Party for which the anti-Communists were clamoring. He went out of his way to underline past achievements of the party.

True, he eventually brought himself to the point where he conceded the Communists were like "rats which have eaten a part of a big cake, and tried to eat the pillar of our house." But he was quick to warn that "in catching the rats we should not burn the house." Soon after, he was praising the Communist Party again for its "contribution and sacrifices" for Indonesia's independence, and asking his listeners, "Was there any other political party, thousands of whose leaders were jailed by the Dutch?" Then he astonished his audience by suggesting he might build a monument in West Irian to commemorate the services of the Communist Party.

To all this the army leaders listened sourly. But if Sukarno had not already crossed the Rubicon in his relations with the army, he must certainly have done so when he dismissed the coup attempt as a "ripple in the ocean of the Indonesian revolution." To the army the slaughter of its generals was no ripple in the course of history, but a national tragedy.

Now the army and Sukarno were drawing further apart. Sukarno seemed to want to rehabilitate the Communist Party, perhaps after some reshuffling of its leadership, and start Indonesia off again on the same course it had been following before the coup. The army, on the other hand, was intent on eliminating the Communist Party and dragging Indonesia back from the leftward slide it had been taking in both internal and foreign policies.

The coup itself, and the unanswered questions about his involvement in it, had cracked Sukarno's stature as a demigod. But perhaps at this stage he could still have retrieved the situation and survived with diminished authority, if not with untarnished reputation. If he had demanded punishment for the Communists, expressed more grief for the murdered generals, and conceded that the Indonesian revolution had swung too far to the left and must be pulled back to a middle course, the army might have forgiven, if not forgotten.

But for Sukarno that price was too high. It would have made him the captive of the army. It would have emasculated his power, leaving him without the balance between army and Communists that had given him room for maneuver and independence—if, indeed, he had not already moved beyond the balance concept and pledged himself completely to the left.

For Sukarno there was really no choice. Rather than settle for curbed authority at the army's behest, he would gamble for a return to total power. For this he needed a revival of the Communist Party, or some force of similar militancy and ideology, to offset the army's gathering influence.

Not only internal factors influenced Sukarno to his dogged rearguard action in defence of the Communists. Sukarno's foreign policy had brought Indonesia's relations with the United States nearly to the breaking point. Moscow was disillusioned with him. Of the major powers, Communist China was now his sole remaining ally. Could he afford to offend China by outlawing the pro-Peking Indonesian Communist Party? The answer, as undoubtedly pointed out to him by the Chinese Ambassador in Djakarta, was no.

The Chinese Embassy had pointedly refused to honor the murdered army generals after the failure of the coup. It was bombarding the Indonesian foreign ministry with a series of scorching protests about hostile actions toward the Chinese diplomatic mission in Indonesia. In Peking, the Indonesian Ambassador was frequently summoned on the carpet by irate foreign ministry officials.

Peking's anger stemmed not only from the treatment afforded its diplomats in Indonesia. It had a vested interest in the two to three million Chinese people living in Indonesia, as indeed it had in all the so-called "overseas Chinese" living beyond the borders of the Chinese motherland.

About a million of the Chinese living in Indonesia had become Indonesian citizens. About another million held passports issued by Communist China. The remainder were officially "stateless," but presumably felt some allegiance to Nationalist China, which Djakarta of course refused to recognize. Nevertheless, any Chinese in Indonesia was never far from the antagonism that lurked close beneath the surface, whatever alliances Sukarno might forge with the men of Peking. Industrious and astute, the Chinese minority had risen to a dominating position in trade and finance. Most Indonesians resented it.

When the army gave the green light for the crackdown on the Communists, it also touched off a witch-hunt against the Chinese. Particularly hard hit were Chinese traders in smaller towns outside the capital. Looters swept through Chinese homes, seizing property. Chinese shops were closed, their owners forced to flee. Some towns in which the Chinese were predominant became deserted overnight, like Nevada ghost towns.

Many wealthy Chinese left the country for Singapore or Hong Kong. Others clustered in Glodok, the Chinese quarter of Djakarta. Still others went streaming back to mainland China in repatriation ships sent by the Chinese Communists to fetch them. In the Sumatran port of Medan, thousands of Chinese were herded into a concentration camp, awaiting places in the repatriation ships.

Their persecutors were not only Indonesians, resentful of relative Chinese affluence. Anti-Communists among the Chinese community launched their own purge of their fellow Chinese who had exhibited Communist sympathies.

One of these anti-Communist Chinese told me, "While the Communist Party was riding high in Indonesia, the Communists among the Chinese made things hot for us. We're only human. We're getting our own back now. And we're going to make sure that Chinese who are Communists never give us a tough time again. There's only one solution for them—go back to China."

These sentiments were echoed by many commanders in the Indonesian Army, charged with responsibility for areas where Chinese were congregated. The garrison commander of the Central Javanese town of Semarang, Lieutenant Colonel Suparno, told Antara, the official Indonesian news agency, that the best solution was to repatriate Chinese aliens to China. To underline the point he ordered all "aliens"—in other words, all Chinese— in Semarang to announce themselves by means of display signs outside their houses. Chinese who were not Indonesian nationals had to paint their names in white on red boards. Even Chinese who were Indonesian nationals had to display signs, but they could paint their names in white letters on blackboards.

If the Chinese were encouraged to leave, they were also squeezed as they left. In Djakarta the garrison commander issued an order, the effect of which was to prohibit departing Chinese from taking valuables with them. It went further, blocking them from selling or transferring their property to anyone else. To the Chinese with money, and therefore influence, there were ways to circumvent such decrees. But the fact that such orders were being issued, coupled with the campaign against China itself and the hounding of the pro-Peking Indonesian Communist Party, did little to assuage Peking's anger.

In his bid to save the tottering alliance between China and Peking that was the cornerstone of his foreign policy, Sukarno leaned heavily on Foreign Minister Subandrio. As always, Subandrio was the willing servant of his master. Such was Subandrio's pliability that while he cooperated with the Communists at home and Peking abroad, and railed against the imperialists and the capitalists, he kept his son studying political science at the University of North Carolina.

Now, however, the Communist Party was in disarray, and Subandrio was apparently scrabbling to save both it and the alliance with China, all upon Sukarno's order. He brought to the task all his skill, his ability to twist and turn, his capacity to roll with the blows of international politics, then come bouncing back. He lashed out at Djakarta newspapers criticizing the Communists, charging that they were aided by, or acting as instruments of, the American Central Intelligence Agency. But two days later, after an avalanche of angry rebuttal on his head, he withdrew the charge. He clucked disapprovingly about the Communist Party's excesses for anti-Communist audiences at home, but quietly implored the Chinese Ambassador to have patience and look to a normalization of relations after the heat was off. He conceded in public that Indonesia's relations with China had become strained, but by December was also talking hopefully in public about "signs of renewed friendship" between the two countries.

For all his industry, however, Subandrio was not in the end to save either Indonesia's alliance with China or himself. The mutterings of criticism against the old way of things in Indonesia were beginning to be heard openly, particularly from the young students who were not of the revolutionary generation of 1945. Of President Sukarno's contributions to Indonesia's nationhood they read in the history books, but the economic chaos of his creating they could see with their own eyes. At first, public criticism of Sukarno was muted and guarded. It took an indirect form—complaints about high prices and economic chaos. But Subandrio was a vulnerable target. The student campaign against him began to roll. The army, too, applied pressure for Subandrio's removal from sensitive positions. Sukarno denied he had any intention of dropping Subandrio as foreign minister. But he did bow to pressure and remove Subandrio from deputy command of KOTI, the Supreme Operations Command. This was the country's highest executive body, of which Sukarno himself was supreme commander. Further, Subandrio lost his control of Indonesia's intelligence network. There were rumours he might be sent abroad on an extended tour.

In attacking Subandrio, Sukarno's right-hand man, the critics were of course indirectly questioning Sukarno's administration, too. Now a group of legislators in Bandung, in a move clearly implying fading confidence in the President, suggested that General Nasution be appointed to the post of vice president, vacant since 1957, to assist Sukarno "in speeding up the conclusion of the Indonesian revolution."

It was in the economic sphere that the Indonesian revolution under Sukarno's management had failed most dismally. Though the army men were not economists or financial experts, they were staggered by the extent of the problem as they moved into positions of increasing responsibility. To boost army morale, the generals by stroke of pen increased the wages of all armed forces personnel by 500 percent. But this did not help civilians, particularly town and city dwellers, caught in the squeeze between soaring inflation and shrinking wages.

To restore some reason to the runaway currency situation, the government revalued the Indonesian rupiah in December by one new rupiah to a thousand old rupiahs, but the basic problems remained. During the twelve months of 1965, prices went up by 544 percent. Foreign trade dwindled. Foreign-exchange reserves shrank to almost nothing. Just to keep up the payments and service charges on the massive foreign debts incurred by Sukarno, the country had to find $530,000,000 in 1965—a difficult task when its foreign-exchange earnings from exports, mainly oil and rubber, barely managed to stagger beyond $400,000,000.

Though Japan had stood by Indonesia long after the confidence of many other nations in the Indonesian economy had been impaired, even Japan now suspended its exports. The Japanese government refused export insurance on goods bound for Indonesia when the backlog of Indonesian debts on previous shipments topped $10,000,000.

To the ordinary man in the Indonesian street the problem was more immediate than dwindling foreign-exchange reserves, shrinking foreign trade, and loss of confidence abroad. His problem was starkly simple: wages were pegged low, prices were going up daily, and he could not make enough to feed, clothe, and house his family.

As the protests mounted, Sukarno abandoned his long-standing detachment from economic problems. Grandly he announced a new cabinet post. He said it would be open to anybody who undertook to lower prices within three months. There was one catch. If the new minister failed, warned Sukarno, he would go to jail for 10 years. If after three months the economy became worse, he would be shot dead. The announcement did not suggest that Sukarno had become any more practical in his approach to the economic crisis, and the scheme faded away.

As 1965 drifted into 1966, Sukarno and the army presided over Indonesia in a sort of uneasy coalition rule. Neither was enthusiastic about the arrangement. The army had assumed sweeping emergency powers; to Sukarno it was an unwelcome poacher upon his authority. In pursuing its anti-Communist campaign it had ignored his orders to desist—the President, whose word was once unquestioned, had been shunted aside. His prestige and authority had been badly eroded. Yet, with the Communist Party on the run, Sukarno had no other instrument at hand with which to cut back the army to size.

For its part, the army leadership was increasingly disillusioned with Sukarno. Generals like Nasution and Suharto were suspicious of his role in the coup attempt and disgusted that he had dragged his feet on the condemnation and punishment of Communists afterwards.

But if disillusionment had set in, there was reluctance on the army's part about direct confrontation with Sukarno. Perhaps in Suharto's case this may have reflected some of the traditional Javanese abhorrence of such showdown scenes, but there were many practical considerations, too. For Sukarno was revered as the father of the nation. About him there was a legendary aura. Could the army challenge his prestige and influence and get away with it? The army was not sure, at least at this stage. The army's own image in the countryside had not been particularly good, and though the soldiers now were considered the heroes of the anti-Communist cause, their massacre of Communists had also made them many enemies.

Sukarno had solid support in large areas of Central and East Java. Throughout the ranks of government were strewn senior officials who had prospered on his patronage and would be alarmed to see him go. Even within the army, many generals owed their positions solely to Sukarno. Though they conceded he had made mistakes, some of them were flatly opposed to any talk of ousting him. Others took the same attitude, but from no standpoint of personal interest. They were genuinely loyal to the President and reluctant to expose the nation to the public humiliation inherent in the destruction of a man it had built into a demigod.

The Sukarno spell still lingered throughout much of the country, it seemed. The army was not yet ready for open political warfare against the man who had stalked imperiously across the Indonesian scene for so many years, so it shared power with him in an ill-defined and irritable alliance. Neither party cared for the other, but neither could rid itself of the other.

But now into this tense political situation was injected a new factor—the teenage students of Djakarta, who were fed up with the economic chaos they were falling heir to, and for whom the Sukarno magic had worn transparently thin. They had been born into a world where they were captive to Sukarno's propaganda and indoctrination, but they had also been born after the revolution of 1945, with no personal experience of Sukarno's role in it. Although they were fired by the spirit of Indonesian nationalism, they were as divorced from those days as were American teenagers in 1966 and 1967 from the drama of World War Il, little more than 20 years before. The world they knew best was one of poverty and hardship, economic chaos, and mismanagement. After twenty years of Indonesian independence, the promised land seemed nowhere in sight.

Now they went into the streets in protest. They demonstrated not openly against Sukarno but against rising prices and government inefficiency. At first, Sukarno was plaintive in his response. "Sometimes," he said in an address to the People's Consultative Congress, "I feel that I am just ignored by some groups. They say they stand behind me and abide by my words, but in fact they push me and kick me about what to do. They say I should do this and that."

As the protest movement picked up momentum, he became angrier. Scribblings started appearing on walls demanding rice instead of national monuments. And one weekend the students rumbled off in trucks, buses, and cars to Bogor, demonstrating so noisily outside Sukarno's palace there that the presidential guards fired several shots into the air to restore order.

Dr. Subandrio took to the radio, calling on the people to defend the President. The demonstrations, said Subandrio, had "really shocked the souls of us all." The President had concluded, he said, that the demonstrations were aimed at overthrowing both him and his government.

The President had indeed so concluded, and he did not like the conclusion he had come to. In a voice shaking with emotion he told one student gathering at Bogor, "I am sick of the secret campaign being launched against me. My present stand is as follows: I, Sukarno, the Great Leader of the Revolution, the Supreme Commander of the Armed Forces, say whoever is still willing to follow me should rally behind me, defend me, build your strength. I now see efforts to topple me. I remind my followers not to act in disorderly manner. Wait for my command."

He said he had seen leaflets accusing him of defending Gestapu. "Although these leaflets were against my assistants," he explained, "they were obviously aimed at me."

As the demonstrations continued through January into February of 1966, Sukarno, the wily and astute politician that he was, could scent serious trouble brewing for him. He determined to head it off with a multifaceted campaign. To Suharto he awarded another general's star in a move that some observers believed was intended to buy the army commander off. Then, although he clearly had not banned the Communist Party, Sukarno had Subandrio publicly imply that he had. "The Communist Party," Subandrio told a student protest meeting, "is already dissolved. Should the President be ordered to stand on the palace steps and say 'The Communist Party is dissolved?'"

Meanwhile, Sukarno himself told students they should form a "Sukarno Front" to check attempts to overthrow him and to prevent the Indonesian revolution's being moved to the right. It seemed a ploy to fill the vacuum left by the eclipse of the Communist Party and to give Sukarno a new instrument for leverage against the army.

Whether Sukarno really believed he had dampened down criticism by these moves, one cannot say. But now he moved sensationally onto the offensive. On February 21 he announced a new cabinet. It was something, he explained, he had been considering doing for some time, but conditions had "not been suitable till now." As he produced the names of his new cabinet, it was clear he was flinging down a gauntlet at the army's feet, for

General Nasution, the army's hero who had barely escaped death in the October coup attempt, was fired from his post of defence minister—was not even in the cabinet at all.

Back in the cabinet, however, was former air force chief Omar Dhani, whose role in the Gestapu affair was particularly offensive to the army. This was the man Suharto had confronted so furiously after the coup attempt, ripping his epaulettes from his shoulders and slapping his face with them.

The changes could hardly have been more provocative to the army.

Two other new ministers objectionable to both the army and the student demonstrators were Basic Education Minister Sumardjo, who had been held by the army for his alleged participation in Gestapu, and Security Affairs Minister Lieutenant Colonel Sjafie, a former mobster whose role was clearly to crack down on the protesting students.

Read with other cabinet appointments, it all seemed clear enough. Sukarno had moved swiftly to hobble the mounting political power of the army, restore himself to supreme and unshared political control, and thrust Indonesia sharply to the left again. But he had miscalculated the tenacity of the students. Now was to be unleashed a campaign of remarkable student intensity which, bolstered by the army, would compel Sukarno to back down.

18. Youth Says No

For a newspaper correspondent covering the Far East, Djakarta was in February, 1966, obviously the place to be, but for American correspondents there was a problem. In January, Sukarno had had yet another of his frequent explosions against the American press and had ordered all American newsmen expelled, their offices closed, their facilities for filing press cables canceled.

Affected by the order were the Associated Press and United Press International, which maintained staff correspondents in Djakarta, and *The New York Times*, which was represented on a stringer basis by an American national.

To make the ban complete, Sukarno also directed that Indonesian nationals could henceforth no longer work for American news organizations. Not only were the Americans to be expelled, but they could not leave behind them Indonesian journalists or assistants who could file stories out of the country.

In addition, the Indonesian foreign ministry announced that the British news agency, Reuter, would also be banned from the country when the short-term visa of its correspondent expired. The correspondent at that time was a Burmese national, who had managed to stay on after the expulsion of the previous Reuter man, an Australian.

But once again, I was holding a visa in my passport valid or Indonesia. When the boom was dropped on American correspondents, no Indonesian official called at my Hong Kong office, no piece of paper arrived, canceling it. Needless to say, I did not raise the matter, but instead cherished my visa carefully for use at the most appropriate moment.

With the firing of Nasution from Sukarno's cabinet, it seemed that the moment had come. I did not know whether I really could get into Indonesia, nor, if I did, whether I could get any of my dispatches out. Even in times of political tranquillity, Indonesia's communications with the outside world are unpredictable. Now, in the midst of the crisis following the cabinet reshuffle, they were nonexistent.

Although the confusion did indeed prevent transmission of my stories by orthodox means, it may have been a factor that assisted my entry into Indonesia. After I had flown into Djakarta on an Indonesian airliner, nobody stopped me at the airport, told me that American newsmen were barred, or put me on a plane flying out again. Instead, I found myself cleared by immigration and customs men and rattling into the city in one of the decrepit taxis whose owners prey on incoming passengers.

Even as we drove through the streets, however, it seemed clear that unless I did something that made me extraordinarily conspicuous, few of President Sukarno's officials were going to have time to worry about me. Seething student unrest and continuous demonstrations had brought Djakarta to chaos. Before we had driven far, the taxi was halted in a mammoth traffic jam as hundreds of teenagers swarmed over the cars, gluing signs to their windshields and scrawling slogans in chalk over their paintwork. In a capital where Sukarno had long reigned unchallenged, these were sensational scenes. "Hang Subandrio" and "Communist Party Must Go" proclaimed the stickers. Smeared in paint across walls were crude drawings of a little dog bearing not its own head, but the bespectacled head of Dr. Subandrio. If any amplification were needed, the words underneath spelled it out: "Subandrio, little Pekingese dog." Other signs labeled Subandrio the President's "durna," a reference to a character known in one of Indonesia's traditional *wayang* shadow plays as an evil adviser to the king.

By night, the army had been compelled to reimpose a strict curfew. By day, in defiance of specific presidential decrees banning demonstrations, the students milled throughout the streets, bringing the work of the capital to a standstill with their protest campaign.

The specific target was the new cabinet, which they quickly dubbed the Gestapu cabinet. Some 14 of its 100 members were pro-Communist, they charged. Throughout Djakarta they distributed a list of 23 members of the cabinet to whom they objected, on grounds either that the cabinet members were sympathetic to the Communist Party or that they were "plin plan"—opportunists who would jump with the Communists if they thought the Communists were going to triumph. The list was headed by Dr. Subandrio and included Chairul Saleh, another deputy premier. Thoughtfully, the issuers of the list included on it the addresses and telephone numbers of the cabinet members they were campaigning against.

Sukarno himself dismissed their objections as "crazy."

But the Gestapu cabinet, as they called it, was merely the provocative symbol of the old order in Indonesia with which the students had become increasingly disillusioned. When you talked to student leaders, they set forth three formal demands. They wanted the Gestapu cabinet, and particularly Subandrio, swept away. They wanted the Communist Party banned. They wanted prices lowered. Beyond this, it was not difficult to detect the desire for a whole new political deal in Indonesia.

At this stage they carefully couched their campaign in the language of support for the President. They wanted "the guidance of Bung Karno [Sukarno]," said one of their broadsheets. Their actions were not intended to topple him, "but to exercise the 'social control' which is called for by the President himself."

Yet in the same breath as the students called on the people "to defend the President," they called on them "to crush the parasites who wallow in luxury." When they demanded to know "Where are the results of a cabinet which has been in power for six years?" it seemed clear their criticism was of Sukarno, who himself headed that cabinet.

Their opposition to the new cabinet, however, was now about to take a dramatic turn. Two days after its announcement, some 50,000 students tried to storm Sukarno's Merdeka palace in the heart of Djakarta. At one point, they broke briefly through the cordon of palace guards. Reinforcements for the Tjakrabirawa were quickly on the scene, and the students were beaten back by soldiers swinging rifle butts and prodding with bayonets. However, the students did succeed in seizing the state secretariat building, not many yards away from the palace entrance, and ransacking offices there before soldiers ejected them. Among other officials, two deputy premiers maintained offices in the building.

In the melee some students were injured. The blood-soaked shirts of two of them were solemnly fastened to a flagpole outside the palace by their fellows.

The next day, February 24, was installation day for the 14 full ministers in the cabinet the students so despised. For the ceremony the presidential palace was turned into a heavily armed redoubt. Sukarno ordered it ringed with crack troops, protected by barbed wire, the approaches blocked by street barricades.

Before marching on the palace again, the students had business elsewhere in the city. At every key intersection they stopped cars and trucks, slewed them across the road, and let the air out of their tires. Hundreds of vehicles blocked the streets for hours as their owners and drivers trudged off in search of air-pumps to inflate their tires. It was a well-conceived plan, and it brought Djakarta to a standstill. The object, of course, was to keep the members of the new cabinet from getting through to the palace to be sworn in.

Among Sukarno's aides there was urgent consultation. Clearly, no cars could bring the stranded cabinet members to the ceremony. Helicopters would have to be sent out to fetch them. In this incongruous manner, most of the cabinet members reached the palace, flown in over a city brought to a halt by protests against them.

Even so, some of the ministers only just made the journey. One was hauled puffing into a helicopter, with pursuing students only yards behind him. The helicopter, its rotor blades already whirling away, whipped up into the air with only seconds to spare. Another minister was seen arriving at the palace in full dress regalia by bicycle. Others disguised themselves in sports clothes to slip through the student cordons.

Inside the palace, Sukarno appeared unruffled as he presided over the installation ceremony. "Do not," he warned in his address, "try to push me. I am not a leader who can be pushed. I know the job."

Outside the palace, however, the students were pushing the presidential guard. As a Tjakrabirawa jeep nosed through the crowds, they turned on it, stoned it, and smashed its windshield, slightly wounding a sergeant.

Now, as Sukarno entertained his guests with biscuits and orange juice, there was the crackle of gunfire. This did not sound like a few warning shots. These were bursts from automatic weapons, and as the guests moved nervously away from the windows, the gunfire sounded uncomfortably close.

The guns were turned on the students, however. One of them, Arif Rachman Hakim, a medical student at the University of Indonesia in Djakarta, was shot dead. In that instant, the student campaign was transformed. Prior to this, the students had marched on the palace, spilled some of their blood in scuffles outside it, and driven Sukarno to the ignominy of airlifting his new cabinet in by helicopter. But now, though the President might have his cabinet, the students had their political martyr. The President's guards had had to keep his people at bay by gunpoint, killing one in the process.

Now the student organization had become a political instrument of significance. It turned bitterly on Sukarno. Arif Rachman

Hakim, observed a student pamphlet pointedly within hours of his death, "was not allowed to sit in luxurious cars or helicopters, and to be guarded by soldiers who are paid by the people themselves. Do not you think that only he who is an enemy of the people is afraid of the people and needs to be guarded against the people?"

In a rage, Sukarno banned KAMI, the university students' action front, and KAPPI, the schoolchildren's action front, which had been organizing the demonstrations. The President even outlawed gatherings of more than five people.

It made no difference. The demonstrations went on. The day after Arif Rachman Hakim's death, 50,000 students turned out and marched in funeral procession through the capital's streets. Among the mourners was Mrs. Yani, wife of the murdered army commander. Her presence gave the students heart and left no doubt where her political sympathies lay. The student was given a hero's burial.

An angry Sukarno ordered the University of Indonesia closed, its Djakarta campus to be taken over by the army. The morning after the ban, there were certainly army tents pitched on the university lawns and armored cars at the gates. But the guns pointed outwards, and the soldiers looked suspiciously protective, rather than preventive. Thousands of students still milled about the campus, organizing, rallying, and blatantly criticizing the old order of things in their country. Each night, 3,000 of them slept in the classrooms.

From a series of clandestine headquarters, the student high command plotted the next moves in the campaign. One well-informed student told me that part of the time they used the mortuary in the school of medicine. There they were usually free from interruption and discovery.

Although the university was theoretically closed, there was a mass turnout for the inauguration of a new student "regiment," named after Arif Rachman Hakim. The dead student's mother traveled from her home in west Sumatra to be present and to give the new regiment her blessing. The regiment was divided into seven battalions, named for the six generals and Nasution's young aide slaughtered in the October coup attempt.

So far as one could see, the regiment was not equipped with firearms, though some of its members may have carried revolvers without showing them. But some kind of military-style discipline was clearly necessary, for the mood in Djakarta was turning increasingly ugly. The KAMI and KAPPI students could not be sure where they would find friends and where they would find enemies. Rival demonstrators from the leftist Bung Karno University were also on the rampage. There were bloody clashes as the two factions met in the streets, flailing away at each other with staves and clubs, and hurling rocks. Then there were the gangs unleashed by the new security affairs minister, Lieutenant Colonel Sjafie, against the KAMI-KAPPI forces, in an attempt to halt their drive against the old order.

Tempers and emotions ran high, and the foreigner attempting to weave his way through the chaos did so at some minor peril. The Western press corps attempting to cover all this was a slender one. I was the sole American correspondent in the country, but also present were Fred Emery, the engaging correspondent of *The Times* (of London) in Tokyo, who had somehow managed to acquire a visa there for Indonesia, and Donald North, a Canadian freelancer, whose various commitments compelled him to move through the crowds festooned with cameras and recording equipment.

It was not always easy to distinguish which group of demonstrators was which. Often our car would be almost into some rioting mob before we could identify it as one of the militant left, looking for just such a group as a trio of Western correspondents to beat up. Then our terrified Indonesian driver would jam on the brakes and go squealing away in a fast turn.

Even among crowds of demonstrating anti-Communist students,

our reception was uncertain. Plunging into them was like passing through eddies of hot and cold water. Here a group would say, "Yes, take pictures, tell the outside world what's going on. They must know." But a few yards farther on, students banded in the identical cause would thump and pummel you, brand you Necolim agents, and tell you to get out. This was Indonesia's business, they would say, and they did not want us there.

Emery and I could sometimes duck and take cover, but Don North with all his cameras was a target hard to miss, and he was beaten up on several occasions. At the end of one particularly exhausting morning we stopped off, battered and sodden, at the American Embassy. After months of harassment, the marine guards there were tense and edgy. As soon as North set foot through the door, one of them seized his cameras and told the Canadian newsman sternly he could not carry them into the embassy. From a supposedly friendly embassy, the timing of the rebuke was unfortunate. North had been bashed around by leftist mobs all morning. Now he exploded and continued in impressive manner till Deirdre Ryan, the embassy's amiable and highly professional press attaché, arrived to make peace and eventually restore smiles all round.

Sometimes students would commandeer cars and trucks to carry them to a rally or protest meeting. Once, when North and I were on our way to a big KAPPI demonstration, students stopped our car, flung open the doors, and piled in on top of us sixteen schoolgirls. Demure and innocent-looking in their white tunics, they were cheerfully on their way to demand that Subandrio be hanged. Then older students clambered on the roof, the hood, and the trunk of the car, and for several sweltering hours we groaned our way a few feet at a time through the mammoth traffic jam to the rally.

As the KAMI and KAPPI students went about their campaign,

they not only had to watch out for sudden attacks by leftist student groups and Lieutenant Colonel Sjafie's gangs. They had to be wary of factions within the military establishment. Openly hostile to the students were the Tjakrabirawa palace guard and the marines. The attitude of the militarized police force was uncertain.

The army was generally sympathetic to the student cause, but the relationship between the student command and the army's leaders was difficult to define. With individual generals the student leaders had a warm relationship. Before major new moves, the students quietly conferred with Suharto or his aides.

Clearly, Suharto must have let filter down the chain of command an order that his troops handle the student demonstrations with restraint. There must have been some covert army support. There was not much doubt, for instance, that when the students went on the air with their clandestine "Radio Ampera," broadcasting the "message of the suffering of the people," they were using radio equipment of military origin.

Yet the army's role seemed largely a permissive one. It allowed the students to wage their campaign. It may privately have encouraged them. But officially the army was uninvolved in it. The army had become the martial guardian of law and order in the capital. Despite the army's basic sympathy toward the students, there were confused and violent scenes when individual army units charged with the protection of government ministries or offices were harassed by students attempting to overrun them.

The real initiative was with the students. They had hammered their platoons of sweet-faced schoolgirls and tousle-haired college boys into a political weapon of considerable significance. With it, they were not only prodding Sukarno to retreat, but also the army to advance.

At this moment, General Nasution exhibited the political indecisiveness in time of crisis that had previously characterized his political career. He had accepted his firing from the cabinet by Sukarno without public demur. Now, although he would talk privately, he took no forthright public stand. For many of his qualities, and for his integrity, the students still had great respect, but for the action they demanded, they now turned to General Suharto. From now on, Nasution would be politically bypassed.

Some students at this time believed that Suharto himself had been bought off by the Sukarno Establishment for another general's star. Sukarno's philosophy certainly is that any man can be acquired for the proper price. By promoting Suharto he may have hoped to dilute the militancy of Suharto's opposition. But as events would prove, this was not to be the case.

In any event, the rolling student campaign had now reached deep into the ranks of Djakarta's elite and influential. One of the girl students who gave blood to a fellow student shot down by the presidential guard at the barricades was Neneng Sabur—daughter of General Sabur, the commander of that same presidential guard.

One of the members of KAMI was the daughter of General Machmud, the newly-appointed Djakarta garrison commander supposedly assigned to quell the demonstrations by this "banned" organization. Another girl student, who helped make the papier-mâché effigies of Dr. Subandrio for hanging, was the daughter of a former cabinet minister.

These were but some of the poignant little human dramas unfolding as the students involved more and more of the community in their campaign, tapping an ever-widening circle of public sympathy.

Night after night, the children of generals and ministers and department heads, as well as of ordinary workmen, were coming home after a day at the barricades, sometimes bloodied, and bringing the stark reality of their protest into the family living room. Hardly a home in Djakarta was unaffected. For many parents these were trying days. Even small children were no longer at school, but out in their thousands in rowdy demonstrations. Older children were gone for days, their parents knew not where.

Mingled with parental concern was growing pride. One mother told me, "We were all involved. We were frightened for our children, but we couldn't have stopped them. What they were doing was dangerous, but it was right."

What the mothers in fact did was launch mass feeding schemes. Their own children they could send off with individual food packages, but thousands of students had flocked to Djakarta from elsewhere in the country to join in the protest. Many were living at the university, others wherever they could. Women of Indonesia's *rukon tetangga*, or neighbourhood associations, quietly started cooking rice in huge bowls and packaging bundles of food, even clothing, for such youngsters. Prominent in the support campaign was Mrs. Yani, wife of the murdered army commander.

Sukarno himself, though cheery and confident, was behind heavy guard, his palace protected by barbed-wire barricades. When he moved, it was no longer by car, but by helicopter.

At one huge student rally in one of Djakarta's squares, a fiery speaker went through the usual cheerleading sequence. "Long live Indonesia!" he cried, and the crowd cheered back in thunderous echo. "Long live the Revolution" and again came the crowd's response. "Long live Suharto!" and this time there was a mighty, approving roar. Then a pause, and "Long live Bung Karno!" For a moment the crowd paused, too, then cheered, with noticeably less enthusiasm. For a moment afterwards there was silence again. Then came a ripple of laughter that swept across the assembled thousands.

It was the first public indication on such a scale that Sukarno had now not only fallen from grace, but was, at least for many in Djakarta, a figure for ridicule. For Indonesia, the classic situation had arrived—the ruler had lost touch with his people.

Between Sukarno and the new generation there lay, dark and angry, the charge of betrayal. He felt they had betrayed him. They felt he had betrayed the Indonesian revolution.

"You must get this straight," one of the students told me. "The revolution is very much a part of us. We were born after 1945, but we're good Indonesians, good nationalists. We haven't become soft. It's Sukarno who has become corrupted, who's moved away from the revolutionary principles. And that's why we're moving away from him."

19. Children on the Barricades

Djakarta was now a monument to disorder and ignored presidential authority. Though Sukarno was still, in terms of one of his grandiose titles, the "Mouthpiece of the Indonesian People," his words were drowned out by the crackle of gunfire and the hiss of exploding tear-gas shells as police and soldiers fought to maintain some sort of discipline.

Day after day, the leaders of KAMI and KAPPI poured tens of thousands of their student members into the streets. They roared their message of protest outside government offices. They pounced on hundreds of cars, leaving them clogging the streets with tires deflated to bring the capital's normal routine to a halt. Walls and fences along every important road were scrawled with painted slogans demanding that Subandrio and the Communist Party must go.

On March 3 the high school students surged into downtown offices of the ministry of basic education, seized the building, and took it over as KAPPI "headquarters." At other offices of the same ministry, thousands of students filled streets for several blocks around, demonstrating against the despised education minister, Sumardjo, whom Sukarno had just appointed.

Favourite targets were the office of Foreign Minister Subandrio, next door to the American Embassy on Merdeka Square, and the foreign ministry itself, several blocks away.

At the foreign ministry, students succeeded in lowering the Indonesian flag and replacing it with an effigy of Subandrio hanging from a rope, before the police mobile brigade arrived in force. When shots over their heads failed to disperse the teenagers, some policemen lowered their rifles, pointing the muzzles directly into the student ranks. At this, one university student flung himself forward, ripped open his shirt, and cried, "Shoot me! There are ten behind me to take my place." The police did not fire.

Meanwhile American Embassy officials and employees watched from the embassy windows with nervous fascination as crowds of students mobbed Dr. Subandrio's office next door. The teenagers flung themselves flat in the street and sheltered behind the embassy gates as steel-helmeted police in full combat gear opened fire above their heads. As I stood watching in the embassy forecourt, police beside me, assigned to guard the embassy, opened up with their automatic weapons, firing over and through the grilled front fence.

There were no casualties, but in the demonstration there was an ominous new note. Till then, the main weapons of the students had been courage, conviction, determination. Now they were ostentatiously carrying knives, iron bars, and other primitive—but lethal—weapons.

Finally, on March 8, the students realized one of their goals. Moving suddenly, early in the morning, they swept into the foreign ministry, ransacked it, and held it for five hours, until police and troops finally routed them out with tear gas. It was an incredible scene. Teenagers pounded through the ministry, smashing furniture, ripping filing cabinets open, strewing papers and documents throughout the building and out of the windows in a fluttering shower to the ground outside. Their slogans of protest they daubed on office walls throughout the entire building. Outside, the whole front of the building was covered by clambering students drawing pictures of Subandrio as a little Pekingese dog, or hanging from a gallows. Across the facade of the building where Indonesia's foreign affairs were conducted was painted in huge letters: "Headquarters of the Suffering of the People." Another slogan branded Subandrio openly the "Murderer of the Generals."

When police and troops arrived on scene, the students rained down rocks and pieces of broken furniture on them from the windows. The melee was further confused by the arrival of other— leftist—students who rushed to the ministry to take on the KAMI and

KAPPI students. Now on the lawns surrounding the ministry there were fistfights and free-for-alls as rival student groups slugged it out.

Police fired volleys over the students' heads, but failed to clear the area. Finally they lobbed tear-gas shells into the ministry. Six of the younger children were overcome by the fumes and had to be taken off to a hospital, but the building was vacated.

The ministry was left a shambles. The whole of its exterior was defaced with slogans scathingly critical of Subandrio. The lawns were cluttered with debris from inside the building and thousands of official documents and papers. Ministry cars, their tires slashed, lay disabled on their wheel-rims.

When we finally reached Ganis Harsono, then the foreign ministry spokesman, by telephone at home, he complained bitterly that secret documents were missing following the demonstration. Even now, he said, they were probably being perused by the British or the American Ambassador. The London *Times* man, Fred Emery, promptly drove around to the British Embassy to ask whether this was so. The ambassador, Sir Andrew Gilchrist, a round, stocky man with a beard and an unblinking Scottish sense of humor, told him, straight-faced, "You may quote me as saying that the British Embassy is reading as many documents acquired from the ransacked Indonesian foreign ministry as were acquired and read by the Indonesian foreign ministry following the sacking of the British Embassy [in 1963]."

Next day Sukarno left his palace to inspect the scene at the foreign ministry. Of the students he said, "Oh God, forgive them, because they do not know what they are doing." He charged that agents of Necolim, his shorthand term for the United States and Britain, were really behind the demonstrations. He warned darkly that he knew of people who were giving money to the students to egg them on.

Sukarno had long since neatly divided the world in his own mind into two factions, the OLDEFOS, or Old Established Forces, and the NEFOS, or New Emerging Forces. But despite his accusations, it was not the hand of Necolim, or of the OLDEFOS, behind the demonstrations. Though Sukarno considered himself a NEFO leader, what he had not realized was that within his own country he had himself become the Old Established Force. What really confronted him was a New Emerging Force in the shape of Indonesia's youthful students, now determined to shrug off the old order. It was a decision they had been brought to not by foreign influences, but by Sukarno's own maladministration and provocative actions.

But now the students were no longer alone. They were fast picking up support. They had drawn their families into the campaign. They were involving the army. For the first time, anti-Communist trade unionists made their appearance at some of the student rallies. After the occupation of the foreign ministry, Djakarta newspapers reported the story with a comprehensiveness and freedom that had been lacking for months. The voice of opposition was gaining strength.

Sukarno's forces, however, were far from on the ropes yet. As the student campaign had gained momentum, so too had a new, officially inspired anti-American campaign, perhaps designed to divert attention from the student unrest. Sukarno's spokesmen erupted in a series of outbursts against the Necolim powers. A flurry of signs appeared, some broadly critical of the United States, some specifically directed at the American Ambassador, Marshall Green.

On the very same day on which anti-Communist students launched their dramatic assault on the foreign ministry, a well organized gang of about two hundred Indonesian youths stormed the American Embassy. Across the front of the embassy forecourt ran a long grilled metal fence. It was goodlooking, and high, but its designer could not have had attacking mobs in mind when he created it. On this occasion, the attackers were up over it in seconds, as if it had been a stepladder, and had dropped down into the embassy grounds. Later that day, when the main gates were still padlocked, I scaled it easily myself. By next morning, the lesson had been learned, and workmen with welding torches were fixing an extra barbed-wire entanglement—inelegant, but effective—atop the fence.

For now, however, the attackers had the grounds to themselves. A grille, built earlier, across the front of the actual embassy building stopped them from getting in. But they bombarded both the embassy and an annex next door with rocks, smashing windows. Three rocks smashed through the window of the Ambassador's office, sending a shower of plate glass across his desk and chair. The Ambassador was not in his office at the time, but lunching at home. Telephoned the alarm as soon as the raid began, he announced his intention of returning immediately to the embassy. Security men ordered him to remain at his residence.

The window-smashing was but a prelude to more serious intent, however. The attackers had come armed with home-made Molotov cocktails, or gasoline bombs. One was flung at the embassy itself, below the Ambassador's office. But beyond blackening the wall, it flared out harmlessly.

Slipping around the side of the embassy, the attackers forced back an Indonesian employee at knife-point, then tried to set fire to an embassy store building. Into three embassy cars parked in the compound they tossed fire bombs. In seconds, the cars had gone up in columns of black smoke, completely burned out. Racing through the compound, the youths hurled rocks and stones through the windshields and windows of other cars, damaging sixteen.

A few hundred yards away, unaware of all this, Mrs. Faye Lynch, wife of the embassy's public affairs officer, was traveling in the direction of the embassy in her car. The car bore diplomatic plates and was easily identifiable as American. Suddenly, crowds blocked the street and swirled around the car. Mrs. Lynch, whose husband was away at the time on business in Tokyo, was politely but firmly asked to get out. Then the car was set ablaze and gutted. She was not harmed.

This incident was clearly connected with the almost simultaneous attack on the embassy. Nor was there much doubt about the inspiration for the attack. One of the trucks carrying the party to the embassy bore a banner from the leftist Bung Karno University. Individuals among the attackers were identified as members of the youth wing of the extreme-left Partindo (Partai Indonesia) party. It looked suspiciously as though the attack might not have come entirely as a surprise to Lieutenant Colonel Sjafie, the security affairs minister.

Before they left, the raiders tore down the American flag from the flagpole in front of the embassy, hoisted an Indonesian flag, which they had thoughtfully brought with them, and cut the halyards. They departed, as they had entered, over the embassy's front fence.

Protocol required that this Indonesian flag should not be lowered by an American. An Indonesian employee of the embassy therefore shinned up the pole to remove it. Upon dropping to the ground he was seized by Indonesian police stationed inside the embassy compound. Their task was to guard the embassy, but throughout the raid they had remained inactive. Now, however, they snapped into life to drag the unfortunate Indonesian who had lowered the flag out of the embassy compound. There followed an angry scene as an embassy official ordered the police to hand back the embassy's employee. But reinforced by other police outside, who had arrived after all the action was over, the officers bundled their captive into a car and drove him away.

Immediately, the embassy took up the matter with police headquarters, and next day the Indonesian employed was returned.

He was bruised, but cheerful. He had only been beaten up with a buckled belt, he said. He had expected far worse.

Speaking of the whole raid, Ambassador Green told reporters it was "outrageous" and said he would lodge a strong protest with the Indonesian foreign ministry. But aside from the fact that its own building was a shambles, temporarily uninhabitable, the foreign ministry was about to be beset by even more problems.

For now it was the turn of the Chinese Communists to defend their premises against raging student mobs. The day after the attack on the American Embassy, anti-Communist students stormed the villa housing Peking's official New China News Agency.

Though the raid was over by the time we heard about it, Emery, North, and I went around to get the story. The gates were locked, and a glowering Chinese refused to let us in. After consultation, we sent in a visiting card with the notation that the Western press corps would like to pay its respects. After a few minutes, down the driveway came Chang Hai-tao, the bureau chief. He let us in, received us politely, and ushered us through the wreckage of an outer room of the villa into a small sitting room where relative order had been restored.

He offered us cigarettes and tea, then in response to our questions told us his story of what had happened. Hooligans, he said, had swarmed over the fence and first cut the telephone line so that the Chinese could not call for help. Then they battered at a door, behind which Mr. Chang had taken refuge, shouting, "If you don't open the doors, you will die." Once in the building, the raiders smashed furniture and windows.

Ten New China News Agency employees lived and worked in the building, said Mr. Chang, and five of them had been injured in the melee, two of them seriously. The bureau had been cut off from help during the attack. The fire brigade had taken half an hour to come to put out a blaze started by the attackers. Troops had not arrived until an hour after the action ended.

Mr. Chang said his bureau had filed a protest with the Indonesian foreign ministry. When I asked whether he had yet filed the story of the attack to Peking, he smiled sadly and said that Indonesian military censors had withheld the report from transmission via Indonesian cable facilities. The bureau may well have had its own radio transmitter, however. As we came in, we noticed an impressive antenna at the rear of the building. And as we chatted, from somewhere at the back of the house we could hear the *beep-beep-beep* of a Morse-cast, though whether incoming or outgoing we had no way of knowing. Even if the Chinese Communist news agency had been unable to get a message out, however, it seems unlikely that the Chinese Embassy would not already have transmitted the news to Peking via its own communications channels.

After tea, Mr. Chang took us on a tour of the garden, showing us two cars in the driveway battered by the invaders, as well as a hole in the roof and various windows through which he said the attackers had hurled Molotov cocktails.

With a straight face and in his best *Times* of London manner, Fred Emery asked the Chinese newsman whether the attackers had not, perhaps, got the idea from the attack on the American Embassy the day before. Was not the U.S. Embassy attack, he prodded, the first occasion on which Molotov cocktails had been used during the current unrest? Mr. Chang refused to rise. However, when asked who he thought was responsible for the attack, he was quick to reply. "Rightist hooligans" had done it, he said, and there was not much doubt that he meant the students from KAMI.

For the anti-Communist students it was a busy day. In addition to the attack on the Chinese Communist news agency, there was yet another massive demonstration outside the office of unpopular Basic Education Minister Sumardjo. Fifteen thousand high school students besieged it, demanding his dismissal.

Meanwhile, some 5,000 KAMI students roared out in truck convoys to the Senajan sports complex on the outskirts of the capital. As we followed them, their destination suddenly became clear. They were headed for the parliament. Whether the army command had been informed in advance, or whether the plan was born spontaneously, was never clarified. But as the trucks clattered onward, the students waving flags and banners and singing old Indonesian revolutionary songs to which they had written new words, an armored column appeared ahead, racing to take up position near the parliament.

The tanks and armored cars stood guard, but there was no attempt by accompanying troops to stop the students swarming over the fences and into the parliament building. For their part, the students were orderly, bent only on a brief occupation, some speechmaking, and presentation of a protest petition, listing their grievances, to the president of the parliament. After he had received it, they withdrew.

Next day, it was the turn of the Chinese Communists again. Students overran both the Chinese consulate-general and a house used by the Chinese commercial attaché. The students apparently had the big Chinese Embassy building, almost hidden behind high walls, on their target list, too, but somebody in authority must have given firm orders to stop that. Armed police and troops beat the students to it, turned them away, and blocked off surrounding streets with barricades. For the rest of the day, the Chinese Embassy remained sealed, barred, and shuttered under the protective guns of Indonesian armored cars.

At the Chinese consulate-general, the raiders smashed their way through the garden gates with a truck and thence into the building—again a large house set in its own grounds. They broke up furniture, ransacked files, strewed papers and documents about, and made sizable holes in the roof by throwing stones through it. They tore down the Chinese flag, and even the flagpole on which it had flown. Then they carried away radio equipment they found inside.

At the residence of the Chinese commercial attaché, the students used a steamroller to smash down the garden gates and a hefty stone wall. Steel concertina gates across a hallway prevented their penetrating the whole house, but they ransacked outer rooms, carrying furniture and papers to a bonfire that was still blazing in the garden when I arrived. Some of the students who had taken part in the attack were still there, but if they had been violent to the twenty-seven Chinese they said they had found inside the building, they were not particularly cordial, either, to a Western correspondent.

No friendlier were the bandaged and bloodstained Chinese who had taken up positions behind a locked gate at the side of the house; they were in an angry mood. At least five of them had been injured as they tried to defend their government's property against the attacking students. Nearby, a car bearing Chinese diplomatic plates had been attacked and burned.

Throughout the capital, hundreds of cars were yet again strewn across the highways, their tires, as usual, deflated by the students. Normal routine was at an end.

Djakarta now seemed on the brink of anarchy. Anti-Communists and leftists clashed in the streets. Capitalist and Communist embassies alike were liable to attack. A Western newsman could get roughed up by Communists or anti-Communists. Even the correspondent from Radio Prague had to run for his life without ever finding out whether his pursuers had mistaken him for a Western correspondent or whether they were chasing him in his own right as a Communist.

20. The Bung Backs Down

A showdown was now obviously only a matter of days, if not hours, away.

Under banner headlines one morning the army newspaper ran a story about the surrounding of the presidential palace and the arrest of key ministers. Not until halfway down the story was the reader informed that the presidential palace referred to was in Accra, Ghana, and the ministers were those of Kwame Nkrumah, whose toppling coincided with the unrest in Indonesia.

In the face of student pressure, the army had become increasingly involved. Truckloads of troops pressing through anti-Communist demonstrations would now join in the cries to "Crush Subandrio." Some would grin at the students and make an ominous, throat-slashing gesture with their hands when Subandrio's name was called out.

Steeling the army to action, too, was evidence emerging from the first trials of ringleaders of the October coup. In February Njono, second deputy chairman of the Indonesian Communist Party, and boss of its more than 3,000,000-strong trade union affiliate, SOBSI, went on trial for treason. Lieutenant Colonel Untung, the Tjakrabirawa battalion commander who led the coup forces, stood trial immediately afterwards, his hearing running into the first week of March. Both were found guilty and sentenced to death. Like most of those to stand trial over the ensuing months, however, they appealed for presidential clemency. Since, under Indonesian law, the President can delay his decision indefinitely, those so sentenced simply languished in jail without the carrying out of the death penalty.

From a Western reporter's point of view, there was much about the initial trials that was unsatisfactory. Foreign newsmen were barred. Only condensed versions of the trial evidence were available from Antara, the official Indonesian news agency. Njono retracted huge chunks of a lengthy statement he had given his military interrogators before coming to trial.

Yet what was allowed to trickle out began to raise serious question marks in the public mind about Bung Karno's own association with the coup—question marks which were to loom larger and blacker over the months as others on trial, and witnesses, told their stories.

Despite all this, Sukarno still seemed a force with which to reckon. As many diplomats saw it in the first week of March, the power play could still go either way. At the American Embassy, there were preparations for the worst. Secret papers were put to the flame. At the Australian Embassy there were similar precautions. We will never know, but it is a good guess that down at the Chinese Embassy, Communist diplomats were doing the same thing.

On 10 March, Sukarno summoned leaders of nine Indonesian political parties for a day-long session at his palace. It was intended as the first act in a three-day marathon designed to restore Sukarno's authority. For the following day he had summoned the cabinet, and for March 12, the day after that, he gave notice that regional commanders of the armed services would be in attendance. The object was to lay down the Sukarno law, cow everybody into submission, smash the mounting tide of opposition.

On the first day, Sukarno tongue-lashed the political leaders, who eventually capitulated in abject surrender. They put their names to a declaration warning against Necolim subversion and the undermining of presidential authority by student demonstrations. They had given Sukarno all he asked.

Various participants have contradictory explanations for their actions that day. Some say that after a blistering oration, during which he smashed a chair against a wall, Sukarno stalked from the assembly room to let them think things over. The implication, they say, was that if they did not sign, they would be physically prevented by the presidential guard from leaving. Others claim they had advance word of pending military action against the President and reasoned that their signatures to a document that would soon be nullified anyway were of little consequence.

The anti-Communist students, however, could not dismiss the declaration by the political parties. They saw it as a betrayal. They feared that Sukarno was steamrollering his way back to total control. Only desperate action, they decided, could bring success for their cause. They planned to cap their weeks of demonstrations on Saturday, March 12, with a mammoth show of force. On the program was arson, the sacking of more government offices and official residences, and the mobilization not only of many thousands of student demonstrators, but of teams of commandos with grim and violent assignments. Some sources say these assignments included the assassination of leftist cabinet ministers.

But now word began to trickle out that Security Affairs Minister Sjafie's gangs were grouping for a new offensive, also scheduled for Saturday. They were to launch terrorist attacks on the anti-Communist students. Further, they were to unleash a new wave of anti-Western—and more specifically, anti-American—violence. Scheduled for a new assault with gasoline bombs was the American Embassy, in retaliation for student attacks on the Chinese Communist consular offices. There were to be bloody attacks on the residences of individual Americans. Also marked down for a going-over, in retaliation for the attack on the New China News Agency villa, was the trio of Western correspondents installed in the Hotel Indonesia.

If all this had come about, there would have been mass mayhem in Djakarta that Saturday. But on the day before, Friday, March 11, events took a sudden and dramatic turn.

This was the second day of Sukarno's three-day persuasive

marathon. With the political party leaders already battered into line, Sukarno set out to impose his will on the 100-man cabinet. The members met at Merdeka palace with Sukarno in the chair, his deputy premiers at his side. Foreign Minister Subandrio slipped off his shoes as the session progressed, relaxing in his stockinged feet, as was often Sukarno's own custom.

A few minutes after 11:30 A.M., General Sabur, the commander of the presidential guard, hurried into the cabinet room to Sukarno's side. He passed the president a hand-written note which Sukarno read then quickly handed to Subandrio. What the note said, according to one cabinet minister who saw it afterwards, was: "Wild troops have the palace surrounded and are advancing." In this sense, the Indonesian word "wild" meant "unidentified."

The note was no ruse. The palace guard had indeed detected troops in full combat gear closing in on Merdeka palace from all sides. The soldiers were stripped of their insignia and the Tjakrabirawa could neither identify them nor be sure of their intent, but there was no doubting the threatening nature of the advance.

In fact, the soldiers were Sarwo Edhy's para-commandos, but, as Sarwo Edhy told me dryly many months later, "We didn't advertise the fact. We weren't wearing our red berets."

Both Sukarno and Subandrio were visibly concerned at the information they had just been given. Some cabinet members watching said later that Subandrio, for the first time in their experience seemed nonplused and shaken, with no suggestion to offer.

Sukarno, however, reacted quickly. He was on his feet and making for the door so swiftly that Subandrio, to keep up with him, had to leave in his stockinged feet and without his shoes. At their heels followed Chairul Saleh, the third deputy premier, leaving Lemeina, the second deputy premier, behind in charge of the cabinet session.

There was no hesitation about the President's progress. He was heading for his helicopter, parked on the palace lawn, which was kept always ready for flight. Within minutes of receiving Sabur's warning note, Sukarno was whirling away from Djakarta, with Subandrio and Saleh safely strapped into seats beside him in the helicopter.

Just how Sarwo Edhy's para-commandos would have acted if Sukarno had remained in the palace is not entirely clear. Indications are that their real target was Foreign Minister Subandrio. Sarwo Edhy told me his men were under orders to shoot down Subandrio that day if he tried to leave or enter the palace.

Certainly Suharto—for the operation could not have been launched without his order—had taken into account the possibility that Sukarno would be flushed out of the palace by news that unidentified troops were advancing on it. One informed source says that the army had already "neutralized" Halim air base that day, and the President would not have been allowed to land there. Whether Sukarno actually ever considered Halim is not known. In fact, the presidential helicopter headed for the weekend palace at Bogor. Members of the Tjakrabirawa, the President's own palace guard, were in control there, but army sources say troops loyal to Suharto maintained a discreet outer cordon around the palace area.

Back in Djakarta, a perplexed Deputy Premier Lemeina closed up the cabinet meeting in five minutes. This, as one cabinet member remarked, "left a bad impression of the President," who had so precipitately left the cabinet in the lurch.

Now came the crucial phase in what was clearly a showdown between army and President. Three generals were dispatched by Suharto, who was genuinely confined to his home by sickness, to deal with Sukarno at Bogor. The three generals were Basuchi Rachmat, the former East Java commander who reported to General Yani about Communist subversion on the night of the army commander's murder, Mohammed Jusuf, a former cabinet minister, and Amir Machmud, commander of the Djakarta garrison.

The official version (leaked at the time) of what transpired at the Bogor meeting was bland and innocent. According to army sources, the three generals simply "clarified" for the President the "political and security situation in the country." Then Sukarno asked whether the generals had any suggestions. Yes, they replied, they had coincidentally brought along a piece of paper they thought the President might sign, transferring authority to General Suharto. After a little badinage, the President took out his pen and signed.

It was, of course, an impossible account of what really happened. But what the army was anxious to avoid was any suggestion that the President was forced to sign at pistol point. Said one high-placed army officer, "The generals were not armed, they were not carrying weapons. There was nothing like that." This is probably true. The generals themselves say emphatically that they did not carry side arms. Probably, under the circumstances that day, the palace guards would not have allowed them into Sukarno's presence if they had been armed. But there is not much doubt that other pressures were applied to induce the President to cooperate.

Long after the event, one of the generals involved, though barring use of his name, filled in some of the details for me.

Before leaving Djakarta, he said, they were briefed by Suharto. They traveled to Bogor by car, drafting as they went the order they wanted Sukarno to sign.

Were they nervous, I asked? "Yes," he replied, "we were praying all the way that things would work out."

They saw the President at about 4:30 P.M., he said. "We told him order had been restored in Djakarta, and appraised him of the whole situation. We showed him the order we wanted signed. At first he was very angry. Later he calmed down. But eventually, after a lot more talk, he called in Subandrio, Chairul Saleh, and Lemeina [who apparently had been summoned to Bogor after the arrival there of Sukarno and his two other deputy premiers]. He asked them to comment. Only Saleh had any additions. He suggested inclusion of a line saying that Suharto should get the advice of other military men about actions he wanted to take under authority of the presidential order. Then the President asked General Sabur to get the order typed up, and he signed it.

"We got back to Djakarta about seven o'clock that evening and reported to Suharto. Earlier Suharto had told us that if we were not back by six, things would start happening."

The implication of this last remark is that if the generals had not returned safely, Suharto would have started his troops moving against the Bogor palace. Whether he would also have used force if Sukarno had refused to sign the order is a question for historical debate. Some observers speculate that if Sukarno at that point had called Suharto's bluff and refused to sign, the army would not, in fact, have taken drastic military action against the President.

Sukarno, however, must have been convinced his personal security was threatened. So he surrendered and signed an order authorizing General Suharto "to take all steps considered necessary to ensure security, calm, and stability of the government." For Suharto, it seemed a blank check. In return, Suharto was instructed by a line in the document to "guarantee the personal safety" of the President.

Knowing the personalities of the generals involved, and of Sukarno himself, I do not believe the generals who confronted the President at Bogor thumped the table and demanded that he sign, or else. I believe that in a typically Indonesian way, they presented him with a typically Indonesian summation, in which the ultimatum was clear for all to see. Djakarta, they probably told Sukarno, was on the brink of anarchy. Rival factions planned arson, murder, and political assassination the following day. The army would have to step in, and the country could well explode in civil war. Then, I believe, they told him that in the midst of all this bloodshed the President's safety could not be guaranteed. Students or troops might attempt to overrun the President's palace. The way to forestall all this, they probably said, would be for the President to give General Suharto sweeping powers, which would enable him to crack down and control the situation.

However it was effected, the transfer of sweeping authority from Sukarno to Suharto transformed the political atmosphere in Djakarta. In the early hours of Saturday—the day on which the capital was to have exploded in violence—a student contact came hammering on my hotel room door. "We've won, we've won!" he cried, excitedly. "The President's given in—surrendered. It's all over."

During the night, Suharto had briefed student leaders on developments at Bogor. Now the news was being broadcast throughout the city. At the Hotel Indonesia the radio speakers in the rooms, which had been cut off during the disturbances, suddenly came to life. In Indonesian they broadcast the gist of the President's order and the announcement that troops would parade through the city later that morning. Crowds began to gather in the streets, smiling, chattering. There was no sign of the leftist opposition. It was as if a pall over the city had been lifted. Now, from the sky, army helicopters rained down hastily printed copies of Sukarno's order giving Suharto extensive control.

Did it mean what it seemed to mean? Finally I reached one of the President's aides by phone. "The President," said the aide, "has given General Suharto full authority for everything." But a few minutes later I talked to a general close to Sukarno. "Yes," he said, "but Suharto still has to consult with the President."

In the streets, however, there were no such subtle distinctions. Thousands of wildly cheering Indonesians lined the roadside as the army rumbled its men and equipment through the capital en route to key positions near the palace.

In official parlance it was a "show of force" by the army. In fact, however, the public treated it as a victory parade, greeting the soldiers like the liberators of an occupied and oppressed city.

Sarwo Edhy was in command of it, and he gave it all the muscle he could muster, with tanks and rocket launchers and field guns and armored cars by the dozen, as well as battalions of infantry in open trucks. At the head of the column he placed thirty truckloads of his own elite para-commandos, after which came paratroopers of the Siliwangi division.

In the cheering crowds were many of the students who had been in the forefront of the anti-Communist campaign. Now they threw flowers at the soldiers, and pretty girls stopped the trucks to kiss the troops. Students clambered aboard the tanks and rocket launchers and climbed into the trucks, shaking hands with the military men and slapping them on their backs.

Student motor-scooter squads wove their way in and out of the military cavalcade, hooting their horns ecstatically. Youngsters who could not scramble onto the military vehicles commandeered trucks and buses. Packed inside, and festooned with students on the roofs and hanging on outside, these buses and trucks were tagged on to the tail of the military column. For the rest of the day, they roared around the streets, many carrying student banners and the Indonesian national flag. Prominent were banners of the student regiment named after Arif Rachman Hakim, the student shot down by the presidential guards.

As one watching Westerner was moved to remark, "It's like V-E Day and V-J Day all rolled into one."

The mission of the parading army forces was not, however, entirely celebratory. They had serious work to perform, too. Around Merdeka palace there was strict security. Antiaircraft guns, mortars, and recoilless rifles were set up in commanding positions.

The palace was the focal point because Suharto had required Sukarno to return there from Bogor and the drama of the evening before. Sukarno had already scheduled a meeting for this Saturday morning with his regional military commanders. Following his meetings with party leaders and cabinet members on the two previous days, he had planned to cap these with a session laying down the Sukarno law, and underlining his authority, to the military. Now, although the circumstances had changed dramatically, the commanders were assembled and waiting at the palace, and the meeting was to be held as scheduled.

The same three generals who had confronted the President the previous evening were sent back to Bogor Saturday morning to return him by helicopter to Djakarta. Again there was emphasis on the fact that the generals were not armed, were not applying pressure to the President.

When I heard that the three generals had gone to fetch the President, however, I suggested to a palace official that this was somewhat unusual. "Yes," replied the official, with superb understatement, "it might seem a little unusual—but this is Indonesia."

Waiting for the presidential helicopter to arrive from Bogor, I stationed myself in the palace grounds just outside a Tjakrabirawa duty room, alongside a path over which the President and his entourage would have to walk after landing. After some while, there was the distant clatter in the sky that announced the helicopter was coming. Suddenly, out of the duty room beside which I stood there burst a familiar figure, with sleek black hair, dressed in white slacks and white shirt with a cabinet minister's insignia on it. It was Dr. Subandrio. He was almost as surprised to see me as I was to find him emerging from such unexpected quarters. With a hasty "Good morning," he wheeled off and away to meet the President before I could ask any of the dozen obvious questions about the important events of the past twenty-four hours.

Sometime after the President had signed the order giving authority to Suharto the previous evening, Subandrio had left the safety of Sukarno's side at Bogor and returned to the palace in

Djakarta. Although Suharto's troops were rumbling through out the city, the palace was still in the hands of the Tjakrabirawa, loyal to Sukarno, so Subandrio had taken up quarters in the security of a Tjakrabirawa duty room until Sukarno returned.

As the President came up the path after the helicopter landed, he looked grim and shaken. At his elbow and behind him there marched the usual cluster of aides and officials. But whereas ordinarily he would nod and often smile at anyone nearby, on this occasion he would not acknowledge the handful of spectators. Instead, he walked past unseeing, with the air of a weary man.

It could hardly have been coincidence that the head of the army's parading column circled the palace just as Sukarno himself arrived. As he made his way to the big reception hall where his military commanders stood waiting, he could hear clearly the roar from the crowds that went up to welcome Sarwo Edhy's para-commandos. If Sukarno at that moment had any thought of countermanding the order he had signed the previous evening, the show of force by army units now surrounding the palace must surely have canceled it out. He went in to address his commanders, and though the session was closed, with reporters barred, the official news agency Antara undoubtedly got the story right when it reported that the President asked his commanders to carry out the instruction he had signed the night before.

For Emery, North, and me, the three Western correspondents who had covered the campaign of student protest, there was one final postscript to this day of student victory.

For North to get pictures of the truckloads of cheering students we stopped not far from a gate at the rear of the presidential palace. Outside it were some thirty or forty members of the Tjakrabirawa, or palace guard. Whether they thought North was photographing them was never made clear, but suddenly they ran for him, seized him, and dragged him kicking and protesting into a building nearby.

There was only one course for Emery and me to pursue—bluster. We found a sergeant and warned him that unless North were returned unharmed within five minutes, we would have to take "serious action." We did not, of course, have the faintest idea what action we could take, but we made an ostentatious show of checking our watches and stamping up and down impatiently. It must have been a good act, for when, at the end of five minutes, nothing had happened, a lieutenant who had appeared on the scene meekly obeyed our demand that we be taken to the guard commander.

There, instead of a battered and beaten-up North, we found our colleague chatting quietly with a colonel of the guard at his desk. The colonel was apologetic. His men, he said, were "simple soldiers." They did not understand. He hoped we would forgive them for the incident. For an officer of the notoriously ruthless palace guard, it was a remarkable attitude to take toward a Western photographer. And it was significant. For though the "simple soldiers" outside were confused by the victory parade, and uncertain of its meaning, their more sophisticated officers had seen the writing on the wall and grasped the fact that the new order had dawned in Indonesia. Their assessment was correct. Within a short while, Suharto would order the Tjakrabirawa regiment to be disbanded, and guard duties to be assumed by regular units of the army.

21. Subandrio Behind Bars

Within hours of assuming his new authority, General Suharto fulfilled the first of the three demands that had inspired the students to their vigorous campaign of protest. He formally banned the Communist Party, a step that Sukarno had dallied over and failed to take.

It was the easiest of the demands to meet. The party was cowed, its apparatus smashed, many of its leaders missing or dead, its reputation discredited. The two remaining demands were more complex. One was for the purging of pro-Communists from Sukarno's cabinet, including the dismissal of Foreign Minister Subandrio. The other was for the lowering of prices.

Suharto moved first toward cleansing the cabinet. But he took a week to lay his plans, and in Djakarta these were days of doubt and impatience for the students. Sukarno had given Suharto sweeping power, but the students wanted it demonstrated. Subandrio was sheltering under Sukarno's wing, first at Bogor, to which Sukarno had returned after his meeting with the military leaders in Djakarta on March 12, and then later at the palace in Djakarta after the President had again returned to the capital. The students wanted Subandrio not under the President's protective wing, but under lock and key. As long as he was allowed freedom of maneuver, they argued, he was highly dangerous.

The army was reassuring, asserting that it had everything under control. It urged the students to be patient. But Sukarno was acting suspiciously unlike a man who had quietly accepted the transfer of his authority to Suharto. Within days of the hand-over, he was proclaiming that he was answerable only to God and the People's Consultative Congress. He tried to subvert individual generals from Suharto's cause. In that anxious week I came upon reliable information that he was secretly inciting factions within the marine corps, the police, and the air force to act against the army. The incitement failed to stir these forces, and the army command, which must have been aware of all this maneuvering, remained unruffled and confident.

Finally Suharto dispatched the same three generals who had confronted Sukarno at Bogor the previous week to Bogor once again to tell the President he was required in Djakarta, and to accompany him back to the capital.

Many months later, one of the generals recounted to me a curious incident that took place that day, which smacked suspiciously of an attempt by Sukarno's guards to seize the three generals and hold them as hostages.

"At first when we arrived at Bogor," said my informant, "the President was willing to come back to Djakarta. But as he was dressing, he got a message from one of his cabinet ministers warning him that when he returned, army leaders would be waiting for him and would force him to dissolve the cabinet." The cabinet referred to was, of course, the one to which the students were so opposed.

My informant went on, "The President asked us about this, but we denied it. Finally he agreed to come, and called General Sabur [the commander of the palace guard] to make the arrangements. Sabur said that we three generals must fly in the Sikorsky jet helicopter ordinarily used by the President. The President was to fly in another helicopter, and some of his aides and ministers in a third helicopter.

"We got into ours, but the pilot said he couldn't start the engine because it had suddenly developed generator trouble. So we got out, and as we did so, we saw the President's helicopter taking off. Then we tried to use another helicopter standing nearby, but the pilots said there was no gas for it. By now we were suspicious. And with reason, for as we stood there, we noticed the Tjakrabirawa, the palace guard, closing in on us.

"One of the other generals said, 'Quick, there's a car. Let's take it and get out of here.' We jumped in and raced away past the Tjakrabirawa As we got to the palace gates, we saw they were closed, but one of my colleagues leaned out of the window and bawled 'Open the gates!' without stopping. The soldiers did, and we went as fast as we could back to Djakarta. On our arrival there, as we raced to the palace, we saw on the grass outside it not only the helicopter the President had flown in, but also the same Sikorsky that was supposed to have had engine trouble a little while before, and from which we had had to get off."

The actions of the presidential guard, as related, certainly sound suspicious. The general who told me the story said he was "really frightened" by what happened—much more so than he was when he had had to confront the President the previous week. Was Sukarno in on the ploy, or was this simply a maneuver by the palace guard? Did the guards mean to do the generals physical harm, or simply hold them hostage? If the latter was the idea, was it simply to ensure that the President arrived safely in Djakarta, or were the generals to be used as pawns in a bid to hold off dissolution of the cabinet? Probably these questions of minor historical interest will remain unanswered. The generals did get away, and the incident was soon to be overshadowed by much more dramatic events. For Suharto was now ready to fulfill the second of the students' demands, the demand for action against those cabinet ministers considered politically objectionable.

At 5 A.M. on March 18, troops loyal to General Suharto took up positions around the presidential palace. Once again, Sarwo Edhy's para-commandos came to the fore. This time they wore their red berets.

Charged with responsibility for the arrest of Foreign Minister Subandrio, who had sought security in a guesthouse within the palace grounds, was the Djakarta garrison commander, General

Amir Machmud. Also scheduled for arrest, at other locations throughout the city, were other wanted cabinet ministers.

With guns trained on the palace, tanks positioned to assault it, and the para-commandos encircling it, Sukarno had little room for maneuver. He agreed to come out, leaving Subandrio behind. One source, however, says that he whispered to General Machmud, "Amir, do not kill him [Subandrio]."

General Sabur, the palace guard commander, came out of the palace to consult with General Sarwo Edhy on the details of the President's departure. As Sarwo Edhy tells the story, Sabur announced that Sukarno would leave by helicopter, but Sarwo Edhy was having none of that. Any helicopter that left the palace that morning would be "shot down for security reasons," he told Sabur. Finally the two generals agreed that the President would leave the palace by car, alone in it except for his driver. This Sarwo Edhy insisted upon in order to make certain that Sukarno did not try to smuggle out the wanted Subandrio.

It was in this manner that Sukarno did leave the palace. A block away, however, he was stopped by the para-commandos, acting on Sarwo Edhy's explicit orders. The President was ordered to alight while the troops searched the presidential limousine to make sure Subandrio was not hidden somewhere in it. Explosively, Sukarno refused to get out. After some parleying, there was a compromise in which the back door of the car was briefly opened. For Sukarno, who had declared adamantly throughout the months that he would not fire, or get rid of, Subandrio, it was a humiliating experience.

With the President out of the palace, Suharto's troops swiftly picked up an unresisting Subandrio, and through the day arrested another fourteen cabinet ministers. Highest ranking after Subandrio was third Deputy Premier Chairul Saleh. The list of ministers included Sumardjo (basic education) and Setiadi (electricity), both of whom had been particularly strongly criticized by the students, and Sjafie (security affairs). Also arrested was Jusuf Muda Dalam, governor of the Indonesian state bank.

As always in times of Indonesian crisis, troops occupied all key installations, cable and telephone communication with the outside world was cut off, and the airport was closed, but by nightfall Djakarta radio was broadcasting an announcement from General Suharto that the fifteen ministers were in "protective custody." New appointees, said Suharto, had been selected to fill temporarily the ministerial posts now vacant. Most notable was the appointment of Adam Malik as acting foreign minister in Subandrio's stead.

Now the students were convinced that victory was really theirs. Two of their three demands had been met. The Communist Party had been banned, and ministers they considered pro-Communist or linked with the Gestapu movement had been expelled from the cabinet. At the University of Indonesia there was a great victory feast to which thousands came.

In the next week, Suharto and his followers hammered out with Sukarno a compromise cabinet reshuffle that was announced March 27. The new cabinet would have twenty-four full ministers, with deputy ministers under them, but there would be an inner cabinet of six deputy premiers. Three of them—Johannes Lemeina, Idham Chalid, and Ruslan Abdulgani—were holdovers from the previous cabinet. The other three were Suharto himself, Adam Malik, and Sultan Hamengku Buwono, the Sultan of Jogjakarta. Despite his feudal title, the Sultan was a good nationalist who had been active in the revolution against Dutch colonial rule and had gained national respect. Now, he had been picked as the man to put Indonesia's crumbling economy somehow back on its feet. He was given charge of economics, finance, and development.

Few people thought the new cabinet was ideal. Suharto himself admitted it represented only "the maximum possible progress in the first stage." Said one newspaper, "We are still far away from our goal, but the first sign of victory is in sight." Commented another, "This is the maximum that can be achieved in the present situation." But it represented a major improvement over the previous one appointed by Sukarno, and the assumption was that it would be replaced by something better, once Suharto had consolidated his position.

If the cabinet changes were not all that the students had hoped for, they nevertheless placed in key roles three men who were to be the guiding triumvirate of the new order in Indonesia in the months to come.

Suharto was to use his new powers and his military forces to maintain security and prevent any Communist resurgence. The Sultan of Jogjakarta was to divine, and try to rectify, the country's economic ills. Malik was to handle foreign policy, but also keep a hand in political affairs at home.

The three tasks were intertwined. With security relatively assured, the most awesome challenge confronting the new leadership was to save the sagging economy from total collapse. This required drastic measures. Most obvious was an austerity campaign at home, but this was far from enough. Indonesia had to have emergency help from abroad, and quickly. Clearly such aid could not come from Communist China, which was snapping and snarling almost daily at the new administration in Indonesia. Meanwhile, Indonesia's relations with the Soviet Union were correct, but cool, and, anyway, Indonesia was already over its head in debt to Moscow, so that not much could be expected from that direction. The aid Indonesia had to have could come only from the non-Communist world—Japan, Europe, the United States. But to get help from those quarters, Indonesia would have to give evidence of reform and a return to political stability. This evidence of good intentions could most dramatically and swiftly be produced by shifts in foreign policy, so Foreign Minister Malik set out to convince the world of his country's intention to climb back to international respectability. In fact, Suharto, the Sultan, and Malik were now engaged in a reversal of Indonesia's policies as they had been under Sukarno.

The facts of Indonesia's economic crisis, as the new leaders began to dig into them, proved chilling. Prices had gone up more than 500 percent in 1965. Now the Sultan calculated that, despite the students' third and unfulfilled demand, that prices be lowered, they would in fact go up by about 1,000 percent in 1966. The cost-of-living index had climbed from a 1958 base of 100 to 90,000 by the time the Sultan assumed his post as cabinet minister in March, 1966.

When the new men took over, they inherited foreign-currency reserves of about $8,000,000. But the country's foreign debts were more than 300 times this amount—some $2,500,000,000. Interest and repayment charges on these debts due in 1966 totaled about $675,000,000, but earnings from exports were steadily sinking and looked as though they would raise only about $360,000,000 during the year. Most of this would be gobbled up by emergency imports, with little to spare for debt repayment.

Meanwhile, industry was working at less than 20 percent of capacity, and the population was increasing faster than food production. Clearly, if Indonesia were a company, it would be in the bankruptcy court.

The new leaders went on an ostentatious cleanup campaign designed to impress countries from whom help was desperately needed. Sukarno's palace guard, the Tjakrabirawa, was disbanded. Communist members of the People's Consultative Congress were formally barred from their seats—if, indeed, any of them had dared show up to claim them. Malik began a screening campaign in the foreign ministry at home and started bringing key Indonesian diplomats back to Djakarta for interrogation about their political views. The Indonesian Ambassadors in Hanoi and Peking refused to obey the come-home orders and were promptly fired. Other Ambassadors resigned, rather than face Malik's questioning.

Then Malik started talking about renewed cooperation with various United Nations agencies and dropping hints that Indonesia might return to the United Nations itself.

Despite rumblings from Sukarno that Indonesia's policies remained "unchanged," Malik's public actions and private assurances were carefully noted in Tokyo, Washington, London—and presumably in Peking and Moscow, too. The new Indonesian leadership wanted to move discreetly, for though it sought to show that it had pulled back from Communism's embrace, it did not want to suggest that Indonesia had suddenly become a handmaiden of the West. Nor had it. The policy was to be genuinely one of nonalignment.

In Washington, too, the approach to helping Indonesia was kept sensibly low-keyed. But the help was needed, and so in April came the quiet announcement that the United States would extend to Indonesia an $8,000,000 credit—not a gift— for the purchase of rice. Even Britain, which had maintained 50,000 troops in Malaysia in defense against Indonesia's confrontation, gave Indonesia £1,000,000 ($2,800,000) of emergency aid. Theoretically, there were no strings attached to the British gift, but it could not have been made, of course, without the substantial decline in Indonesia's military activity against British and Malaysian troops that had taken place in the preceding months. It was clearly intended to encourage a formal end to confrontation.

With the new leadership in Djakarta, Britain's desire for an end to the idiocy of confrontation found a sympathetic echo. Foreign Minister Malik had soon determined that Indonesia's pocket war with Malaysia was a pointless, Sukarno-inspired extravagance the country could not afford. Internally, there was the cost of maintaining troops on the alert in remote border areas. Externally, the image of Indonesian belligerence against little Malaysia had cost it millions of dollars in loans, investment, and aid that had been choked off until Indonesia leaned toward more rational policies.

Initially, Malik had to move cautiously on the issue of peace with Malaysia. Confrontation had after all been the cornerstone of Indonesia's foreign policy. Sukarno had whipped his country over the years into a frenzy of anti-Malaysian feeling. Indonesian paratroopers had been dropped over the Malayan peninsula, Indonesian saboteurs had exploded bombs in Singapore harbor, Indonesian jungle troops had ambushed Malaysian and British forces in Borneo. In Djakarta, huge posters had savagely caricatured the Malaysian leaders, and massive rallies had called for their blood.

So the new leaders at first paid lip service to the confrontation policy, and pledged that it would continue. In the new cabinet announced in March, General Nasution was even brought back as deputy commander of KOGAM, the Crush Malaysia Command.

But the starkness of the economic crisis outweighed the political risks attached to peace moves. In May, Sultan Hamengku Buwono succeeded in extracting a $30,000,000 loan from Japan. It would tide Indonesia over with emergency imports, but much more dramatic assistance than that was needed. Before it could start flowing, Indonesia would need to have made peace with Malaysia.

As the month drew to an end, Malik flew with an Indonesian negotiating team to Bangkok, the city of golden spires and tinkling temple bells, in Thailand, there to meet with a Malaysian delegation headed by Deputy Premier Tun Abdul Razak. The Indonesians went despite sputtering protests from Sukarno back in Djakarta. But to make sure the Malaysians understood that the new leadership in Djakarta was serious about peace, Suharto dispatched, on the eve of his negotiating team's departure for Bangkok, a military goodwill mission to the Malaysian capital of Kuala Lumpur. It was a historic little scene as the Indonesian airliner touched down and high-ranking officers who had been conducting the confrontation campaign set foot on the soil of the nation they had in theory been trying to "crush."

But they came in friendship, and as Tun Razak told one reporter at the Bangkok negotiations, "That mission really paved the way for these talks, and provided the right atmosphere. It was a real demonstration of sincerity on the Indonesians' part. Because of the visit, we clearly assumed they were sincere in wanting to bring about peace."

The Bangkok peace talks did not end in quite the same rosy glow as they began. The participants refused to admit that confrontation had officially ended. Instead, they said they were taking back peace proposals to their respective governments for ratification. Part of the hedging seemed to be intended to provide some face-saving for Sukarno. After three years of sputtering war, the Indonesian delegation had to preserve the appearance of some negotiation and bargaining at the peace table.

There was some negotiation about sampling of public opinion in Malaysia's two Borneo territories of Sarawak and Sabah. Sukarno had consistently opposed the inclusion of these two territories within Malaysia and had demanded a new referendum to determine whether the people really wanted to be part of Malaysia. Malaysia argued that opinion had already been adequately tested under United Nations supervision. At the Bangkok negotiations Malik waived Sukarno's long-standing demand, but discussion lengthened over some suitable alternative.

However, at the end of the talks, as Malik and Tun Razak clinked celebratory glasses and linked arms and beamed at the photographers, it was obvious that confrontation was all but over. During the three years of hostility, Indonesia had lost 580 men killed, while 220 were wounded and 750 captured by Malaysian and British forces. The Malaysians had lost 82 dead, the British 22 soldiers killed, the Gurkha troops under British command 39 killed, and the Australians and New Zealanders 5 killed.

Although a formal peace treaty would not be signed for another two months, the fact that confrontation had been brought to an end in defiance of Sukarno's wishes was striking evidence of his political eclipse. His wings were now literally being clipped. His helicopters were no longer available, except for trips approved by Suharto. He was not allowed to slip away to Central Java, where he might stir up trouble. Telephone calls out of the palace were controlled, and his visitors regulated.

Though he had been stripped of his power, the army treated him courteously, if firmly. Malik and Sukarno frequently exchanged heated words at private sessions of the cabinet, but others present say that Suharto, perhaps with his Javanese antipathy for strident scenes, engaged in no table-thumping or angry harangues.

There were other, extremely practical, reasons why Suharto elected to retain Sukarno in what was supposed to be a figurehead presidential role. First, the President was a useful political lightning rod, who could be used to deflect criticism that might otherwise be directed at the army itself. Suharto was acutely conscious of the fact that the third of the protesting students' demands—the lowering of prices—was unfulfilled. To retain the sympathy of the students, and broaden its political support among the people, the army was under pressure to produce swift progress on the economic front, now that it was in charge. Yet as the army dug deeper into the facts of the economic mess, it could see that far from being able to lower prices, it would have to live with increases in the cost of living, no matter how efficiently it could administer the country. In the eyes of visiting experts and of economists at the University of Indonesia, about the best the new leadership could hope for over the next two or three years was an inflation rate of 30 percent a year.

It was not inconceivable that the students who had so wildly cheered Suharto's assumption of authority in March might in several months' time be out on the streets again demonstrating against lack of progress in the economic field. If Sukarno were deposed, the army would have to bear the full brunt of that criticism.

Then again there was Suharto's own genuine insistence on constitutionality and dignity in the handling of the President. Privately he told friends he wanted no Latin American-style power takeover in Indonesia. If the army simply fired Sukarno, he argued, then that would set a precedent for the future. Anybody disenchanted with successive leaders could oust them with similar lack of legal process. If the President was to be dismissed, then it must be by constitutional means.

Suharto argued for the resuscitation of the 1945 constitution and the reactivation of the People's Consultative Congress (MPRS) as a genuine policymaking institution. Though Sukarno's gradual assumption of power over the years had blurred the original concept, the Congress was supposed to be the supreme constitutional authority in Indonesia, to which the President was subservient. In practice, Sukarno had vested all policymaking authority in the hands of the President, himself. Now the army argued for reversion to the original concept under which the Congress would determine constitutional matters and set broad guidelines for Indonesian policy, while the President, his cabinet, and the parliament would execute the administrative details of such policy.

Another restraint upon Suharto in his dealings with the President was his own patriotism and national pride. True, the outside world had to be convinced that Indonesia had embarked upon more reasonable policies, but Suharto hoped to avoid presenting the world with the spectacle of Sukarno's political crucifixion. Sukarno was, after all, the father figure of the Indonesian revolution. He had played a major role in giving

Indonesia pride, unity, and independence. In all these things, Indonesians still believed. For them to face up to Sukarno's shortcomings and admit that their demigod was human and vulnerable, after all, had been a traumatic experience. Now Suharto sought to retire Sukarno with relative dignity and avoid further humiliating of Indonesia's image abroad by humiliation of the man who had been Indonesia's voice for two decades.

Beyond this there was yet another important factor, namely, that Sukarno retained blocs of genuine political support, particularly in Central and East Java. His provocative dismissal could spark violence among his still considerable supporters, perhaps even civil war.

Despite the impatience of students and even of some of his own generals who wanted the President fired, Suharto set about the difficult and dangerous task of destroying Sukarnoism while retaining Sukarno.

22. Return to Respectability

With its new accent on constitutionality and legality, the Indonesian leadership now scheduled a session of the People's Consultative Congress for May 12. The aim was to revive the constitutional process, breathe new life into the Congress, and transform it from an instrument of Sukarno into the genuine policymaking body it was originally intended to be.

General Nasution, now speaking out increasingly critically of the old Sukarno order, had already left little doubt about what was expected of the Congress. Several years before, at a session dominated by Sukarno, the Congress had elected Sukarno President for life. But this, said Nasution, was "clearly a deviation from the 1945 constitution, which unmistakably states that the tenure of office of the presidency is five years. And five years does not mean a lifetime." Nasution also talked of holding elections within three years.

To Sukarno himself, it was all clear enough. His opponents were calling the Congress into session to curb him still further and formalize the figurehead role for him the army intended. He balked, and Suharto compromised, postponing the Congress session till August. But anti-Sukarno students put on a fiery series of demonstrations against the postponement, and the session was finally set for June 20.

The Congress met for two weeks in the Soviet-built sports palace at Senajan within a protective ring of troops and tanks. During most of the session, students staged forceful demonstrations throughout the capital to make sure Congress delegates understood their opposition to Sukarno and his policies. There was now no longer any pretence about the real target of their criticism. "What is in Sukarno's heart?" demanded the student banners. "He is trying to revive Communism. He is flirting with China. He likes building monuments." One student truck in a procession through the capital carried a dummy of Sukarno sitting on a throne, his arm around a man clad in a Communist flag, taking money from a Chinese. On several occasions, troops broke up crowds of students demonstrating outside the Congress hall and near Sukarno's palace.

One of the first actions of the Congress was to appoint General Nasution its chairman, in place of imprisoned Deputy Premier Chairul Saleh. For Sukarno, who had thrown Nasution out of his cabinet only four months before, it was an obvious snub.

Nasution was sworn in as chairman just before Sukarno arrived to deliver a 40-minute address. In it, Sukarno said he would give up his title of lifetime President if the Congress so decided. With his hand on his heart, and apparently at one stage close to tears, he said, "Everyone has the right to serve the country. The body can be jailed, the body can be overthrown, the body can be shot, but not the cause of freedom.

"The cause of freedom is a deathless cause, the service of freedom is a deathless service, and for forty years I have dedicated myself to that service. I leave it to God if He wants to give me strength to carry on that service."

With a disdainful reference to the new leadership's quest for foreign help, he emphasized his own *berdikari* policy of self-reliance. "Economics," he told the delegates, "cannot be separated from politics. Emphasis should be placed on self reliance."

In a plea for a new lease on his authority, he declared, "I will give leadership to Indonesia, to all of you, excellent leadership."

Neither the Congress nor the demonstrating students outside were inclined to give him the opportunity. The students labeled the President's speech unsatisfactory. KASI, the action front of graduates and intellectuals, came out flatly demanding Sukarno's resignation. Thousands more demonstrators demanded that Suharto should form a new cabinet to tackle the country's problems.

Commenting on the presidential address, the independent daily,

Operasi declared in a headline, "Bung Karno Let His People Down."

Said another newspaper, "Populace dissatisfied, displeased, discontented ... It's the same old story. It does not meet the wishes of the people."

In closed session, the Congress went purposefully about its business. It ratified the March 11 delegation of emergency powers by the President to General Suharto. It ratified the dissolution of the Communist Party, and ordered a ban on Communism, Marxism, Leninism. Finally, it approved a string of decrees formulated by various Congress committees during the two-week session.

To thunderous applause from the 500-odd delegates, the decisions were reeled off. The Congress decided there should be free elections in Indonesia not later than two years hence—by July 5, 1968. It instructed General Suharto to form a new cabinet by August 17, Indonesia's national day. It directed that Indonesia's foreign policy should be non-aligned—the end of the Djakarta-Peking axis.

It set up a special committee to review the President's political teachings and called upon him to explain the nation's "economic and moral decadence," as well as circumstances surrounding the coup attempt of 1965.

Then came the decision: Sukarno's title of President for life was revoked. For the moment, he would remain Great Leader of the Revolution, but the title would carry no power. And he was to stop issuing presidential decrees.

On the face of things, Sukarno appeared to accept the decisions of the Congress calmly. As a matter of fact, he said, as far as elections were concerned, he would be prepared to hold them right away. He wanted "to know the real will of the people of all Indonesia from Sabang [on the northern tip of Sumatra] to Merauki [in West Irian. I know," he went on, "that the will of the people is not only that reflected in Djakarta."

It was an obvious reference to his support in Central and East Java. But the armed forces *Daily Mail* took swift issue with him. The Congress, said the newspaper, consisted of delegates from all parts of the country, and it was an insult to them to doubt whether they represented the voice and will of the people.

The Congress had instructed Suharto to form a new cabinet. Now the General began a round of negotiations and bargaining to produce one. Sukarno put on a brave show, intimating that his hand was a strong one in the selection and molding of the cabinet, but when the names were announced, it was clear that he had suffered another defeat.

Heading a five-man presidium, or inner cabinet, was Suharto himself. Alongside him, in the same triumvirate which had run the country since the previous cabinet changes in March, were Adam Malik (foreign affairs) and Sultan Hamengku Buwono (economic affairs).

The two other members of the presidium were Idham Chalid, retained from the old presidium, and Sanusi Hardjadinata, a former Indonesian Ambassador to Cairo and minister of internal affairs.

Out of the cabinet went two old Sukarno cronies, former Deputy Premier Johannes Lemeina, and Ruslan Abdulgani. Anti-Sukarno students had maintained a vigorous campaign against them on the grounds that Lemeina was a "yes-man" and Abdulgani an "opportunist."

Of the twenty-seven ministers in the new cabinet, twelve were military men. The new ministers included such strongly anti-Sukarno figures as Major General Sutjipto (agriculture), and Burhanuddin M. Diah, recalled from his post as Ambassador to Thailand to become information minister.

Key Sukarno supporters were dropped, and some figures militantly opposed to him were brought in. Particularly galling to Sukarno was the retention in a vital role of Adam Malik, a Sukarno foe whose campaigns to end Indonesia's confrontation with Malaysia and to wean Indonesia away from Peking had particularly infuriated the President.

There was criticism of the new cabinet from various political and religious groups who had not fared in it as well as they believed they should. But probably its most serious defect was its paucity of skilled technicians—economists and administrators so badly needed to set the Indonesian economy back on its feet. Perhaps of necessity, Suharto opted heavily for military men in key roles, whose loyalty and political reliability was beyond question. Though filled with the best intentions, they did not necessarily know anything about running their complex ministries.

After the installation of the new cabinet, Sukarno spluttered and fumed in an hour-long speech. Looking at Lemeina, who stood with tears rolling down his cheeks, Sukarno declared, "I am deeply hurt that youth has branded Lemeina a yes-man, and no good. I know Lemeina is a true patriot. Those slogans which said 'Reject Lemeina' were an insult."

Meanwhile, though General Suharto had earlier declared that Sukarno was no longer Prime Minister as well as President, Sukarno rumbled angrily that he really was still Prime Minister, too. "I tell foreign correspondents," he said, "that I am still Prime Minister because I am the President. In accordance with the 1945 constitution, the President is the Prime Minister." The constitution did not specifically say this, he added, but it was an established fact.

Then referring to his March 11 order bestowing executive power on Suharto, which had been confirmed by the People's Consultative Congress, he said, "I stress it is not a transfer of authority."

As if to convince his listeners that he was still really in charge, he announced that the confrontation with Malaysia would continue, but when reporters scurried along to question Suharto about this, the General took it all calmly and would only say, "Wait two more weeks."

Suharto had cause for quiet confidence. He knew what he was talking about. Two weeks later to the very day, Foreign Minister Malik and the Malaysian deputy-premier, Tun Abdul Razak, sat alongside each other in Djakarta and with a flourish of gold pens signed the peace treaty ending confrontation between their two countries.

On August 11, Tun Razak flew into Djakarta with a 50-man delegation from Malaysia. Precisely at noon, with a ceremony at the foreign ministry, the undeclared war between Malaysia and Indonesia came to a formal end. The terms of the treaty were straightforward. First, the Malaysian government agreed to give the people of its two Borneo territories, Sabah and Sarawak, the chance to "reaffirm as soon as possible their position in the Malaysian federation through independent and democratic general elections." This was the face-saving clause for Sukarno, which cost the Malaysians nothing, for elections would ultimately be taking place in the Borneo territories, anyway.

Second, the two governments agreed to restore diplomatic relations. Third, they agreed to cease hostilities.

Prior to the signing ceremony, Tun Razak sped to the presidential palace and in a swift little ceremony presented Sukarno with a silver tea service, a gift from the king of Malaysia. The day after the ceremony, Foreign Minister Malik flew with an Indonesian delegation to the Malaysian capital of Kuala Lumpur for a one-day return goodwill visit.

Clearly, the peace treaty had been signed over the President's vigorous opposition. He tried to put the best face on it, declaring that the treaty signed in Djakarta differed "in content and spirit" from the agreement worked out in Bangkok two months earlier. The inference was that Indonesia had stiffened its terms and extracted concessions from Malaysia, and that he had agreed to the signing of the treaty for these reasons. But when Malik got back from Kuala Lumpur, he bluntly and decisively shot down the presidential assertion. It was, said Malik, the "very same accord, intact," that had been agreed upon in Bangkok. "There is no difference from or modification to the Bangkok agreement."

Five months had now elapsed between Sukarno's order bestowing executive authority on Suharto and the signing of the peace treaty with Malaysia. After a cautious start, the new leadership had begun to issue a flurry of announcements of its good intentions. At home it had announced a new austerity program. To listeners abroad, it indicated Indonesia would return to the United Nations and rejoin a string of international organizations like the International Monetary Fund and the World Bank. The Indonesian leaders dropped hints that they would like their country to be invited to the December Asian Games in Bangkok—and would seek forgiveness for past sins. At the 1962 games in Djakarta, Indonesia's refusal to invite Nationalist China and Israel had touched off a major political row.

Indonesia announced it would make reparation to the British government of more than $1,840,000 for the sacking of the British Embassy in 1963, and would pay for damage caused to American diplomatic property.

Political prisoners of the Sukarno regime were released, among them Mochtar Lubis, the crusading Indonesian journalist jailed for nine years for his opposition to the government.

Though the army kept newspapers at home in check, and censored the outgoing cables of foreign correspondents, reporters and editors began to enjoy more room for maneuver. Some brutally frank cartoons began to appear, mainly mocking Sukarno but occasionally prodding the military, too. The newspaper run by the foreign ministry carried one cartoon blasting Sukarno for his addiction to monument-building while the people went poor. Sukarno raged at Foreign Minister Malik over that—and Malik leaked the story to reporters.

KAMI students put on a public display of more than a hundred political cartoons. The opening ceremony was delayed for two days until student leaders agreed to withdraw eight cartoons the military regarded as over-critical of Sukarno. Even so, the ones exhibited left no doubt about student contempt for Sukarno and the old order.

For many Indonesians this contempt was underlined by their sudden discovery of the contrast between living standards in Indonesia and in the Asian countries around them. With the end of confrontation, Indonesian delegations of students and communications experts and trade officials went trundling off to Malaysia. They came back stunned by the development and economic progress there. Said one such Indonesian official to me bitterly, "What have we in Indonesia been doing for twenty years? We've just frittered things away."

As the new leaders started the country on the long climb back to international respectability, however, they were beset by a lingering problem. Its name was Sukarno. The President was not playing the game by the rules the army believed it had laid down, back in March. With the transfer of executive authority to Suharto, confirmed by the People's Consultative Congress, the army thought the future was clear: Sukarno would retain his palaces, his cars, his women, his funds, but would keep his hands out of politics and become a figurehead President. In exchange for the surrender of power, he would retain his niche in Indonesian history, his earlier contributions to the nation would be stressed, and eventually he would pass from the scene without any public exhibition of embarrassing disgrace.

Sukarno, however, was not willing to become a sort of Grand Old Man of the Indonesian Revolution. He fought back, clawed at the new leadership, contradicted its reassuring statements to the outside world.

On August 17, 1966, came his opportunity to tell the nation

and the world of his frustrations. He grasped it with both hands. The occasion was the anniversary of Indonesian independence, the national day. Every year for twenty years on this day he had emerged to give a sort of state-of-the-nation address with all the dazzling display of verbal fireworks that was his speciality.

For two hours now, he addressed a huge crowd under the broiling sun in Djakarta's Merdeka Square. The new leaders listened tight-lipped and grim. Some students booed and left. For in his speech Sukarno roared out all the clichés of the old order.

Shouting with all his old fire, gripping the microphone, brandishing his clenched fists, he said Indonesia would not immediately recognize Malaysia, nor would it rush to rejoin the United Nations. Those declarations, of course, cut right across Foreign Minister Malik's laborious efforts to make Indonesia internationally respectable again.

Once more, Sukarno declared he had agreed to the peace treaty with Malaysia only after it had been radically changed. He had given Suharto "some backbone" in his negotiations with the Malaysians, he said. And Indonesia would not recognize Malaysia until after the elections promised in the Borneo territories.

As for the United Nations, Sukarno said that though Indonesia would eventually rejoin in order to "reorganize" the international organization, he planned first to intensify his reorganization campaign outside the United Nations. He indicated he would push ahead with his scheme for a Conference of New Emerging Forces (CONEFO), a sort of rival to the United Nations, in an ambitious complex of buildings he had begun at Senajan in Djakarta.

Perspiring in the sun, Sukarno declared he was working night and day to step up the battle against imperialism and colonialism. In a slashing attack on the United States, he said imperialism killed, burned, bombed, and spread poison gas in Vietnam. "Please, America," he said, breaking into English, "please get out of

Vietnam."

He was at pains to stress that he was still the Great Leader of the Indonesian Revolution, that he was still Prime Minister, and that he had not transferred power to General Suharto.

In justification of his policies, he said rocketing inflation was not caused by his projects, but by heavy expenditure on the military.

"I am not over-ambitious. I do not seek private gains. I am not driven by self-interest," he assured the listening crowds. Then, more sternly, "Follow my leadership, obey all my directives. March onward to continue the revolution along the path of my direction."

Within hours there were rumbles of angry reaction. A statement from KAMI, the university students' organization, said students regarded the speech as a guarded command to the Communists and their sympathizers to consolidate their strength for further upheaval.

Five Moslem mass organizations expressed no confidence in Sukarno as head of state and said his speech divided the people and did Indonesia great harm in the eyes of the outside world.

Several Djakarta newspapers criticized the speech, and in the West Java city of Bandung, students called on Sukarno to step down. They carried effigies of him through the streets and burned one that depicted Sukarno surrounded by pretty girls, with the Indonesian people before him in slavish postures. Some of the banners they carried warned him, "Don't call yourself Great Leader if you do not understand the will and hearts of the people."

Pro- and anti-Sukarno students clashed violently in Bandung, fighting for several hours. One anti-Sukarno student, Julius Usman, was killed in the melee and Major General Dharsono, the new commander of the area, who had himself been outspoken in his criticism of Sukarno, ordered the student buried with hero's honors. Sukarno was furious, and summoned the general to Djakarta to explain. According to a version of the conversation published later by an army newspaper, Dharsono told the President: "I'm convinced, sir, that the struggle of those students was pure and in line with the demands of the people's conscience. It is proper to appoint Julius Usman a hero."

Sukarno then, according to the newspaper, told Dharsono he had heard there were "attempts to disinter Julius Usman" from the special heroes' cemetery in Bandung. Did not this indicate, he asked, that the presidential followers were considerable in number?

Yes, Dharsono is supposed to have replied, it was true. "Your followers are considerable in number. They are hooligans and hoodlums operating around the square and the station in Bandung," he is quoted as saying.

When Sukarno asked him whether he did not want to revoke his decision giving the dead student hero status, Dharsono replied flatly that he did not.

The account may be somewhat embroidered, but such was Sukarno's deteriorating status at that time that Dharsono may well have spoken in roughly those terms.

To stem the criticism following Sukarno's August 17 speech, and to reassure the outside world, Information Minister Diah told correspondents that Sukarno could say anything he liked, but it would have no effect whatsoever on decisions taken by the cabinet.

As if to underline the point, Indonesia returned with a flourish to the United Nations in September, despite Sukarno's opposition, and announced that joint Indonesian-Malaysian patrols would soon be operating in Borneo "to check the Communist menace."

Malik and the Sultan of Jogjakarta went off on separate tours around the world to seek emergency extensions of the deadlines for foreign debt repayments and to raise whatever financial help they could. Suharto stayed home keeping a watchful eye on the security situation and on Sukarno.

23. President No More

When the army assumed power in Indonesia, it was reluctant, for reasons already explained, to oust Sukarno completely. The argument was that it could not afford to do without him, albeit in a figurehead role. But by now, many Indonesians had come to the conclusion they could not afford to go forward with him.

His August 17 speech, and other, similar, outbursts threatened to sabotage all that the new order was trying to achieve. The students of Djakarta demanded his dismissal. They were supported by individual generals who urged Suharto to act firmly against Sukarno once and for all.

Suharto was no less disillusioned with the President than they. There were rumors several times that his patience was almost at an end and he was near to sending Sukarno flying out of the country to exile. But in fact Suharto kept to a moderate course. Though there were generals urging him to get rid of Sukarno, there were others with strong personal allegiance to the President. Aside from differences within the army, there was the fact that the marine corps and elements of the police, air force, and navy were firmly loyal to Sukarno. Outside the armed services there was division of opinion, too. The big Partai Nasional Indonesia (PNI), founded by Sukarno himself in 1927, had come out with a pledge of support for him despite serious internal differences of its own. The clash between pro- and anti-Sukarno students in Bandung, as well as tension elsewhere, underlined Suharto's fears that firing the President might spark civil war.

Proponents of the Suharto policy argued that the new leadership was making impressive progress despite Sukarno's heckling. It was an argument of considerable validity. As thousands of students marched at the end of September to keep a night long anniversary vigil beside the well at Lubang Buaja, it was clear that Indonesia had become a changed country in the year since the army's generals were done to death there.

Twelve months before, Indonesia was swept by a campaign of poisonous hatred toward the West. British and American diplomats locked themselves in their offices as Indonesia rushed past pell-mell in a Communist-encouraged slide toward the left. Sukarno had whipped the country into war fever over Malaysia, implying that Indonesia's real enemies lay in Washington and London. In petulant isolation, Sukarno had withdrawn Indonesia from the United Nations and the world community. Not even toward Moscow, which had poured millions into Indonesia's military establishment, was there much cordiality. Instead, it was to Peking, and the most militant apostles of Communism, that Sukarno looked for his inspiration.

Now, a year later, and not much more than six months since Suharto had acquired executive power from Sukarno, Indonesia was back in the United Nations, and the war with Malaysia was ended. The country had certainly not become a satellite of the West, but it had pulled back from Communist China's embrace to a more genuinely non-aligned stance. The Communist Party was crushed. The wind of reason was blowing through the corridors of government, and if stability was a long, long way away, the new leadership had given many indications that it was serious about attempting the grueling climb back to it.

Sukarno himself, Suharto's supporters argued, was boxed in. He had been stripped of his power. Now his influence was being eroded by a carefully graduated campaign designed to discredit him. A prominent factor in the campaign was the September trial of Jusuf Muda Dalam, the former governor of the Indonesian state bank, who had been swept up with former Foreign Minister Subandrio and a string of other wanted cabinet ministers in the army's series of March arrests.

In court, Dalam told a story of easy money and easy women that was immediately the hottest gossip of Djakarta. A parade of Indonesian movie actresses, pretty secretaries, and singers peeled away the layers of a national scandal that eventually laid bare the *dolce vita* of Sukarno's administration. A shapely girl who won Sukarno's favor, the country learned, could bustle along to Dalam and acquire credits and import permits worth huge amounts. It was not a question of thousands of dollars, but millions, which had been swindled and misappropriated. Besides his massive mismanagement of state funds, Dalam was charged with having six wives instead of the four allowed by Moslem law. As also was made clear, he maintained more than twenty mistresses about the country.

Sukarno's name was mentioned several times during the trial. Fascinating were some of the stories which emerged. One businessman related how Sukarno had given him a special deferred payment license, worth about $10,000,000, to import yarn. In return, he said, he gave the President $600,000. Though Sukarno did not appear at the trial, he admitted the deal in a public speech, but said he had planned to use the $600,000 to build a planetarium for the Indonesian people. As a matter of fact, he added, he had also wanted money to build a large theater.

Many Sukarno critics, however, felt that evidence of Sukarno's involvement was not pressed at the trial, and that the judges backed away when they could have gone further.

Despite the army's assurances, the anti-Sukarno students watched the President's continued maneuverings with suspicion and apprehension. They listened to him declaring, "I am a Marxist. Marxism is in my chest," although the People's Consultative Congress in July had banned Marxism. They listened to him insisting on the old formula for Indonesia of Nasakom—nationalism, religion, and Communism—although Communism had similarly been outlawed. "We don't have to call it Nasakom," Sukarno announced grandly. "We can call it Nasasos [for nationalism, religion and socialism]." But, he added, "these three factors are still essential." They listened when he warned that the imperialists were behind the campaign to make him step down, and that snipers were waiting to kill him, apparently under orders of the American C.I.A. It was a charge for which he produced no evidence, of course. The students knew, too, that the campaign to remove him was inspired not from outside Indonesia, but from within.

Meanwhile, he consistently contradicted Foreign Minister Malik's assurances to the outside world. When Malik, for instance, announced in New York that Indonesia would honor its pledge to hold a plebiscite in West Irian in terms of its international obligations, Sukarno denied it.

For the students opposed to him this was not good enough. They poured on the pressure to get rid of him. KAPPI, the high school students' action front, in a public statement called him "a bloody liar, twisting the facts of history." Indonesians, the statement continued, "are condemning the Marxist Sukarno who has deviated from the revolution and is dreaming in broad daylight. He only thinks of himself, turns his people into slaves, and organizes lavish parties for himself and his closest associates."

At a KAPPI rally, student leaders shouted, "Do you know that Sukarno gave the order to kill the generals?" They charged that Sukarno's politically conscious second wife, Hartini, installed in the Bogor palace, had subversively channeled funds to Communist Party officials who had gone underground in Central Java after the coup.

Criticism of the President now thundered in hourly from the students and other anti-Sukarno factions. They demanded that he explain Indonesia's economic collapse and his links with the 1965 coup attempt. From South Celebes came a call from five student action fronts that he stand trial. A Moslem student association urged that he leave the country "because he calls himself a Marxist at heart." Others demanded a ban on publication of his writings. One student organization criticized Sukarno's art collection and asked the new leadership to remove all nude statues from his palaces, because they were "clashing with the rules of morality in Indonesia." KAMI suggested the withdrawal of banknotes and postage stamps bearing Sukarno's picture. The KAMI newspaper explained that it was "disgusting to lick the reverse side of President Sukarno's picture for anyone who wants to send mail." The anti-Sukarno newspaper *Karya Bhakti* stated flatly that Sukarno was involved in the Gestapu movement. "Bung Karno," said the paper, "obviously violated military laws by committing desertion, by going over to the enemy not for fear or because he was forced to do so, but because Bung Karno was himself the leader." It concluded ominously, "The punishment for desertion is death."

The vehemence of this campaign put the alliance between the students and the military men to severe strain. The students wanted immediate action to depose Sukarno. The army command sought much more gradual and cautious movement. The next step in Suharto's plan was the trial of ex-Foreign Minister Subandrio. With dramatic flair, the army scheduled the trial for October 1, a year to the day after the murder of its generals.

But even as the Subandrio trial got under way, thousands of students staged a massive demonstration outside the presidential palace. If Sukarno failed to give an account of events leading up to the 1965 coup, they threatened, they would storm the palace and occupy it. Though the army had long been sympathetic to the students, it was not prepared to allow this. Orders went out that the student masses were to be dispersed. The man charged with the assignment was Major General Kemal Idris, the KOSTRAD chief of staff, who ironically was one of the anti-Sukarno students' heroes.

Later he told me his side of the story. "It all began with a ceremony at KOSTRAD headquarters," he explained. "A delegation from KAMI was due to attend, but I heard that the students planned to come in force. We'd been keeping them away from the President's palace, but KOSTRAD headquarters is close to the palace, and they thought if they could get a few thousand students to KOSTRAD, it wouldn't be difficult for them to go on after our ceremony to demonstrate outside the palace.

"I got hold of the student leaders and told them the army just wouldn't stand for anything inside the palace. But they said they only wanted to put up pictures of our murdered generals outside the palace. I agreed to let them do that, provided there was nothing else.

"Well, they put up their pictures, but then they camped there, right outside the palace. Suharto got on the phone to me and told me I had to clear them. 'Why me?' I asked him. 'Because,' he told me, 'the whole thing started with your KOSTRAD ceremony. So you've got to move them out of there.'"

General Kemal Idris gave a little smile as he recalled his predicament, and then continued the story, "I called the student leaders over and said, 'Be reasonable. I'm under orders to get you out of there, but I'd rather you do it yourselves. Now, I'll give you twenty-four hours. If you haven't moved by then, I'm going to have to act against you.'"

"Next morning," he said, "they were still there. This time I told them if they hadn't moved in an hour, my troops would go into action. I waited four hours, but they still hadn't budged. There was nothing for it, then. I told the commander of my soldiers there not to fire. The soldiers were to use rifle butts, and if they had to use anything more, bayonets. It was a bad business, but it had to be done."

The business was done, and dozens of students were wounded as the soldiers charged them. There were screams and chaos as the first line of students, some of them girls, buckled under the glittering line of bayonets. Students were slashed, and others were battered with rifle butts.

For both students and soldiers it was a moment of great anguish. Yet despite the injuries, there was remarkably little ill-feeling afterwards. Said one student, "I guess we had it coming. But we'll go on with our campaign." For its part, the army leadership was publicly apologetic, but still determined that student demonstrations would be kept under control and that students would not be allowed to occupy the presidential palace.

"We want to work closely with the students," one general told me, "but they can't take over. They've got to understand that we're in charge, and we must decide how the game is to be played."

The next card in the army's game was the Subandrio trial, but despite the big build-up, it proved something of a disappointment to those expecting dramatic revelations. The former foreign minister was charged with plotting against the government and subversion, but as the evidence developed, it seemed mainly to prove what everybody knew, namely that Subandrio had helped Sukarno swing the country's foreign policy to close alliance with Peking. Although this was now unpopular, Subandrio's lawyers argued that it was not illegal at the time he did it. The prosecution, however, demanded, and eventually got, the death penalty for Subandrio on the grounds that all this represented "crimes against the state."

In a Western court of law the evidence against Subandrio would have seemed scant and circumstantial, but it was, of course, a political trial, and Subandrio's real crime was that he was a key figure in Sukarno's "old order."

At one stage the prosecutor charged Subandrio with being an "old order" architect. Subandrio replied that he was "too small for that title. Only a greater man deserves it. I was only an assistant of the President."

Subandrio's comment raised the great unanswered question of

the trial, namely, if Subandrio was being tried for implementing these policies, what about Sukarno, whose policies they really were?

Nevertheless, Subandrio remained reasonably loyal to the President throughout. He admitted he had received reports of a pending Communist coup, but said flatly he had not passed them on to the President. Nor was any evidence produced directly linking Sukarno with the coup. In fact, the military tribunal heard a statement from Sukarno read out in which he specifically denied foreknowledge of the coup or of the training of Communist assassination teams at Lubang Buaja.

There were some fascinating aspects to the trial. Evidence emerged, for instance, of Aidit's correspondence with Sukarno after the coup, when Aidit was hiding in Central Java. Questions were raised about Subandrio's calm reaction to the coup, when he got news of it in northern Sumatra. But though these had a bearing on the possible foreknowledge of, and involvement in, the coup of both Sukarno and Subandrio, they raised only suspicions and produced no facts.

At the trial's end, those who had anticipated that Sukarno himself would stand convicted of a master participating role in the coup were disappointed.

When Foreign Minister Malik returned home in November after his world travels, he could scent mischief. Besides foreign policy, he had been given broad responsibility for political affairs at home. In both tasks he was suffering from Sukarno's maneuvering, dabbling, contradicting. Malik, a direct and spunky little Sumatran, did not share Suharto's apparent confidence that the new leadership could glide on with Sukarno neatly trussed up in a figurehead role. "I've known Sukarno for 30 years," Malik told a friend, "and if he's allowed room to maneuver, he'll use it. That's just the way he is."

Thus the problem of "dualism" in Indonesia's leadership had to be resolved, declared Malik. It was a polite way of suggesting

Sukarno had to go. One way would have been for the President to take a long foreign trip. It was suggested that he might like to fly off to Tokyo, where his Japanese wife, Dewi, had gone to prepare for the birth of a child. Those who thought presidential travel might be the ideal answer to the problem speculated that after the baby's birth he could go on to Vienna for a medical checkup, perhaps spend a little while in Europe. Then somebody discovered that Sukarno had been invited to visit Cairo, and that a visit with President Nasser might be the solution. The reason for the invitation was something of a mystery—until someone remembered that Adam Malik had included Cairo on his recent itinerary. When Malik politely inquired of Sukarno whether he could inform Nasser of his acceptance, however, Sukarno gave the foreign minister a knowing smile and declined.

If Sukarno refused to throw in the towel so easily, however, he was soon to face a new assault. In December came the trial of former air force chief Omar Dhani. As with previous sessions of the *mahmillub*, or military tribunal, trying those involved in the 1965 coup, there was tight security. Roads were blocked off for hundreds of yards around the square white building used for the sessions. Tanks and armored cars were drawn up defensively. Troops checked the documents of anybody entering. Key witnesses, and the accused, were driven to the sessions in bullet-proof military vehicles.

Dhani had been at Halim air base during the crucial hours of the coup. Now, from his own testimony and that of witnesses, there began to emerge the clearest picture yet of the sequence of events there, and of Sukarno's own actions. This time, there was no reticence on the part of the prosecution or the military judges in extracting information about the President's behavior. The trial was broadcast live. The listening nation discovered that when General Supardjo, one of the ringleaders of the coup, reported to Sukarno about the arrest and death of the army's generals, the President accepted the news with remarkable equanimity. He did not order Supardjo punished, or the co-plotters arrested. In fact, there was the suggestion that he may even have given Supardjo a congratulatory pat on the back.

There was also Dhani's revelation that he had talked with the President on the eve of the coup, warning him of trouble, and that Sukarno knew Supardjo was in town, having secretly left his post in Kalimantan—a fact that had been withheld from the then KOSTRAD commander, General Suharto.

Another startling piece of information that emerged from the trial was that Dhani in the very month before the coup had flown secretly to Peking, using Sukarno's personal plane. His mission had been to try and tie up, among other things, the delivery of 100,000 small arms to Indonesia—a transaction that was not to be brought to the attention of the army or regular defense ministry channels.

For his part in the coup, Dhani, as expected, got the death sentence. But now for Sukarno, wily though he might be, the end was also drawing near. Like hounds on the hunt, his critics began to close in. He was subjected to increasing pressure. Some wanted him tried. Others wanted him brought before an investigating session of the People's Consultative Congress. Still others were prepared to settle, at least initially, for an explanation of his role in the coup, which in fact had already been requested by the Congress.

Fifteen months earlier, generals and cabinet ministers had turned somersaults at the crook of Sukarno's little finger. Now he was the subject of widespread contempt and ridicule.

At a major Moslem celebration he was called by one speaker a "humbug." It was very difficult, the speaker went on, "to include him among genuine Moslems, because he can be classified only as a hypocrite."

Mochtar Lubis, the journalist freed from Sukarno's jails, went on an Asian speaking tour and talked frankly and critically about the old order. In Tokyo he bluntly criticized some Japanese who had "supplied Indonesian leaders with money and women." To make sure nobody missed the point, the armed forces *Daily Mail* in Djakarta ran its report of the speech next to an item about Sukarno's Japanese wife Dewi.

Even Dewi herself had some admonishments for her husband. In an interview with a Dutch newspaper she was quoted as saying, in Tokyo, "I have long since warned him. I tried to explain that he would make a mistake if he continued to be angry and stubborn. But he is a man of political principles who does not know of retreat. He does not like compromise.

"I told him, 'Others have principles, too, but they are far more diplomatic. You, too, must be like that. If not, you will not advance. Why, if you make speeches, must you always put forward questions of malicious jealousy? That's why you always create jealousy.'

"Sukarno lost contact with his people. He does not know what is in the mind of the people, what they feel, say, and want for their individual and family lives," she concluded.

There was even an extraordinary public debate in Djakarta newspapers as to whether Sukarno, the head of state, had raped a 14-year-old girl on one trip abroad. There were statements from the foreign ministry, and the palace, and even one from Sukarno himself, denying it. Foreign Minister Malik said he was asking Indonesian embassies abroad to look into reports of Sukarno adventures in countries where the President had traveled.

Much more ominous was the statement of the chairman of the Indonesian Lawyers' Association. After examining the evidence at the Dhani trial, he concluded that Sukarno had encouraged the coup movement. If others had been given the death sentence for encouraging the coup, he said, "the same thing should apply to Sukarno."

As 1966 drew to its end, the commanders of the army, navy, air force, and police issued a joint statement. The armed forces, they said, would "take firm steps" against anybody, no matter who, who tried to deviate from the constitution, or who refused to implement the decisions of the People's Consultative Congress. The decisions the military leaders had in mind, of course, were those of the previous July curbing Sukarno. The offender at whom they aimed their statement was the President himself. After issuing the statement, the military leaders went into a series of meetings with Sukarno.

If it all seemed a little vague, KAMI, the university students' action front, left little doubt about what it thought needed discussing. Welcoming the armed forces statement, KAMI called on the military men "to discipline Bung Karno, who so far has shown neither intention nor willingness to implement the decisions of the People's Consultative Congress." Sukarno had failed, said the students, to account for the economic and moral deterioration of the country, while "juridical facts" had shown him to be involved in Gestapu. KAMI urged the armed forces to "curb the activities and speeches of Bung Karno."

As the conferences with the military leaders progressed, it became clear that Sukarno was still in no mood for surrender. At one stage, according to one of the participants, he angrily threatened to dismiss the cabinet, block any session of the Congress, fire almost everybody, and plunge the country into chaos. The military men responded in pointed manner. They staged a show of force, in which units from all services rumbled into Merdeka Square and up to the front gates of the presidential palace.

Two days later, Foreign Minister Malik emerged from a joint session between Sukarno, the cabinet, and the military leaders, and said, "After the New Year, the Congress and the people will have their way."

Malik had earlier casually remarked to Indonesian reporters that unless the political crisis were resolved, it might not be possible to prevent students demonstrating in the streets again.

Sukarno thought things over. As 1967 dawned, he indicated that he would comply with the request from the People's Consultative Congress for some explanation of the circumstances surrounding the coup, and the country's economic and moral decline. When the explanation came, however, in a written statement on January 10, Sukarno airily dismissed suggestions that he was in any way responsible for any of the country's ills.

The arrest and murder of the generals, he said, was a "complete surprise" to him. The whole affair had been caused by a "conjunction of three causes." The first was the "wrong way" taken by the leadership of the Indonesian Communist Party. The second was the cunning of Necolim (Western) subversion. The third was the involvement of people who were "nuts."

In his statement he asked why he was the only one called upon to account for the coup. What, he asked, about the responsibility of General Nasution, who was minister of defence and security at the time? As for the economic crisis, he declared it was unfair to make him alone responsible. The trouble was not the fault of one person, but the result of actions taken by the "whole of government apparatus and society." As far as the nation's moral decline was concerned, again he denied that he alone should be held responsible. This was the result, he explained, "of the behavior of a society as a whole."

Sukarno's statement was, of course, unacceptable to his critics. Thousands of students gathered in the streets shouting, "Hang him, hang him!" At one rally, a speaker explained that resignation would now be too mild a punishment for the President. "We want him to be hanged in public," he shouted, "because he was the mastermind behind the 1965 abortive Communist coup." Many demonstrators carried banners, some reading: "January is ringing the death knell to the old order and its main architect, Bung Karno."

Two days after Sukarno's cavalier statement of "explanation," the army announced a dramatic haul. At 5:30 in the morning of

January 12, troops captured General Supardjo, one of the leading plotters in the coup, who had managed to evade arrest for more than fifteen months. Arrny sources said he had been picked up in the Lubang Buaja area, at Halim, not far from the spot where the generals were murdered and buried.

Supardjo had been the coup leaders' liaison man with the President. He, perhaps better than anybody else, knew exactly what was Sukarno's involvement in the plot. The timing of his arrest, two days after the President's exasperatingly inadequate "explanation" to the Congress, might have been pure coincidence. On the other hand, army sources admitted that troops had been shadowing Supardjo for three weeks prior to his capture. Some observers speculated that Sukarno's non-explanation might have been the last straw for the army and that army leaders now had determined to throw the book at the President.

The ferocity of attacks against him, plus the arrest of Supardjo, may finally have convinced Sukarno that the game was up. In one little speech in striking contrast to the arrogance of his earlier "explanation," he said: "There is no human without faults." He asked "the Indonesian people and even the whole world" to forgive his "conscious, as well as unconscious, faults."

But it was too late. On January 20, leaders of the People's Consultative Congress announced that the Congress would meet in full session to consider the problem of the President. On January 23, General Suharto told army officers there was a limit to his patience and that he would take strong action against any person who failed to follow Congress decisions. On January 24, the Djakarta garrison commander, General Machmud, went on the radio and announced he was ready to arrest President Sukarno, if given the order.

The army was now busy interrogating General Supardjo. He defended the President, insisted that there really had been a

Council of Generals, and denied that he had been a key figure in the assassination plot. But from the investigation the army extracted some fascinating details. It learned, for instance, that Supardjo while hiding had received at least one letter from Sukarno apparently urging him to marshal pro-Sukarno groups.

The manner in which Supardjo had escaped detection for so long after the coup was also interesting. Apparently, he had been most of the time in Djakarta. Various people in whose homes he had hidden now declared under interrogation that he had carried a letter from Sukarno asking everyone to give the bearer protection. A corporal who gave Supardjo refuge in his home said he understood that Supardjo was "Sukarno's man."

Again there was corroboration of that shoulder-patting incident between Sukarno and Supardjo. Supardjo's version was that Sukarno, when he clapped him on the shoulder after being told of the generals' fate, said, "That sort of thing will happen in a revolution."

Supardjo's trial was scheduled for February 23. During the preceding week, Suharto began a flurry of showdown meetings with his own advisers, the military leaders, and Sukarno. The atmosphere was grim and tense. Finally, on the eve of the Supardjo trial came the terse announcement that Sukarno, "after realizing that political conflict in the country needs to be ended for the sake of the people, the state, and the nation," was transferring "the authority of the government" to General Suharto.

About the handover there appeared to be contradictions. Since March 11 of the previous year, for instance, Suharto had already had executive power. In one sense, the new development seemed only to be underlining the existing situation. There was speculation about a secret deal in which Sukarno, in exchange for his agreement to the transfer, had extracted a guarantee from Suharto that he would not be brought to trial.

But all this was soon to be overtaken by the climactic session of the People's Congress that began March 7, 1967. In the Istora Hall at Senajan, where Sukarno had so often whipped up the masses with his oratory, there was this time no Sukarno, not even a picture of him, as the delegates gathered soberly to go about their business. With the exclamation "Bismillah!" ("In the name of Allah!"), General Nasution, the Congress chairman, opened the session.

General Suharto delivered an hour-long speech in which he seemed to be calling on the Congress to get rid of Sukarno without excessive humiliation. The decision had to be reached, he said, "authoritatively, but tactfully." Suharto in his speech criticized Sukarno's defense and protection of the Communist Party. But he declared that "unless there are indeed still facts we haven't been able to find until this very day," it did not appear that Sukarno was "the mastermind, or even an important figure" in the Gestapu plot. Undoubtedly, Suharto was inspired to this moderate speech, defensive of Sukarno, by his concern lest civil war be touched off by any harsh action against the President.

But it also put the onus for action squarely upon the Congress members. Nobody later could say that Suharto had led the attack on Sukarno, or that the President had been toppled by military maneuver that was unconstitutional.

While the Congress was scheduled to finish its deliberations on March 11, there was bitter wrangling between hard-line opponents of Sukarno, who wanted to press the campaign against him to the hilt, and those apparently heeding Suharto's appeal who wanted Sukarno let down lightly. There was no disagreement over Sukarno's ouster. The argument was over the manner in which it was to be effected.

Finally, after taking an extra day to agree, the Congress on March 12 stripped Sukarno of all his powers, without actually stating that he had been sacked. The question of trying him was left to General Suharto. Suharto was sworn in as Acting President.

In official terminology, the Congress announced that Sukarno had "failed to meet his constitutional responsibilities." Therefore Congress "withdraws its mandate" from him, "and all his powers." The Congress said Suharto was appointed Acting President until a new president was elected by Congress after general elections (scheduled for 1968). The solution to the "judicial problem involving Dr. Sukarno" was entrusted to the Acting President. Meanwhile, Sukarno was-"banned from political activities" until the elections.

To the perspiring correspondents from abroad it seemed an odd way to change rulers. They pressed for a straightforward interpretation and clearcut confirmation that what they thought had happened had actually happened. But as Indonesia's smiling new leaders explained, this was the way things were done in Indonesia.

There was, however, no doubt about it. For Sukarno this was the end of the political road. Finally he had been dragged down by the sequence of events triggered on that night in 1965 when the murder gangs set out to exterminate the army's generals.

24. New Order

In government offices and in Indonesian embassies around the world, the portraits of Sukarno came tumbling down. New ones—of Suharto—went up.

Now Sukarno was simply "Doctor Engineer" Sukarno, a title acquired with an engineering degree in his youth. His golden presidential standard was furled. The presidential trappings were gone; the old splendor was no more. Suddenly, he cut a pathetic and broken figure.

If Sukarno had ever had any provisional claim to greatness in the history books, that, too, was now gone. The drama of his going seemed certain to overshadow his earlier achievements. Future generations seemed much more likely to remember him as a degenerate demagogue than as a dynamic revolutionary.

Somebody, after his toppling, remarked that Sukarno served his country well in war, but sabotaged it in peace. Perhaps unjustly, he seems destined to be recorded in history not as the man who united Indonesia, but as the man who nearly wrecked it.

When he squandered the country's opportunity and resources after independence, he squandered also his own claim to greatness.

Herein lies the tragedy. Sukarno did play a major role in giving Indonesia unity, a sense of nationhood, pride, and identity. But his story is the sadly familiar one of a charismatic leader whose sense of grandeur for his country became blurred and overtaken by his inflated sense of personal grandeur. Spurred on by his dream of leading not only Indonesia, but the whole "New Emerging Forces" (NEFO) world of Afro-Asian-Latin America, he lost touch with his own people.

When they needed rice, he gave them battleships and submarines, mortgaging the country's economic future for years to pay for them. When the people's need was the opening up and irrigation of land for cultivation, Sukarno poured millions into concrete monuments of stupefying uselessness and dubious artistic taste. He built department stores, but had nothing to put in them for his people. He built luxury hotels, but these were for the foreign visitors and delegations he sought to impress. In the shadow of these hotels, tattered Indonesians begged for shirts and handouts.

Organized opposition he eliminated by introducing his own concept of "guided democracy." Restlessness and doubts among his people he subdued by the invention of foreign threats, such as the menace of Malaysia and the perfidy of Necolim. Carping criticism seemed unpatriotic, and was stifled, as Sukarno kept the nation called to arms and in a state of perpetual political emergency.

Eventually the spell which he wove around all this, and which had kept Indonesia bemused for so long, wore off. After nationhood, the people had been led to expect the promised land. What they got was empty talk. They needed sewers, but Sukarno gave them speeches. After two decades of Sukarnoism, their country was bankrupt at home, almost friendless abroad. Its sole major ally was Communist China, whose leaders probably held Sukarno in secret contempt.

The tragedy is not the tragedy of one man's downfall, but of a nation's missed opportunity. Sukarno could have given Indonesia happiness and prosperity as well as identity. Instead, he despoiled the country's resources. At his peak, Sukarno had the stature to demand anything of his people, to lead them anywhere, while they followed unquestioning. If sacrifice were needed for patient construction of the economy, Sukarno could have asked for it and gotten it. But he was not that kind of a builder. Instead of such mundane activity, he took his people down a road which, though full of adventure and excitement, led eventually to despair. For Sukarno they did shed their sweat and tears, and finally their blood, too, but he in return left them a legacy of chaos.

The coup of 1965 was the beginning of Sukarno's end. Thereafter, suspicion of his involvement in it loomed like a question mark across his hitherto undefaceable image. But the real crisis for him was the assumption by the army of rival authority. Under the emergency conditions created by the coup, military men were thrust into control in many areas, shunting aside the governmental machinery ordinarily responsible to the President.

It is arguable that at various stages after the coup, Sukarno might still have saved himself. His best opportunity came immediately after the coup, when the army looked to him for a lead. He could, at this time, have made a show of condemning the Communist Party. He could have put himself in the vanguard of mourners for the army's generals, demanded punishment for the plotters, declared that Indonesia would look with harder eye at its alliance with Peking. If he had done so, he might have nipped off the anti-Sukarno campaign before it blossomed.

Instead he went on to reshuffle his cabinet provocatively in February of 1966, firing General Nasution and appointing ministers held to be pro-Communist. Even after that, he could have bowed to the people's will as manifested in the militant student street demonstrations in Djakarta. Instead, he was unyielding; his stubbornness brought on the confrontation with the army and his transfer of executive authority to General Suharto on March 11.

Probably, after that, he could never have reacquired real power by process of public reform. But he could have retained the presidency with some stature and respect for his earlier services to the nation. However, he refused to obey the rules, and though it took twelve months more to steadily slice away his reputation and discredit him, he was ultimately toppled. Even during that year, the army offered him ample opportunity to make his exit a graceful one. He rejected it.

Perhaps it is unrealistic to suppose he might have acted otherwise than he did. To have taken any of the opportunities offered would have meant meek acceptance of the diminution or eclipse of his power. Such concession was not in the character of the man. As one Western diplomat once perceptively remarked, "If you give Sukarno a choice between humiliation and war, he'll choose war." Sukarno gambled for all, and lost. It was in keeping with his megalomania. He was, after all, a man who had publicly compared himself at various times with Buddha, Jesus, Mohammed, Jefferson, and Stalin.

I do not believe Sukarno intended to make Indonesia a subservient satellite of Communist China. This is not to say that Peking would not have out-maneuvered him and made it so. Indeed, one can argue that such a subversive process was already well under way. But a conscious decision by Sukarno to bend his country to Peking's whim is unthinkable. Sukarno had too monumental an ego to play second fiddle to anybody. He clearly welcomed an alliance, but a servant-to-master relationship he could not have tolerated. Even in an alliance between equals, Sukarno would not have jumped to obey orders from Mao Tse-tung. One cannot avoid the suspicion that, as Sukarno saw it, it was he who advised Mao what to do.

Sukarno throughout his reign claimed he was not a Communist, although he clearly favored and protected the Communist Party. He admitted he was a Marxist. He certainly was oriented toward the extreme political left. All the evidence is that in the months preceding the 1965 coup he had been moving faster and faster in that direction. Overshadowing all of his political philosophy and actions, however, was his egotism. Sukarno used the techniques of Marxism as an instrument for his own ends. Foreign holdings might be seized, investors be driven away, private enterprise be cut back, and the nation's energy, resources, and means of production be channelled toward the state. But the state was Sukarno, without whom nothing was permitted to run in Indonesia. Marxism may have been its basis, but Sukarnoism was Sukarno's policy.

Happily for Indonesia, nationalism proved stronger than either Sukarnoism or Communism.

Basically the reason for the younger generation's revolt against Sukarno was that he had betrayed the revolution. With the idealism of youth, the students believed the revolution should be kept pure and incorrupt. Guarded thus, the revolution would produce the affluence at home that they were told had gone funneling abroad in colonial times.

But Sukarno had not responded to these aspirations, or fulfilled them. Indonesia was actually worse off than it had been in colonial days. Though Sukarno preached in the name of Indonesian nationalism, he had in fact come perilously close to losing his nation's birthright.

Indonesia had become so blatantly badly run that the visitor from abroad, be he liberal or conservative, could in all conscience hardly forbear to lambaste its leadership. In the Western world Sukarno had made himself a figure of fun; to much of the Afro-Asian world he sought to lead he had become an embarrassment. Only in the ranks of China's militant Communists did he find support, and even this was inspired by political expediency and the opportunism of China's leaders, not by their respect for him.

Though Indonesians themselves had permitted all this to happen, indeed had often applauded Sukarno in his destructive adventures, the new generation could not accept as a good nationalist the man who had brought economic and political disgrace to their country and placed it, for whatever reasons, within the alien embrace of Communist China.

The lesson of misplaced trust that Indonesia has had to learn is a bitter one. But in Sukarno's fall there is an important lesson also for the outside world, and particularly the United States, locked as it is in competition with Communism. The lesson lies in the resilience and durability of Indonesia's nationalism and in its ability, without foreign intervention, to reject the forces that sought to dilute and sully it.

From this painful period, Indonesia's new leaders have emerged with justifiable pride in one thing: Indonesians them selves purged their country of Communism. They had no outside help, made no plea to Washington for an expeditionary force, or the Seventh Fleet. In the days when the outcome hung in the balance, direct American intervention or involvement would have been an embarrassment and hindrance to the new leaders, undermining their position and giving credence to Communist charges that they were instruments of the West.

The anti-Communist campaign in Indonesia succeeded not in spite of American nonintervention, but perhaps because of it. In fairness to Washington, it must be said that the State Department saw this as readily as did Indonesians themselves. In this situation there was to be no American tub-thumping. If the United States really wanted to help, went the analysis, it would keep quiet. And it did.

As a result, United States diplomacy toward Indonesia has proved one of the most successful chapters in the contemporary history of American foreign policy in Asia. Even the timing of the changeover of American Ambassadors in 1965 could hardly have been better. Former Ambassador Howard Jones has been criticized for identifying himself too closely with Sukarno. Certainly his friendship with Sukarno would have been a liability to the United States had his ambassadorship overlapped the advent of the new order in Indonesia.

As Jones saw his mission, it was to keep the lines of communication open to Sukarno. This he did, and when other ambassadors in Djakarta wanted to know what was in Sukarno's mind, it was to the door of Ambassador Jones that they came pattering. When the anti-American campaign flared in Indonesia, the State Department resised petulant criticism that it should break relations and hung grimly on. It was a good decision, for when the mood in Djakarta finally changed, the American Embassy, though battered and scarred, was still in business and able to take advantage of the situation.

Back in 1965, however, when it became clear that Sukarno was no longer listening to what the United States had to say, the value of being able to reach him became doubtful. When Jones retired, he was succeeded by Marshall Green. Green, too, was criticized. Where of Jones it had been said he was too soft, of Green it was said he was too brusque and lacked the sensitivity to deal effectively with Indonesians. Green certainly was swift to show he was a no-nonsense ambassador. Though he could not reach Sukarno, his red head bobbed angrily around the Indonesian foreign ministry as he protested the latest anti-American incidents. But he, too, held grimly on, and though he was still new when the coup erupted, he had already laid the groundwork for detachment from the old order, which served him well in his relations with the new. In the months to come he had need of cool nerves. As events swirled about, he showed he had them.

If all this had been planned, the anonymous genius behind some desk in Washington who masterminded it all should be sought out and given charge of the whole Asian policy of the United States. However, though credit must go to the State Department for accurately assessing the situation, the fact is that the United States pursued its commendable policy of restraint in Indonesia because there was no alternative. There was no call for intervention, nothing the United States could have done except what it did—sit tight until the dust settled.

Thus, without any loss of American life, without the expenditure of any United States dollars, the local nationalists in Indonesia showed themselves strong enough to block the path of

Communism's advance. With American intervention, it is just possible that they might have failed.

If the lesson is worth remembering, it is also important to understand that it cannot be applied to every country threatened by the Communists. Inevitably there will be some attempts to suggest that the same United States policy applied to Vietnam as applied to Indonesia would have been similarly successful. There is no justification for such an argument, for the two situations are entirely different.

Indonesia is a vast country with a huge population of 105,000,000 people where the Communists, though well-organized, were nevertheless in a minority. In addition, Indonesia is an island nation relatively safe from incursions across its borders. It has one of the sturdiest military establishments in Asia, whose leadership has been consistently non-Communist.

South Vietnam, on the other hand, is a tiny country with a small population where the Communists launched a dangerous guerrilla war. Its own forces are inadequate to meet the guerrilla menace, and its borders are wide open to incursion and infiltration.

The lesson of Indonesia is that before the United States leaps to embroil itself in any and every country threatened by Communists, it should pause and consider whether it might not be doing more harm than good. The lesson of Indonesia is not, however, that inaction is everywhere desirable.

It is also important for the United States to remember that the nationalism that swept away the Communists and was responsible for Sukarno's toppling still burns brightly in Indonesia. The men who defied China's ambition of making their country a Communist satellite are no more anxious to make Indonesia a ward of Washington. Relations with the West are friendlier now. There is trade, and there is aid. But Indonesians are still hypersensitive and ultranationalistic. They will pursue their own policy. Capitalists who forget this are just as likely to get singed by the flames of Indonesian nationalism as are Communists.

Indonesia's new leaders are confronted by some awesome problems, and it is easy to be pessimistic about their solution. The most urgent challenge is in the economic sphere. Austerity measures at home are designed to curb the primary problem of galloping inflation. Motions are being made toward repairing and restoring the transport system and other economic services.

Abroad, the Indonesians have gone frankly to their creditors and told them they simply cannot, at the moment, pay the country's $2.7-billion foreign debts. About a billion dollars of this is owed to the Soviet Union, Indonesia's largest creditor. Through separate negotiations with the Soviets, and a roundtable conference with its other creditors in Paris at the end of 1966, the new Indonesian leadership succeeded in buying time for the repayment of the most pressing of these debts. The creditor nations rescheduled, or in other words postponed, the payment due.

But Indonesia needed more than this. From individual nations the new leadership sought emergency credits to cover vital imports. In Amsterdam early in 1967 various nations interested in helping Indonesia overcome its financial difficulties met to decide on new credits that would help plug Indonesia's foreign exchange gap for the year, estimated at about $200,000,000.

All these measures were vital, but of course they only gave Indonesia breathing space. They could not in themselves resolve the basic problems. In the long run, Indonesia will have to repay its debts, not postpone them. It will have to make up its balance-of-payments deficit by increased production, not emergency credits and handouts.

The task before the new leaders is the rebuilding of the whole economy. Indonesia is being given a second chance, but in one sense the odds are more unfair now than they were 20 years ago. In

Java, the key to the whole Indonesian economy, there are still, as there were 20 years ago, too many people on too little land. Except now, with the soaring birthrate, there are even more people trying to scratch an existence from the same amount of overcrowded land. Moreover, the new leadership did not take over with the books clean; it is saddled with an enormous backlog of debt.

As the hard-headed international economists see it, Indonesia faces a long, hard grind, if it is to return to economic stability. The experts mark the various milestones in terms of years. But some Indonesians expect results in months. The balance of payments may be all very well, but the *betjak*-driver and the student grinding his way through college have more basic and personal interests. They want the price of rice lowered now.

The pressure on the new leaders to produce tangible progress is intense. Undoubtedly there will be a tendency in some less-sophisticated quarters to look upon Suharto as a miracle-worker. But miracles are unlikely. What the new leaders most need are patience and an understanding on the part of the populace that Indonesia faces a long period of sweat and tears.

During that long period, the new leaders will not be able to produce the diversionary fireworks of the Sukarno era. Suharto has none of the Sukarno charisma, and neither do the practical Sultan of Jogjakarta and Foreign Minister Malik. There will be no flashy monuments, no foreign adventures to distract from the frustrations at home. Indonesia will be face to face with the harsh facts of reality. This is a confrontation that the Javanese, in particular, have often sought to avoid.

There are, of course, other problems besides economic ones.

Sukarno may no longer rule, but there is lingering support for him in Central and East Java. This could cause the new leaders trouble. Similarly, the Communist Party is smashed, but there are Communists enough still at large, some of them reorganizing the party underground.

There is the traditional suspicion harbored by civilians of a military regime. Indonesia has not known military government before, and if the slide toward militarism hastens, this suspicion could be translated into outright opposition.

Even if military authority is accepted, confidence in it could be eroded by the army's misuse of power, corruption in the officer corps, and the bestowal upon army leaders of big houses, luxury cars, and all the trappings and perquisites of the old order.

There is antagonism between religious groups, and rivalry between political parties and factions. Among the latter, the lure of elections is hastening the in-fighting and maneuvering in the vacuum caused by the eclipse of the Communist Party.

There may be new strains on the nation's unity, for whatever Sukarno's failings, he managed to keep the disparate peoples of Indonesia together. Without him there may be a tendency toward fragmentation.

Though it would be unrealistic to underestimate the problems, Indonesia has exhibited a remarkable resilience in the face of adversity. Despite all the gloomy predictions, its basically peasant economy did survive Sukarnoism, and its people can probably squeeze through several more years of hardship.

For a Javanese, who might well prefer to side-step issues, and a military man, who might well not understand the intricacies of economics, Suharto has moved practically and swiftly on the economic front. Repair work on the economy required the abandonment of most of Sukarno's foreign policy. The issue was faced, the step taken without question. Told that only emergency help from abroad could save Indonesia, Suharto gave the green light to go out and get it. He authorized new legislation to encourage foreign investors and sanctioned reparations to foreign companies that had had their property seized. Soon the aid men and the business representatives were cluttering Indonesian hotels. Oil company representatives were bidding for important new offshore exploration and development rights.

If Suharto showed a necessary directness in the economic sphere, he has blended with it caginess and deftness on the political front that have served him well. Eighteen months it took to remove Sukarno, and during this time the pace of Suharto's advance was often under attack. On several occasions it looked as though Bung Karno had slipped from Suharto's gentle grasp and was bouncing back to power. Yet the Suharto way succeeded, and the country was not plunged into the civil war that might have been. Suharto skilfully juggled different groups and factions. Despite Sukarno's ploys and struggling, the toppling of the national leader was accomplished with a certain grace and dignity. During it, Suharto established a reputation for constitutionality that undercut criticism that Indonesia had been seized by a military dictator.

Of course, the whole situation could still explode in his face. Any one of half a dozen factions could be out on the streets again, this time demonstrating against the army and the new leadership. But Indonesia's capacity to confound the outside world is almost unlimited. Despite the formidable problems, it could emerge successfully from its present time of trial. It is important that it should do so, for though American attention is riveted on little Vietnam, Indonesia with its 105,000,000 people and 3,000 miles of strategically placed territory is of much greater long-term importance.

With the fall of Sukarno, Indonesia has won a second chance. Not all countries get that opportunity. Now the challenge for both Indonesians and their friends is to see that it is not squandered like the first.

Index

Page numbers for photographs are in *italics*